THACKERAY *and his* DAUGHTER

The Letters and Journals of ANNE
THACKERAY RITCHIE, *with*
Many Letters of WILLIAM
MAKEPEACE THACKERAY

Anne Thackeray Ritchie.
From a drawing made in 1914
by John S. Sargent, R. A.

THACKERAY
AND HIS DAUGHTER

The Letters and Journals of ANNE
THACKERAY RITCHIE, *with*
Many Letters of WILLIAM
MAKEPEACE THACKERAY

Selected and Edited by
HESTER THACKERAY RITCHIE

With Unpublished Drawings by
THACKERAY *and* LADY RITCHIE

Publishers
HARPER & BROTHERS
NEW YORK AND LONDON
1924

Contents

List of Illustrations

PREFACE

In making this selection from our family papers my aim has been to give a full account of my grandfather's home, and to record the story of my mother's life.

So little is known, so little has ever been heard, of Thackeray's married life that it has been decided to publish some of those letters which reveal how greatly he was devoted to his wife, and the magnitude of the tragedy that deprived him and his children of her companionship and help. Here my grandfather is seen from an entirely fresh point of view, and we find, too, much information concerning his own and his children's daily life, his work, his outlook on the world, and his inner thoughts. A few passages in which my grandfather alludes to his books, as well as the Christmas sermon, and the description of his breakdown in the Manchester lecture, were quoted by my mother in her Biographical Introductions. A word should be said about the copying of his letters. It has seemed of importance to transcribe them exactly as they were written with their amusing and unexpected spelling, contracted words, and peculiar punctuation. His letters to Mrs. Frederick Elliot and Miss Perry were given to me for publication by Mr. Arthur Elliot: I also thank my mother's other friends for all their help.

Of my mother's letters to her father unfortunately only the two printed in this collection have been preserved. In these, and in her early journal which gives such a vivid picture of Thackeray in his own home, we see her power of description and mastery over words, but not the depth of sympathy, the clear and wide vision, which are afterwards so striking. It was always a keen pleasure and rest to her to take up her pen and write to her friends. She did not require solitude, but she enjoyed writing surrounded by "eager life"—its noise and clatter. She gives no hint in her correspondence of the constant ill-health from which she suffered and how she

> . . . ever with a frolic welcome took
> The thunder and the sunshine.

To the last my mother was working for others, her mind remaining alert and brilliant. She writes: "Who says 'Youth's a stuff will not endure'? It lasts as long as we do, and is older than age. For those moments of eager life of seeing and being come back to us, and we babble of green fields and live among them to the very end."

HESTER THACKERAY RITCHIE.

Freshwater,
January 9th, 1924.

PRINCIPAL DATES IN THE LIFE OF ANNE THACKERAY RITCHIE

1837. Born June 9th, at 18, Albion Street, Hyde Park.

1840. She was sent to Paris with her infant sister Minny, to be brought up by her grandparents.

1849. She and her sister returned to live with their father at 13, Young Street, Kensington.

1852. October 13th. Thackeray's first visit to America. His children stayed at Paris with their grandparents during his six months' absence.

1855. October 8th. Thackeray's second visit to America. His children again went to their grandparents in Paris.

1862. She published her first book, *The Story of Elizabeth*.[1]

1863. December 24th. The death of Thackeray.

1867. June 10th. The marriage of her sister Minny to Leslie Stephen.

1875. November 26th. The death of Minny Stephen.

1877. August 2nd. Her marriage to her second cousin, Richmond Ritchie (third son of William Ritchie, Legal Member of the Council of the Governor-General of India), by whom she had one son and one daughter.

1903. She was elected a Fellow of the Royal Society of Literature.

1906. August 8th. The marriage of her son to Margaret, second daughter of the Right Honourable Charles Booth, D.C.L., D.Sc., F.R.S.

1912-13. President of the English Association.

1912. October 12th. The death of her husband.

1919. February 26th. Her death at The Porch, Freshwater, Isle of Wight.

1919. March 4th. Her burial in the churchyard of Hampstead Parish Church.

[1] For chronological list of books see Appendix.

THACKERAY *and his* DAUGHTER

I

1837—1840

ANNE ISABELLA, the eldest child of William Makepeace Thackeray, was born on June 9th, 1837, the year Queen Victoria came to the throne. She was christened Anne Isabella after her two grandmothers. Her godmother was Mrs. Sterling, wife of the *Times* "Thunderer" and mother of John Sterling.

One of the earliest recollections of her childhood, she would say, was the gift of a pair of red shoes from her godmother. She was then two years old; she has told me of the rapture she felt, and how she sat upon the floor and gazed at her shoes in speechless delight. Another remembrance she would describe was the joy of being drawn along the streets in a little wooden go-cart by "Old John," an ancient family retainer who had followed her father from Devonshire to Great Coram Street.

Of her father and mother in these early days Anne Ritchie has written: "Almost the first time I can remember my parents was at home in Great Coram Street on one occasion, when my mother took me upon her back, as she had a way of doing, and after hesitating for a moment at the door, carried me into a ground floor room, where some one sat bending over a desk.

"This some one lifted up his head, and looked round at the people leaning over his chair. He seemed pleased, smiled at us, but remonstrated.

"Another impression remains to me of some place near Russell Square, of a fine morning, of music sounding, of escaping from my nurse and finding myself dancing in the street to the organ with some other children.

"Some one walking by came and lifted me up bodily on to his shoulder, and carried me away from the charming dance to my home, which was close by. As we went along, this stranger as usual became my father whom I had not recognised at first.

"Then I can remember standing at his knee asking him to tell me the name of my doll, and my father said: 'This is Miss Polly Perkins, I think.'

"I had a fine time of it. My mother used to give me chocolates, and play prettier dance tunes even than the organs outside. I was but little over two years old. I liked the world at that age. The house seemed to me a splendid house upstairs and downstairs and there were organs constantly playing outside." [1]

William Makepeace Thackeray was twenty-five years of age and his wife twenty at the time of their marriage. He would sometimes tell his children that he lost his heart to their mother when he heard her sing. A lovely voice and perfection of technique distinguished her as a musician. She was Isabella Gethin Creagh Shawe, a daughter of Colonel Matthew Shawe, C.B., of Doneraile, Co. Cork. The marriage took place at the British Embassy in Paris on August 20, 1836.

Isabella Thackeray's portrait drawn by her husband at this time hangs in my brother's home. It is a water-colour sketch delicately tinted. The whole picture is very harmonious and serene. She stands erect, a small slight figure, dressed in the flowing draperies of the day.

Knowledge of her character can be gained from her

[1] Biographical Introduction to *The Hoggarty Diamond.*

own letters. One is struck by her gaiety and quickness of understanding, her gift for friendship and the way in which all turned to her for advice, help and sympathy.

In a letter to Edward FitzGerald soon after his marriage, Thackeray says: "Dear Edward, do come and see me, it would do your heart good to see how happy I am."

And to his mother he writes: "DEAREST MOTHER,— Here is a short scrawl written at midnight, write to us plenty of long letters, though I repay them so badly, but they make me happy for the rest of the day. I am sure I love you better since I was married than before, perhaps it is because, being so happy, I am grown a little more *good*. God bless you dearest Mother. I am as well as possible and Isabella as well as can be expected.— W. M. T."

Thackeray's letters to his mother form almost a complete autobiography, so important a part did she play in his life and in the lives of his children.

Before her marriage, she was Anne Becher, a daughter of John Harman Becher, and was celebrated for her good looks. At sixteen she went out to India, became a "reigning beauty," and to quote my mother's words, "was destined to be married, to be a mother and a widow, and to be married again before a decade had gone by." [1] Her first husband, Richmond Thackeray, died at Calcutta in 1816; he was the father of her only child, William Makepeace Thackeray. In 1818 she married Major Henry Carmichael-Smyth of the Bengal Engineers. She lived to the age of seventy-two and died on the 18th of December, 1864. She was serious, fervent and deeply religious. She adored her son, but it was

[1] Biographical Introduction to *The Newcomes*.

always a sorrow to her that upon certain questions of religion they did not see alike.

Early in 1837 Thackeray and his wife left Paris and came to London. In June my mother was born at 18, Albion Street, Hyde Park, the home of the Carmichael-Smyths.

Soon after the birth of his daughter, Thackeray moved to 13, Great Coram Street, Brunswick Square, where he spent the next three years. The illness of his wife in 1840 brought the home to an abrupt and cruel end.

How happy a home it was the old letters in our possession still tell, and it is from these letters, chiefly written to Mrs. Carmichael-Smyth, that it is possible to reconstruct a little the story of these early days and learn something of my mother's childhood.

The first mention of "Anny" occurs in the following letter which bears the postmark of 1839. She was then two years old, but seems already to be a personage, and to have taken her place in the world.

Isabella Thackeray to Mrs. Carmichael-Smyth

13, Great Coram Street
[1839].

Upstairs I can hear Anny playing with the squirrel and her "brooms to sell." She has very little childishness about her, not that she is beyond her years, but there seems a kind of reasonableness in all she does. Her love of pictures is very great and she can distinguish the forms of things ever so minute. I have been trying to teach her the names of colours but everything is either red or white. She knows not only the names of animals but the noise they make, so that when William called her a little donkey to-day, she immediately began to hee-haw hee-haw!

Isabella Thackeray to her sister Jane Shawe

[1839].

Where do you think William, William Ritchie, and Charles and Arthur Buller and half-a-dozen others went to the other day? Do not scream—to a boxing match! and I had only ordered a leg of mutton for dinner, and in they all poured at six o'clock, not the boxers but the gentlemen. "I gave them no encouragement, my dear," said William, "but they would come," at which there was a hearty laugh as if they thought it a very good joke. Nothing suffered but the leg of mutton. I could not help thinking William and Arthur had been engaging in pugilistic exercises themselves, they ate like famished wolves. . . . I wish you would give me a list of airs in *La Sonnambula,* I sang that one that everyone admires so much, *"Ah non giunge uman pensiere."* I only like Bellini's solemn and plaintive music. Do you sing *"Come per me sereno"* and *"Ah! non credea"*?

Now what will you give me in return for this long letter? Another. In the meantime love to you and both our loves to Mama. William works hard all day.

In 1839 a second daughter was born, who died in infancy. She left a tender and lasting memory. I have been told that my grandfather could never speak of her without emotion, and that his eyes would fill with tears.

W. M. Thackeray to Mrs. Carmichael-Smyth

[1839].

MY DEAREST MOTHER,—Isabella will tell you how we have been gadding to Gravesend, and how dear little Pussy enjoyed the trip; it was delightful and the wind and the sunshine have made me pleasantly tipsy as it were; for I am not used to them in London which generates sluggishness of body and often mind too—I wish I could afford more frequent trips, one to Paris above all for profit as well as for pleasure, but it is not improbable that something may turn up to keep me in London for the whole of the Summer at least within reach of it.

What shall I say to you about our little darling who is gone?—I don't feel sorrow for her, and think of her only as something charming that for a season we were allowed to enjoy: When Anny was very ill, dying as I almost thought, it seemed to me wrong to pray for her life, for specific requests to God are impertinences I think, and all we should ask from him is to learn how to acquiesce and now I would be almost sorry—no that is not true—but I would not ask to have the child back again and subject her to the degradation of life and pain. O God watch over us too, and as we may think that Your Great Heart yearns towards the innocent charms of these little infants, let us try and think that it will have tenderness for us likewise who have been innocent once, and have, in the midst of corruption, some remembrances of good still. Sometimes I fancy that at the judgement-time the little one would come out and put away the sword of the angry angel. I think her love for us and her beautiful purity would melt the Devil himself—nonsense you know what I mean. We have sent to Heaven a little angel who came from us and loved us, and God will understand her language and visit us mildly —why write you this mad stuff, dearest Mother? God bless you and all besides. I shall write G. M.:[1] and thank her for her money and use it too.

Your afft.

W. M. T.

[1] G. M. = Grandmama.

W. M. Thackeray to Mrs. Carmichael-Smyth

Sunday, Monday, December 1, 2, [1839].

MY DEAREST MAMMY,—Isabella seems to have written an enormous letter to Mary,[1] and I suppose in all those pages and crosses has given you the whole news from Great Coram Street which amounts exactly to O. We have had a succession of pleasant yellow fogs: one to-day so bad that one can hardly see. We have led a tolerably sober and regular life, always up before nine, breakfast over by ten, books, books, books all day until night when to my great consolation FitzGerald has been here to smoke a segar and keep me company until one or so.

Well, what else is there? Mrs. Brody[2] has gone to visit her relations at Wapping—from six o'clock until 10 last night Miss Thackeray roared incessantly, which would have done your heart good to hear. I don't know what it was that appeased her, but at the expiration of these four hours the yowling stopped, and Miss began to prattle as quietly and gaily as if nothing had happened. What are the mysteries of children? How are they moved, I wonder? I have made Anny lots of pictures, and really am growing quite a domestic character.

The little child is perpetually prattling about you all, and walks in the "Shondileasy" with "Granny and Aunty and Polie" just as if she were in France instead of here. There's a great power of imagination about these little creatures, and a creative fancy and belief that is very curious to watch; it fades away in the light of common day: I am sure that horrid matter-of-fact child-rearers, Miss Edgeworth and the like, with their twopenny-half-penny realities, do away with the child's most beautiful privilege. I am determined that Anny shall have a very

[1] Mary Graham, a niece of Mrs. Carmichael-Smyth's.
[2] Anny's nurse.

extensive and instructive store of learning in Tom
Thumbs, Jack-the-Giant-Killers, etc. What use is there
in the paltry store of small facts that are stowed into
these poor little creatures' brains?

I have just turned off a thundering article against
Bulwer, and yesterday had the misfortune to read the
Comic Almanack—anything worse or more paltry cannot
well be imagined—it is as bad, very nearly, as the prints
which illustrate it; and these are odious. Cruickshank I
suppose is tired of the thing and bends all his energies to
the illustrations of Jack Sheppard—I have not read this
latter romance but one or two extracts are good; it is
acted at *four* theatres, and they say that at the Cobourg,
people are waiting about the lobbies, selling *sheppard-
bags*—a bag containing a few pick-locks that is, a screw-
driver, and iron levers: one or two young gentlemen have
already confessed how much they were indebted to Jack
Sheppard, who gave them ideas of pocket-picking and
thieving which they never would have had but for the
play.

Since writing the above I have been out to take what
they call fresh air here: and am come home half-choked
with the fog: the darkness visible of Great Coram Street
was the most ghastly thing I have seen for a long time.
O for smiling Paris and sunshine! If I can make some
decent engagement with a bookseller, I will pack off my
traps, let the house again, and come somewhere at a
decent distance from my dear old Mother. I have been
reading a power of old newspapers and reviews concerning Napoleon, and very curious the abuse is of that
character. Old Southey is one of the chief mudflingers,
and it is good to read the *Quarterly Review* that settles
he was "no gentleman."

I wish you could get Carlyle's *Miscellaneous Criticism,*

now just published in America. I have read a little in the book, a nobler one does not live in our language I am sure, and one that will have such an effect on our ways and thought and prejudices. Criticism has been a party matter with us till now, and literature a poor political Lackey—please God we shall begin ere long to love art for Art's sake. It is Carlyle who has worked more than any other to give it its independence.

Here are three pages of nothing as I promised. We propose to get up at eight to-morrow and are at this very minute in the act of going to bed. God bless my dearest Mother. Anny particularly told me to send her love and had proposed to write too. Love to all.

W. M. T.

Isabella Thackeray to Mrs. Carmichael-Smyth

13, Great Coram Street
Dec. 1st, 1839.

. . . Arthur Buller has been here since Saturday, which I am glad of on William's account, he romps with Anny like a second baby of two. You may suppose she is in high glee and exclaimed "Such a funny gemplem Papa." They figure away at cachuchas and mazurkas, she singing "Look how puty I dance!" and it is with great difficulty I can get her to bed. She talks a great deal about dear Granny and all at Paris. She has excellent reasoning faculties which *you* will believe though others might laugh.

To-day is a nice wholesome day with sunshine, and Anny and I are going to pay visits. Did William tell you how she was invited to a party at the Kembles' on Christmas day? She was such a little Queen. She was made much of by everybody, she danced and sang what she called her "totch song"—"Charley Charley."

Isabella Thackeray to Mrs. Carmichael-Smyth

[1839].

. . . I need not tell you Anny wins everybody's heart. Mrs. John Kemble begged me to bring her to visit Miss Gertrude, who was very jealous of Anny and at last gave her two hard smacks on the head, to which looking greatly astonished she merely said "Why you spoil my pretty bonnet." Mrs. Kemble then taking her daughter behind the door did what she was correcting the child for doing, and Anny in the generosity of her heart forgetting her head, rushed after her saying, "Don't hurt poor lickle girl." You see as I have little space I fill it with what chiefly concerns ourselves.

Anny dictates the following letter to you: "I have a number of play-toys and have pleasure, pleasure's happy. I send Granny my loves, my loving loves."

Isabella Thackeray to Mrs. Carmichael-Smyth

April 20 [1840].

Here is Miss Anny—"Say I am very fond of writing. I have a great many play-toys and I send my love to Granny and say I have been to the Zoololigan gardens to-morrow." Did William tell you how she declared the rhinoceros's skin was tied on and that it was not smooth like her own?

William is full of his Dionysius. I want him to run no risks and be content with half profits, for it has yet to be proved that there will be profits. He says I am a *coward* but I think we are properly balanced. The engravers spoilt his designs in the most cruel manner. They are something in the style of M. Vieuxbois, and he proposes bringing twelve out for sixpence. I do not like to send you any until they are properly got up. It is a kind of pastime for William, for you know it gives him no trouble to sketch.

I am sure you are longing to hear more about Anny. We have been reading out loud, and you know how she will listen to the same story over and over and over again. Her great delight is to hear the History of Dame Hubbard and her dog, amplified by long conversations between the two which have to be invented. William was drawing little Red Riding Hood, but he was obliged to substitute a dog for the wolf, for Anny got very angry at the notion of wolf eating up the grandmother with which true version Mrs. Dowling who was here would annoy her.

She now salutes her father with "What a funny fellow you are Papa!" She is delighted to be employed in carrying messages and knows every letter in the alphabet except E and F.

W. M. Thackeray to Mrs. Carmichael-Smyth

The Reform Club
April 30 [1840].

MY DEAREST MAMMY,—Look at the stamp on my writing-paper and you will see to what a pitch of enjoyment I have been elevated. I came down here solely to have the pleasure of dating my letter from Whitehall, and of knowing the day of the month, which is before me on a great card that these luxurious reformers alter with the day. Anny and I began a letter to you yesterday, hers was "Granny, Here is a letter. I wish my love some day to her. I been Zoologilan Gardens, see eflums and camelo leopards and monkeys and ostriches and everything." This is all Miss Thackeray's letter. She is very well this bright weather as is her Mamma, who will want consolation earlier than June, as I fancy. Why won't my dearest Mammy come over for a month or so? She would be a great comfort to us, and who knows but we might at the end of the time take her back to Boulogne, and there pass a summer month or two? Lettsom told me that you thought of coming, and surely it is wrong not to come from the mere dread of parting. A wise old lady of forty-seven ought to be more philosophical.

My book [1] has not got on much since I wrote last nor indeed I have done much, but I am in a ceaseless whirl and whizz from morning to night, now with the book, now with the drawings, now with articles for the *Times,* Frazer, here and there, and though its such a long time since I did write, indeed and indeed I have nothing to say, the days pass away to me like half hours, or rather like no time at all, clean forgotten as soon as spent; one being exactly like the other and passed in a kind of delirium.

I have just done a huge article on G. Cruikshank for the *L. and W.*[2] which I will send you when it appears. And furthermore am bringing out of my own account a weekly paper, the *Foolscap Library.*[3] I think it will take: and the profits of it are so enormous if successful that I don't like to share them with a bookseller: there is no reason why I should not make a big lump of money by it.

The new Boz [4] is dull but somehow gives one a very pleasant impression of the man: a noble tender hearted creature, who sympathizes with all the human race. You will see in the Cruikshank article, some remarks against myself: I fail by sneering too much: but I think

[1] *The Paris Sketch Book.*
[2] *London and Westminster Review.*
[3] On publication the name of *Foolscap Library* was changed to *The Whitey-Brown Paper Magazine.*
[4] *Master Humphrey's Clock* by Charles Dickens.

Anny as a child.
From a drawing by
W. M. T.

Foolscap will succeed, it begins with the adventures of Dionysius Diddler all in pictures like M. Vieuxbois, quite fabulous, but a good likeness of Lardner and Bulwer introduced.

John if you please has got a new coat and weskit, and is as deaf as a stone. I don't know that I shan't have to borrow from Father for *The Foolscap:*—the thing is a fortune but wants about £30 to start it: however I have some and shan't want yet. Why shouldn't I sell 5000, 10,000 copies?—they will pay me 40 or 80 a week: 80 a week is 4000 a year of which I would put by 3 at the very least per an: see Alnaschar in the *Arabian Nights*. And so God bless my dearest Mammy: and all at number 4: how bright it must look now. My dear old Paris!

W. M. T.

It was after an illness following upon the birth of a third daughter, Minny,[1] in May, 1840, that Isabella Thackeray's health failed. This made it necessary for Thackeray to break up his home and send his children to Paris to be with their grandparents. He himself remained with his wife. The devotion and tender love with which he nursed her, and the unfailing courage with which he faced misfortune, are revealed by his letters to Edward FitzGerald and Mrs. Procter, the friends to whom he turned in his trouble.

My mother writing of this time says: "One cure after another was prescribed, foreign baths and home treatment in turn, all of which my father saw carried out, but of course the expenses were very great. So was the anxiety and the difficulty of earning an income to meet it all." [2]

[1] Mrs. Leslie Stephen.
[2] Biographical Introduction to *Barry Lyndon*.

Long after, speaking of these days to his children, their father told them that one day he was at his desk writing when the servant came and asked him for some money, and he changed the last five pounds he had to give.

Isabella Thackeray never sufficiently recovered from her illness to return to normal activities, and eventually it was found advisable for her health that she should lead a life away from home. Her husband until his death, and then her children, saw and corresponded with her constantly up to the very end.

She lived with two devoted friends, first at Epsom and then at Leigh, Essex, where she died on the 11th of January, 1894, aged seventy-six.

In a letter written in 1852 to his friend W. F. Synge, Thackeray wrote: "Though my marriage was a wreck I would do it over again, for behold love is the crown and completion of all earthly good."

II

1840—1846

IN an introduction to *Barry Lyndon* my mother writes of the time which followed my grandmother's illness, and says:—"My baby sister and I were deposited with our great-grandmother, Mrs. Butler, who certainly thought us inconveniently young. But we had a friend; a faithful and loving-hearted Scotch nurse called Jessie Brodie, who, rather than quit my father in his troubles at that time, broke off her own marriage, so she told me, shyly, long years after. She helped my father to nurse my mother at first, then he left her in charge of the nursery."

After staying with Mrs. Butler for some time the children went to Mrs. Carmichael-Smyth, with whom they spent the next six years. The Carmichael-Smyths lived in an apartment in the Rue d'Angoulême, a cheerful little street turning off the Champs Elysées.

During these years Thackeray's headquarters were in London, but he was constantly moving and travelling from place to place. Wherever he happened to be, he never failed to write to his children.

W. M. Thackeray to Anny aged 3[1]

[1840].

I have nothing to send my dearest Anny but a little picture:—The picture is of some little girls I saw going to church, and one of them I thought was like Anny.

[1] This letter is printed out in big type.

15

Well, this is all I have to say: for there is no time, because the person is waiting who is going to take this. God bless the little girl to whom he is going to take it,

I have nothing to send my dearest Anny but a little picture. — the picture is of some little girls I saw going to church, & one of them I thought was like Anny.

Well, this is all I have to say. for there is no time, because the person is waiting who is going to take this. God bless the little girl to whom he is going to take it, & her little sister. Do you know their names and that their Papa loves them?

and her little sister. Do you know their names and that their Papa loves them?

W. M. Thackeray to Anny aged 4

[1841].

Though I have not written to my dearest Nanny, since I came away, I think about her many times; and pray God for her and Baby and to make them both well and good. You will be well I hope in the spring when we will take a house by the seaside, and you can go into the fields and pick flowers, as you used to do at Margate: before Mamma was ill, and when Baby was only a little child in arms. Please God, Mamma will be made well one day too. How glad I shall be to see all my darlings well again: and there is somebody else who wants to see them again too, and that is Brodie who longs to come back to them.

I have been to see your God-mamma who gave you the red shoes but she is very very ill.

The other night as I was coming home I met in the street two little girls, and what do you think they were doing? Although one was no bigger than you, and the other not so big as Baby, they were singing little songs in the street, in hopes that someone would give them money: they said their mother was at home—that is the elder one said so, (the younger one was so little that she could not speak plain, only sing) their mother was ill at home, with three more children and they had no bread to eat!

So I thought of my two dear little girls, and how comfortable they were, and how their Granny gave them good meals, and their Grand-mamma a nice house to live in; and I brought the little girls to Mr. Hill, the baker in Coram Street, and gave them a loaf and some money, and hope soon to give them some more. And this is all I have to say except God bless my dearest Nanny and that I always say.   PAPA.

I am just come home and have your letter and thank my dear little girl for her good news.

W. M. Thackeray to Anny aged 7

27, Jermyn Street
June 11, [1844].

MY DEAREST NANNY,—Thank you all for your little letters. I am always made glad by the sight of them; and by hearing from Granny that you are well and good. I shall come and see you very soon, and you must tell me

in your next letter if you and Baby want anything that I
can bring.　Mamma I hope will soon come and live with
me in England, at a very pretty village called Twickenham which is by the river Thames.　There are beautiful
walks there, meadows and trees and handsome houses
in parks and gardens.　How I should like to walk there
with my dearest little girls.　God bless them prays Papa.

W. M. Thackeray to Anny aged 8

December 30, [1845].

MY DEAREST NANNY,—Your letter has made me and
Mamma very happy and very sad too, that we are away
from our dearest little girls.　But I for one shall see you
before very long, I hope in a week from this day, and
only write now to wish you a happy New Year.　On
Christmas day I dined with Mamma and she was very
well and happy, only she grew very grave when she
talked about you; and there were tears in her eyes the
meaning of which I knew quite well.

How glad I am that it is a black puss and not a black
nuss you have got!　I thought you did not know how to
spell it en-you-double-ess.　But I see the spelling gets
better as the letters grow longer, they cannot be too long
for me.

Laura [1] must be a very good natured girl—I hope my
dear Nanny is so too—not merely to her schoolmistress
and friends but to everybody:—to her servants and her
nurses.　I would sooner have you gentle and humble-
minded than ever so clever.　Who was born on Christmas
day?　Somebody who was so great that all the world
worships Him; and so good that all the world loves
Him; and so gentle and humble that He never spoke
an unkind word.　But I hope my Nanny is proud with no

[1] Laura Collemache, a play-fellow and life-long friend.

one. And there is a little sermon—and a great deal of love and affection from Papa. May God send my dearest children many happy New Years. I wonder who will kiss Minny for me? [1]

THACKERAY'S CHILDREN ON A DONKEY
Drawn by Thackeray

W. M. Thackeray to Mrs. Carmichael-Smyth

1st January [1846].

MY DEAREST MAMMY,—I had intended to set off for a week's pleasuring with you to-day and have come in upon the New Year's day dinner: but I was a day behind-hand in my work, and as I see there is no chance of being with you, shall wait till Saturday and cross by a Brighton or Southampton boat. It is blowing a tempest here to-

[1] This letter was printed in the Biographical Introduction to *Contributions to Punch.* Vol. 1.

day too and I'm not sorry for the three days' delay. My dearest Nanny's letter set me longing so to see you all that I must come, though it's not worth the while— though the pain of parting is much greater than the pleasure of meeting—at least to my ill-regulated mind.

Tell my dear little Nanny, I have got some books for her and some pictures for Minny. My heart is with them all day and with my dearest old Mother.

In one of Anny's letters she wrote, we have got a black *Nuss* not puss I thought it was a natural yellow-plushism —and was in truth very much disgusted at the idea of the nigger bonne. God bless all: and give you and me and dear old G. P.[1] a happy New Year.[2]

[1] G. P. (for grand papa) was the name by which Major Carmichael-Smyth was known in the family.

[2] In another letter to his mother Thackeray writes: "I had a letter from Anny the other day. 'Papa' she says, 'I am very unhappy and don't know Y.' She's the true daughter of Mr. Yellowplush isn't she?"

III

1846—1852

IT was in the autumn of 1846 that my mother and her sister came back to live with their father. He had given up his rooms in St. James's Street and had taken 13, Young Street, Kensington Square, a pleasant old-fashioned bow-windowed house.

"Once more after his first happy married years," my mother writes, "William Thackeray had a home and a family, if a house, two young children and a little black cat can be called a family."

In the following letter we find a description of the new house.

W. M. Thackeray to Mrs. Carmichael-Smyth

13, Young Street, Kensington
July 1 [1846].

MY DEAREST MAMMY,—G. P. writes me a word that you are unwell and that a change of air wd. do you good; what such a good change as to come here with the little ones? and I hope & pray in God that we shall be able to live together and that I may not be deprived of my Mother & my children. There are 2 capital bed-rooms & a little sitting room for you & G. P.—a famous bedroom for G. M. on the first floor—2 rooms for the children on second, very airy and comfortable; a couple of rooms big enough for servants, & 2 little ones quite large enough for me—There's a good study down-stairs & a

21

dining room & drawing room, and a little court yard
& garden and a little green house; and Kensington Gardens at the gate, and omnibuses every 2 minutes. What
can mortal want more?   If I ask my friends I can ask
them to my own quarters.   We may all be independent
and together.   At all events I ask it as a favour that the
experiment should be tried: and am sure that we shall all
be the happier & better for it.   I'm not ready for you
yet: but hope in a fortnight's time to be prepared—I
have been opening the trunks to-day full of the lumbering
useless old books: and woeful relics of old days.

God bless my dearest little women.   It will be a
comfort to me to see them, and I look to Kensington
Gardens & to breakfasting together; and to many a happy
day please God.   Their Mother is so well and calm; that
when they are of an age sufft. she will be quite able to
come back to us—and I can't be sufficiently thankful for
that famous old Mrs. Bakewell's admirable care of her.
Gloyne too has been as good as can be.

I find the greatest comfort and enjoyment in the quiet
of this place after the racket of St. James's street.   I am
going to quit the *Chronicle* very likely, but if I do it
will be for something better.

God bless my dearest Mother,

W. M. T.

W. M. Thackeray to his sister-in-law Jane Shawe

[1846].

What shall I tell you about my dear little girls?   I
see as little of them as you do almost.   I have just taken
a house big enough for the whole family: but I cannot
get Major Smyth to come to England, and so I lose my
Mother and my children too for some time at least.   It
would break her heart to part with them: and I can't

bear that she should be alone and separated from us all. Here is the last report just come from Paris about Anny. "I assure you Nanny wants a firmer hand than mine. She fights every inch of her way—if it's only to wash her face or put on her stockings, she will not do it without an argument—She is so clever: so selfish: so generous: so tender-hearted yet so careless of giving pain." I am afraid very much she is going to be a man of genius: I would far sooner have had her an amiable and affectionate woman. But little Minny will be that, please God,— and the sisters love each other admirably. As for me I am child-sick, and when I see in Kensington Gardens & in my friend's houses a pair of little girls at all resembling my own, become quite maudlin over them.

In my trade I am getting on very well: and doing everything but saving money. Goodbye my dear Jane, and remember I am always as in old times

Affectionately yours,
W. M. THACKERAY.

Notes on Family History
(Written by my Mother in 1894)

We came to Young Street when I was nine and Minny was six. Papa was not at home when we arrived, but early next morning when we were half dressed and the maid was tying our strings, he tapped at the door and came and took us in his arms.

Everything seemed so strangely delightful. The volumes of *Punch* on the drawing-room table, the delightful keepsake books in their red covers, the old schoolroom with the book case and the cupboards, and Papa's room with the vine round about the windows, and the sun pouring in.

Papa called Minny Min, and me Nan very often, and

when we were little he used to call Minny Finniken
and me Buff, and sometimes Frederica and Louisa.

He called Pussy Louisa and gave her his fish at breakfast, and took her up very gently and put her outside the
door when she would not leave him alone.

When Papa was a tall young man with black hair and
an eye glass, I can remember how we used to hold his
forefinger when we walked out with him. He always
talked to us very gravely as if we were grown women.
Later on, when we grew up, he spoke to us as if we were
children and would say, "Come along, my little dears."

Papa used to talk to us a great deal, and tell us about
the Bible and Religion. He would talk to us of a morning after breakfast in his study, and of an evening after
dinner smoking his cigar, and we generally sat on the floor
and listened to him. And then we would give him a
chair for his legs and a little table for his candles, and he
would presently nod to us and go to sleep.

Papa could not bear the story of Abraham. He used
to say that one day when I was a little girl, he came in
and found Mamma telling me in her sweet voice about
Isaac, and that I burst into tears, and stamped and flew
into a passion. I can remember it quite well too, and
Papa taking me on his knee and Mamma looking a little
shocked.

One night Papa told us he was lying in the dark with
one hand outside the bed pointing up in the air. And
he thought to himself, "Now what would happen, I wonder, if the Devil were to come with a pair of nippers
and take hold of my finger?" So then he put his hand
under the bedclothes again, but he suddenly remembered
that he was not safe, for the Devil might still come with

a pair of nippers, and take hold of his nose. We asked Papa if he put his nose under the bedclothes. He laughed and said, "No, not his nose."

When I was a little girl I was dreadfully frightened by a story he told me, of a man whose nose had been broken for years, and one day when he was blowing it, it came off in his hand. Then Papa waved his hand. I felt a little thrill of horror and thought Papa's was coming off.

W. M. Thackeray to Mrs. Carmichael-Smyth

Friday, *Decr.* 4 [1846].

MY DEAREST MAMMY,—Now the children are with me I am getting so fond of them that I can understand the pang of the dear old Mother who loses them: and who by instinct is 100 times fonder of them than ever a man could be. But it is best that they should be away from you:—at least that they should be away either from you or me. There can't be two first principles in a house. We should secretly be jealous of one another: or I should resign the parental place altogether to you, and be a bachelor still. Whereas now God Almighty grant I may be a father to my children. Continued thoughts of them chase I don't know how many wickednesses out of my mind: their society makes many of my old amusements seem trivial and shameful. What bounties are there of Providence in the very instincts wh. God gives us. To talk about such things though is wrong I think and engenders pride. Best think about them and be humble.

Only I write so far to give my dearest old Mother a consolation in her bereavement. Remember the children are in their natural place: with their nearest friend working their natural influence: getting and giving the good, let us hope, wh. the Divine Benevolence appointed to result from the union between parents & children. May I hold fast by it I pray to God our Father.

And how thankful this makes me to you & my dear old G. P. who have kept the children for me, and watched them so nobly and tenderly—kind and affectionate hearts —dear & affectionate friends, for this I thank and bless you as the father of my children.

Goodbye dearest old Mother—Venables is coming to dine on Tuesday—my old schoolfellow who spoiled my profile.[1] Should you like to come?   W. M. T.

Major Carmichael-Smyth to Mrs. Carmichael-Smyth (who was staying at 13, *Young Street)*

Paris
April [1847].

Annie is now of an age when she can receive a great deal of useful information with much advantage, and she has a mind thirsting for knowledge. William should have a very respectable female to look after the children when he cannot be with them, and he should also devote as much time as he can spare to their instruction.

I had just written so far when I received a letter from Mrs. Collemache, and she tells me Bess [2] is preparing to go to England, and will probably be with you before the end of this month. So we may consider this matter as settled for the present.

Give the children many kisses from their old Grand-

---

[1] *Notes and Queries,* August 5, 1911, contains an account of the fight at Charterhouse in which W. M. T.'s nose was broken. Mr. Roupell, who had been his fag-master, writes: "It was a wet half-holiday, when a boy named Gossip asked leave for Thackeray and Venables to fight. We wanted some amusement, so I let them fight it out in Penny's room, with the important result to Thackeray's nasal organ. Thackeray bled so profusely as to stop the fight, but he and Venables remained friends for life."

[2] A protegée of Mrs. Carmichael-Smyth's, who was engaged as governess to the children.

Thackeray and his daughter
Anny.   Drawn by himself

papa, who will often regret the loss of their merry faces. God bless you, dearest, and with kind love to William.

I am ever your most affectionate
HENRY CARMICHAEL-SMYTH.

W. M. Thackeray to Mrs. Carmichael-Smyth

The Reform Club
[1847].

MY DEAREST MAMMY,—A line just to wish you—though I know it's a humbug—a merry Xmas. Next year please God, you shall have such a one really, and your old eyes will be gladdened by the sight of the children. They are meanwhile doing the greatest good to their father. That must be the poor dear old Mother's only consolation.

My prospects are very much improved and *Vanity Fair* may make me. The thought thereof makes me very humble and frightened—not elated.

Bess is great in the household affairs and the best & briskest of all managers. She manages the children admirably: she gives me too good dinners, that is her only fault.

Mrs. Perkins is a great success—the greatest I have had—very nearly as great as Dickens, that is Perkins *500*, Dickens *25000*, only that difference! but we are selling out our edition very fast, near 1500 are gone out of 2000 already—and this is a great success for the likes of me.

God bless you my dearest old Mother & G. P. When you get this Anny and her old dunce of a father will be at church praying heartily for us all.   W. M. T.

To Mr. Alan Cole I am indebted for the following letter from my mother, written at the age of eleven. Echoes of the revolution of 1848 had evidently reached

the Young Street nursery, and a society was formed by
Anny and her playfellows with no less an object than the
"stoppation of starvation all the world over."

Anny Thackeray to her friend Letitia Cole, aged ten

MADAM,—After having duly considered the subject
to-day proposed by you, to me, I feel it my duty to bring
before the Honble board of Juveniles, a few of the pro's
and cons, towards my accepting of that important office
of secretary. 1st, Mrs. Carmichael-Smyth, having been
informed of the favor to-day conferred upon me, started
an objection, which though *I* am perfectly sure of its
voidness, yet I cannot in any sincerity refrain from men-
tioning it, namely that she was not quite sure whether
my honoured father would entirely approve of my writing begging letters to my friends, and though I (vainly)
represented to her that it was not I who wrote, but the
Society, she replied that she thought I had better write
and ask my father whom I suppose you are aware is at
present at Paris.

Of course I shall be most happy to accept the secretary-
ship (if I can get it) but as to asking for subscriptions
I would feel most deeply grateful to the board if they
would allow me the time for an answer from my Papa.

If I were you I'd post a prospectus to the Prince of
Wales, he might send us 50£ and as his father is the
patron of the great one, why should he not be the patron
of the little one?

In the prospectus of our Society I would propose
something of this kind—The uses of this Commity are
many. They firstly not only further the commerce of
England herself but of all the world's children; think of
this and be proud and happy to send in your little sub-

scription, and by stoppation of starvati ɔn—save millions of people from death, deliver countries from bloody wars excited by starving populaces etc.

My grandmother says I must not write any longer so, Madam

Your obdt. servant
A. THANAKINS TITMARSH.

W. M. Thackeray to his sister-in-law Jane Shawe

Kensington
19 *September* [1848].

I write a line just to shake you by the hand and wish you a happy voyage to your brother. I ought to write and thank him too, for he wrote me the kindest letter about his nieces, and you will be able to give him a good report of them thank God. If ever I make a decent drawing of the little woman he shall have it; but I hope he will judge for himself in England before long, and to see him here, where those who have been good to my wife and children are always welcome.

Won't you write to us and tell us that you are well and happy? I hope you will do so, dear Jane, and after the grief of parting with your Mother for a little, enjoy a grand voyage and a sight of new countries and people. I wish I had the journey before me, and could see the place where I was born again.[1]

It is about this time eight years that the Jupiter came into Cork with our poor little woman on board. My dear, I can't forget how tenderly you always loved her: and look over often in my mind that gap of time since she has been dead to us all, and see that dear artless sweet creature who charmed us both so. What a whirl of life I've seen since then! but never her better I think. *"N'est-*

[1] Calcutta.

ce pas mourir tous les jours"—don't you recollect her singing and her sweet sweet voice? Her anxious little soul would have been alarmed at my prosperities such as they are. She was always afraid of people flattering me: and I get a deal of that sort of meat nowadays.

Here comes Anny with a pair of letters of which Minny's is the best: and Anny's by no means over-burthened with affection, but sincerity is the next best thing. The child has a very warm heart and wd. love you if she knew you. She says at the end of her letter "Give my love to Uncle Charles"—and I say so too. Give my love to him with all my heart. I wish him and you a good voyage. We have had a difference, I know how it began— but I hardly know what it is—and I remember that he and Mary were once very kindly and warmly disposed towards me, and helped me and mine at the time of our greatest need. So give him my love and Farewell dear Jane.

W. M. Thackeray to his brother-in-law Arthur Shawe

13, Young Street, Kensington
May 27 [1849].

This is your niece Harriet's (or Minny as we call her) birthday—and as she was seated at the window yonder just now I made a drawing of her, and bethought me that you and Jane would be glad to hear about the children. Minny is 9. Anny will be 12 on the 9 June— and is a great sensible clever girl, with a very homely face, and a very good heart and a very good head, and an uncommonly good opinion of herself, as such clever people will sometimes have. Minny is very well for cleverness too as children go: and both have a great deal of spoiling and fondness from my Mother, who supplies to them the place of their own—now nearly nine years removed from them. She is at Epsom very well. So you see there are pretty good accounts of all this family, including your brother-in-law the writer of the present: who is become quite a lion within the last 2 years, and is rather prosperous as times go. But though I am at the top of the tree in my business and making a good income now, near upon £2000 a year let us say—yet it is only within the last few months that I have got to this point: and was abominably hit by an unfortunate railway speculation of which I have still not discharged the obligation—so that I am in debt.

W. M. Thackeray to his daughter Anny

June [1850].

MY DEAREST NAN,—I am so busy with my work [1] and so tired of writing that I can only write you a line or two. I'm delighted that you are so happy and that you enjoy yourself & that your friends are so kind to you. The way to have friends is to like people yourself, you see: and I hope you will have and keep a plenty.

I have been at home 3 whole days think of that, not going out at least not until near 8 o'clock to dinner: so that my work is pretty well advanced and will be done by Sunday evg I trust. Then comes printing and proof correcting & so forth, and by Thursday I hope to see you young folk again and bring you back. I must dine with the Chief Baron on the 31st May. Or can Mrs. Fanshawe afford to keep you till Saturday? when I would come down and would take a small trip to the Isle of Wight or somewhere? Please Mrs. Fanshawe write me a word on this subject.

[1] *Pendennis.*

Miss Trulock[1] has had a good offer of £100 a year and I'm afraid must leave us—there will be the business to do over again, the same perplexities botherations uncertainties, why don't you get a little older and do without a governess? You will some day when you'll spell excursion with an S not a T.

Don't make doggrel verses and spell badly for fun. There should be a lurking prettiness in all buffoonery even, and it requires an art wh. you don't know yet to make *good* bad verses—to make bad ones is dull work.

And don't scribble faces at the bottom of your letters to ladies—they shouldn't be done unless they are clever— they are not respectful or ladylike, do you understand? I like you to make jokes to me because I can afford to tell you whether they are bad or good, or to scold you as now: but Mrs. Brookfield is too kind to do so: and when you write to her or to any other lady, you should write your very best. I don't mean, be affected and use fine words, but be careful, grateful and ladylike.

I did not dine till 9 o'clock last night and went to the Opera afterwards, but the ballet bored me and I came away pretty soon. I think that's all I know. And so God bless you and my dearest Minikin: and our friends who receive you so affectionately, & farewell.

W. M. T.

The following note was added to this letter by my mother in 1898:

"I never write an untidy letter but I think of this one. Alas! it has not yet made me into a tidy woman."

A. I. R.

[1] The children's governess, successor to "Bess."

W. M. Thackeray to his Daughters

[1850].

MY DEAREST ANNYMINNY,—As I have not written a single word this day, I think I may have a five minutes' talk to your ladyships. You went to St. Mary's Church [1] I suppose. I recollect it in the year 1817, when I was a miserable little beggar, at school at the Polygon, under an olivey little blackguard who used to starve and cane us. Times are changed since then, and you young women have not had much starving or scolding in the course of your easy lives.

Whilst you have been at church, I have at least been doing no manner of work: for I have been at Richmond all day, dawdling in the sun under a tree, or making sketches for the Miss Berrys [2] with my "goold" pen. The ease and tranquillity were very refreshing, after the hard work of the past 4 or 5 days.

I looked about to see if there were tempting looking lodgings anywhere about. But the prices are very heavy for good rooms, and if Miss Trulock is going away, what the deuce are we to do?—A plague upon such misadventures. As I think over matters just now, I shan't be able to go to the I of Wight with you, and I don't see why you shouldn't travel back as safely as you went. So you must please to write and say by what train you'll come away on Thursday, and the carriage and your Papa or else James [3] his Viceregent upon earth, shall be at Waterloo Station to meet you.

I am going out of town to-morrow evening to stay over Wednesday, & to return on Thursday—Shall I get a new Governess or shall I send you to School after the mid-

[1] Southampton.
[2] Horace Walpole's friends.
[3] Thackeray's servant.

Hélas, madame et cousine, Je suis engagé
a dîner à Newgate demain avec les Chérifs
de Londres — nous irons voir les prisonniers
les treadmills et les jolis petits condamnés
qu'on va pendre

Après je vais dans plusieurs soirées élégantes

(Surtout chez cette dame, Miladi Gordon, que votre mari aime tant) – Ainsi je ne serai de retour à Kensington qu'à minuit, bien trop tard pour venir frapper a votre petite porte si tranquille de votre Cottage si calme où tout ce grand et petit monde

sera couché..

Mess demoiselles sont guéries maintenant de leur chickenpock – Elles envoient mille salutations d'amitié à la colonie de

Litt' Olland Ouse.

Adieu Madame et chère Cousine
votre affectionné
Chevalier de Titmarsh.

summer holydays? I do believe the latter would be the
best plan—and then you'd learn something, as it is—
ballottées from one Governess to another, now at London
and next at Aix-la-Chapelle, your young days pass away
without any larning—and in fine I'm in a great puzzle
concerning you.

This is all I have to say I think. It ain't very amusing
or very wise is it? Give my love to your Mrs. Fanshawe
and a kiss to Totty: and remember young ladies that I'm
always your affectionate father.   W. M. T.

W. M. Thackeray to his cousin Mrs. Irvine

[1850].

Hélas, madame et cousine, je suis engagé à diner à
Newgate avec les chérifs de Londres—nous irons voir
les prisonniers les treadmills et les jolis petits condamnés
qu'on va pendre.

Après je vais dans plusieurs soirées élegantes (Surtout
chez cette dame, Miladi Gordon que votre mari aime
tant). Ainsi je ne serai de retour à Kensington qu'à
minuit, bien trop tard pour venir frapper à votre petite
porte si tranquille de votre Cottage si calme où tout ce
grand et petit monde sera couché.

Mes demoiselles sont guéries maintenant de leur
chicken pock. Elles envoient mille salutations d'amitié à
la colonie de Littl' Olland Ouse.

Adieu Madame et chère cousine,

Votre affectionné,

CHEVALIER DE TITMARSH.

W. M. Thackeray to his Daughters

Hotel de Suède, Brussels
Sunday, 15 *Sept.* [1850].

MY DEAREST YOUNG WOMEN—I am so far on my way
home and my journey has been but a dull one: only to

Homburg and back again where we stopped for 5 days
pretty pleasantly doing nothing, reading novels, making
sketches, seeing the people drink the waters and gamble
at the tables. I tried my luck once or twice, and I think
I won about 5 shillings altogether: but I'm glad I came as
it has given me what I wanted for my Xmas book.[1]
What I should have liked best wd. have been the society
of Miss Anny & Miss Minny—no of Minny some 2 years
later.

In 1852, when I'm back from America and you are
grown even bigger stronger & fatter than at present,
please God, we'll make a tour together, and admire the
beautiful works of Nature together. You may be very
thankful both of you for possessing that faculty, the world
is not ½ a world without it, and the more you indulge
this pleasure the better you are. O, I saw such grand
phenomena of sunrise at Cologne the other morning as
I looked out of my window upon the river! It's useless
to try and describe the scene in writing, but those magnificent spectacles of Nature are like personal kindnesses
from the Maker to us—and make one feel grateful.

I wandered about the town yesterday, wh. is smaller,
but handsomer and richer than Paris, looking for something to buy for you young ladies: but I could hit on
nothing that I thought wd. be useful or that you would
like very much, and I daresay I shall come back empty
handed.

On Thursday or Friday you may look out for me
I think—I shall try for the next 2 or 3 days to be quiet
here (my companion leaving me to-day) and to come
back with some of my month's work done—That's why
I'm writing very early in the morning, that I may go
breakfast quietly, and have a quiet day's work afterwards.

[1] *The Kickleburys on the Rhine.*

Meanwhile you two young ladies will go down on your knees at Church, & say your prayers for me—Won't you? and so good bye and God bless all.

W. M. T.

If you get this on Monday I should like an answer— It will be here on Tuesday afternoon: and I shan't go till Wednesday evg. or Thursday.

Notes on Family History
(Written by my Mother in 1864)

On Sunday mornings in Young Street we had no lessons, and we used to sit with my father in his study, and help him with his wood blocks, and it was often our business to rub out the failures and to wash the chalk off the blocks.

I can still remember a dreadful day when I washed away a finished drawing, for which the messenger from *Punch* was at that moment waiting in the hall.

Upstairs in the school-room at the top of the house we used to do our lessons of a week day, and sometimes to our joy we would be called downstairs by my father, and he would pose us as models for his drawings to *Punch* or *Vanity Fair*.

Then when I was fourteen my father first began to make use of me as his secretary and to dictate his books to me. That was in 1851, the year of the great Exhibition, and one wonderful and never-to-be-forgotten night my father took us to see some great ladies in their dresses going to the Queen's fancy-dress ball at Buckingham Palace. We drove to some big house (it is all very vague and dazzlingly indistinct in my mind). We were shown into a great empty room, and almost immediately some doors were flung open, there came a blaze of light, a burst of laughing voices, and from a many-twinkling

dinner-table rose a company that seemed, to our unac-
customed eyes, as if all the pictures in Hampton Court
had come to life. The chairs scraped back, the ladies
and gentlemen advanced together over the shining floors.

I can remember their high heels clicking on the floor;
they were in the dress of the court of King Charles II,
the ladies beautiful, dignified and excited. There was
one, lovely and animated in yellow; I remember her
pearls shining. Another seemed to us even more beautiful as she crossed the room, all dressed in black, but she,
I think, was not going to the ball; and then somebody
began to say Sir Edwin Landseer had promised to rouge
them, and then everybody to call out for him, and then
there was an outcry about his moustaches that "really
must be shaved off" for they were not in keeping with his
dress.

Then, as in a dream, we went off to some other great
house, Bath House perhaps, where one lady, more mag-
nificently dressed than all the others, was sitting in a
wax-lighted dressing-room, and just behind her chair
stood a smiling gentleman, also in court dress, whom my
father knew, and he held up something in one hand and
laughed, and said he must go back to the house from
whence he had come, and the lady thanked him and called
him Sir Edwin. We could not understand who this Sir
Edwin was, who seemed to be wherever we went, nor
why he should put on the rouge. Then a fairy thunder-
ing chariot carried off this splendid lady, and the nose-
gays of the hanging footmen seemed to scent the air as
the equipage drove off under the covered way. Perhaps
all this is only a dream, but I think it is true: for there
was again a third house where we found more pictures
alive, two beautiful young pictures and their mother, for
whom a parcel was brought in post-haste, containing a

jewel all dropping with pearls.   That evening was always
the nearest approach to a live fairy tale that we ever
lived; and the ball more brilliant than any we ever
beheld. [1]

W. M. Thackeray to Mrs. Carmichael-Smyth

March 15 [1852].

MY DEAREST MAMMY,—I was going to write on this
very little sheet of paper when your letter came in. M. de
Wailly is the very man of all France I would like to
translate [2] me, but is it possible he can give as much as
4,000 francs to me?—there must be some mistake I fear.
Nevertheless I empower you to act, and get what you
can for me.

I have given up and only had for a day or two the
notion of the book [3] in numbers. It's much too grave and
sad for that, and the incident not sufficient. You will
dislike it very much. It was written at a period of grief
and pain so severe that I don't like to think of it, and
am ashamed now to be well so soon and rid of my
melancholy.

The house in the Square has been long since given up.
It is delightfully comfortable, but would cost 500£ and
I should be no better off. About Sloane St. must be my
mark when I move.

I went and sate with poor old Miss Berry last night,
and amused her with a comic story which I was quite
astonished as I told myself as I don't generally perform
the wag or talk much.

Eyre Crowe is not Elliot's secretary, but mine for
the nonce, and Professor of drawing to the young ladies.

[1] This description was used by my mother in an article on Sir Edwin Landseer.
[2] The translation of *Esmond* into French.
[3] Esmond.

I can quite utilize him and like dictating to him: and Miss Holmes [1] has arrived and been here 3 days. There's something very natural and good in her. She seems to me to play very soberly and finely; she says Minny takes to learning the theory of music surprizingly, and that they both may play very well, and have been taught very well by Miss Trulock, who is mortified at the new professor,

A MUSIC LESSON
Drawn by Thackeray

but bears her mortification very kindly. She's a good woman. Poor Miss Holmes is not a lovely object to look upon with red hair and nose, the lady of Babylon is scarcely more scarlet. I have told her she must come and give her lesson, and be off without much talking, else she will be theologizing, but I shall be glad if the gals can be taught music by an *artist* who has the brains and heart as well as the fingers of her art. And so my little

[1] Music mistress.

page is full, and I am my dearest old Mother's & G. P.'s affte W. M. T.

When Mr. Gray goes to Paris you'll have the use of the bag again.

W. M. Thackeray to his daughter Minny

Brighting [1852].

MY DEAREST MINNIKIN,—Kensington is so gloomy without certain young ladies that I can't stand it. How dismal it must be for poor Eliza who has no friends to go to: who must stop in the kitchen all day—as I think of her I feel a mind to go back and sit in the kitchen with Eliza! but I daresay I shouldn't amuse her much, and after she had told me about the cat and how her father was, we should have nothing more to say to one another.

Last week I was away at Manchester, and I thought what a state my dear little women would have been in, when I broke down in a speech before 3000 ladies and gentlemen.—I felt very foolish, but I tried again at night and did better; and as there's nothing more wicked in breaking down in a speech than in slipping on a piece of orange peel and breaking one's nose, why I got up again—and made another speech at night without breaking down. It's all custom and most people can no more do it than they can play the piano without learning—I hope you and Anny are learning hard to play me to sleep, when I come back from America.

I believe I am going to Birmingham next week with the lectures, and then to Manchester & Liverpool, and then Steward: bring a basin. Well that will be over soon, and my dearest children back to me please God. Meanwhile young women you are in luck to have 2 homes, and to be happy in one while t'other is being painted and made more comfortable—for I shall be immensely more comfortable, when I have some money to leave you; and so will you too some day when you get it. I wish you may. Have you read—never mind: I won't go on with that sentence.

This place always makes me better you know, and I'm quite a different man to the individdiwidyouall who came down on Monday—and yesterday what do you think I goes to see?—another marriage, William Hankey Esqre. to Cecile Charlotte d'Estamper, daughter of etc.—Fanny was there looking very pretty and happy and she sent her love to you, and talked of both of you very kindly indeed—and seemed to be as pleased with her father's marriage as he was almost. Well I think I shall marry Tishy Cole if she will have me, and say: 'Tishia my daughters are so anxious for me not to be alone no more, that just to please them I appoint you Mrs. T."—then we will have the fly (the large one, not the brougham) from Ottways, and we will drive to the Starringarter at Richmond, and Tishy shall take the head, and you shall sit right and left of the table, and we will have whitebait and fiddledididdlidydiddledydie—there's enough of that.

Mrs. Yorke was so kind at Birmingham: almost everybody is: so was the Mayor of Manchester with whom I went to stay. It seems about a year ago: but it was only this day week: I spose the time that passes idly passes slowly, and I have not been able to settle anything since I came back, and I can't go out of the reach of London till my novel [1] is through the press. I like it better in print than in writing, and hope the public will like it too.

I think the Fanshawes are very likely coming to Kensington in my absence. Mr. F. is ill again, and London air does good to his *hashma.* I had written a long

---

[1] *Esmond.*

letter to Anny but it is in my pocket, and I don't think
I shall send it. And O I forgot! there's one from the
Thackerays on my table at home—And Major Bob is
here and what do you think? He has written a pam-
phlet and sent it to the president who has acknowledged
it very kindly, there's news! And so God bless and keep
you my darlings & God bless Granny & G. P. says you
don't know who. I shall be back home on Monday.

W. M. Thackeray to Anny

[1852].

MY DEAREST A.,—At last I get your 6 lines. I was
coming to Zurich after Berlin and had hoped to have a
week's quiet there with you all—but now, who nose where
I'll go? Write to me at Berlin P. Restante. Have you
got my letters, Granny hers, G. P. his from Lubbocks?
Answer these queries please.

I haven't had any news of my poor pocket-book:[1] nor
have I been able to write a word and scarce to stir in
this heat, but I shall travel at night and sleep through
it and not stop at the buggy Prague but go straight to
Dresden and see if I can paint a bit. Here it has been
like a little London with fine dinners every day, only
they are over at 7 and I go to the play or the opera.
Nothing can be hospitabler than Ld. Westmoreland.

I am glad I have seen the places, Tyrol and Salz-
kammergut, Munich and the Franconian towns, but
there's no book to be made about 'em: and we 3 couldn't
have made the journey comfortably: you 2 are too big
to sit 3 on a side—Ah me, I wish I was back from America! My darling women must work hard in my absence,
and be able to play polkas and waltzes to set me asleep

[1] This pocket-book had been stolen.

doucement after dinner. It's too hot to move here almost; I read all day, and can't bring myself to write.

Last night I was at another open-air play, quite as good as the first I wrote you about—and I saw the Authoress who admires my works. Mon Dieu qu'elle était laide! but her husband adores her luckily, and what matters, so long as he is happy? It seems about a year since I have been on my travels. I suppose it was wholesomest for me not to work: and I must soon get back to it and see whats to be done and fill up the hole made by the loss of the £90 in the pocket-book. A week's work will do that easily.

God bless my dearest Min and my little Nan and my dearest old Mammy and G. P. This is only to tell you where a letter will find me.

W. M. T.

Wednesday, *July* 14.

IV

1852—1854

IN October, 1852, Thackeray went to America to lecture on *"The English Humourists of the Eighteenth Century."* He was away six months, during which time his daughters stayed at Paris with their grandparents.

Anny Thackeray aged fifteen to W. M. Thackeray in America

Paris
[*November,* 1852].

As usual, I have nothing to tell to my dearest of Fathers except that on Wednesday (to-morrow) his Imperial Highness [1] will arrive from St. Cloud and be received at the Tuileries by the Senators, who will acknowledge him their Emperor, and the Tuileries are all gilt and furbished up for him. Mrs. Corkran says it will be called "République Française No. 3 Emp." and Pauline says she read in an old book his name isn't Louis Napoleon but Louis Charles! Grannie had rather relented after Abd-el-Kader, but now he has spoilt all by reducing the Protestant Conclave to half its number, and by the Bishop of St. Denis.

To-day we have been to M. Monod's Cours and presented our "analyses" tied with red ribbon, but next week we shall get purple for the Empire.

There are about twenty girls and twenty mothers all

[1] Napoleon III.

46

round the room. There is Blanche Girot, the beauty, beautifully dressed, and Miss Stumff, the stupid one— isn't it a good name?—and Zélie de Marville (Oh! if I had been called Zélie de Marville) and Marie Petit, the tall one, and Lucie de Latouche, and a great many more.

We were half as happy at your letter, as when you came back, dear Papa. It came just as I was reading out the most dreary passages of *Iphigénie,* and the maid came in with "Connaissez vous cette écriture-là, Mademoiselle?" Mrs. Collemache sent us the *Globe* with some verses of yours which Grannie said were like Lord Byron and which I thought were like you, as melancholy as Agamemnon in *Iphigénie,* and Grannie and I both burst out laughing at seeing ourselves both crying a little. I wonder what makes people cry when they are unhappy, and when they are happy too, and when they are neither the one nor the other?

To-day is the first cold day; it was so delightful out, with a nice brisk fog, and the little school-boys running to school, that Laure and I could hardly help dancing, and we bought some chestnuts which made us perfectly happy. The dandies have got most elegant cloaks over one shoulder, all braided and arranged with hoods and tassels, and I don't know what, and we meet splendid ladies in velvets driving, negros giving placards, and such quantities of dirty priests. Yesterday we had a race with the little Corkrans in the Tuileries. "I will fall down and break my nose," said little Mary so prettily, and fancy Minnie bursting out into German with their maid. Now it is eight-thirty and I must go and drink my tea and go to bed presently. Good-night, my dearest Papa.

A. THACKERAY.

Anny Thackeray to W. M. Thackeray in America

Paris
[1852].

MY DEAREST FATHER,—To-day at church we had to
pray for His Majesty the Emperor and all the Royal
Family, and on Thursday we had a holiday to go and
look at His Majesty riding into Paris. Minnie prepared
a purple cockade, which she put upon G. P., and you
may guess how disgusted Grannie was. There were
soldiers all down the Champs Elysées and splendid aides-
de-camps with feathers galloping about. Generals with
their staffs trotting off to St. Cloud, regiments dashing
by, all in the drizzling rain, and opposite a whole regiment of Dragoons, there was sitting one of Mrs. Doyle's
little dogs looking up at them, and nothing would induce
him to move. After waiting about four hours (we were
in an entresol) there came more regiments and elegant
aides-de-camps, and I determined that that is what I
should like to have been born. And Jerome on horseback very unsteady and fat, and then all alone in front
of a Regiment his Royal Highness, who was too far off
for me to see plainly, on a prancing horse with a red velvet saddle and golden bridles, and I forget what coat
Louis Napoleon wore, but he had a fine red ribbon across
his body. They cried "Vive l'Empereur" a little, not
very much. Grannie says she counted twelve, but I
assure you there were more. The only way the
Champs Elysées were adorned, was by a piece of calico
stretched across the Rond Point, which was not half long
enough to reach from one side to the other.

I think I am a Napoleonist, for he has done so many
good-natured things; all the poor who have pawned their

mattresses and any other things within four days may
take them back for nothing, and all debtors under I don't
know what, are let out of prison,—the warnings to the
newspapers are taken away, and little crimes are forgiven, and the soldiers got an extra day's pay. Yesterday
we saw him, but as I couldn't see his face I didn't know
who it was, till a little man rushed up to Grannie and
said "C'est l'Empereur!" "Phuiff!" says Grannie, and
walks on. Minnie was with the Corkrans at the Bois de
Boulogne and told me that Sutton set up a loud cheer,
and got a bow.

I am afraid Grannie is still miserable about me, but
it bothers me when the clergymen say that everybody
ought to think alike and follow the one true way, forgetting that it is they who want people to think alike,
that is, as they do. Monsieur Monod tells us things about
the Garden of Eden, which he proves by St. Paul's
epistles. I don't understand how God can repent and
destroy His own work, or how He can make coats as He
did for Adam, or shut a door, as they say He shut Noah
in, and it is things like these that they think one must
go to hell for not respecting and believing. I am sure
when Christ talks about "My words" He means His own,
not the Bible, as Grannie says, but I don't know what it
means when He says that He did not come to destroy
the law but to fulfil it, and so I suppose everybody is
right and nobody knows anything. Minnie and I can
love you and Grannie with all our heart, and that is our
business. Good-bye, my dear Papa, I daresay you are
thinking of us now, and we send our love to you over the
sea.

ANNIE THACKERAY.

Anny Thackeray to George M. Smith

19, Rue d'Angoulême, **Paris**
[1852].

MY DEAR SIR,—I write to tell you how much obliged we are to you for your kind offer. It would give us all the greatest pleasure to have my father's picture,[1] and we thank you very much for proposing to send it. I think (if it is the same to you) that we should like best to have it here, so as to be able to look at it instead of him.

He writes very often to us, and says he gets on famously.

Believe me,
Very faithfully yours,
A. THACKERAY.

W. M. Thackeray to A. Fonblanque

Richmond, **Virginia**
March 4th [1853].

MY DEAR FONBLANQUE,—I hope you have kept carefully all those "Letters of a traveller in America" which will form the basis of my future work in 6 volumes— the drawings are not the least valuable part don't you think so? *entre nous* young Crowe touched them up and —enough of this small joking which may reach you about the First of April, and which please put down to the compliments of that waggish season. I've not written a word that's the truth. I've seen and remarked nothing: in the great cities I had hardly leisure to write to my family, and those one or two kind female correspondentesses to whom a man writes, not about the country he is travel-

---

[1] Before Thackeray started for America, George Smith, the publisher of *Esmond*, commissioned Samuel Laurence to draw his portrait. Two copies were made; one George Smith gave to Charlotte Brontë, the other to Thackeray's children.

Anny & Minny.
From a water-colour
sketch by W. M. T.

ling in, but about himself—and all I have to say about
this great country that's worth saying might be put down
on the remainder of this side of [the] paper.

What could Dickens mean by writing that book of
American Notes? No man should write about the country under 5 years of experience, and as many of previous
reading. A visit to the Tombs, to Laura Bridgman and
the Blind Asylum, a description of Broadway—O Lord
is that describing America? It's a mole or a pimple on
the great Republican body, or a hair of his awful beard
and no more. I have hardly seen as much as that; and
gave up sight-seeing at once as impossible to a man in
my position here. Your room is besieged all day by visitors, you go about from dinner to tea-party and ball, and
the people don't talk to you but try and make you talk.
"Well Sir, how do you like our country Sir?" that's
the formula, and as you are answering this query, the
host comes up and says: "Allow me Sir to introduce you
to Mr. Jones of Alabama, Sir"—shake hands with Jones
of Alabama, query as before; it is not answered when you
are presented to Mr. Smith of Tennessee. "We know you
very well Sir," says S. of T. "your works are extensively
read among us, allow me to present you to my Lady,
Sir, who is a great admirer of" etc.—Mrs. Smith of Tennessee then commences: "How do you like our etc. Sir"—
and, by Heaven, evening after evening passes off in this
way. I know 100 people more every day, and walk the
street in terror, lest every man and lady I meet should
be my acquaintance of the night before. It makes one
half crazy the constant representation—and what must
it have been in Dickens's time when deputations met him
daily and his life was watched by myriads of admirers?
I have refused to be a personage with all my might, nor
indeed has there been much of that sort of honour thrust

upon me, and though I have had plenty of praise from
the newspapers, I have had plenty of assaults too which
were quite refreshing. Ah Monsieur! if one might but
hit again, here and on t'other side of the water, how invig-
orating and pleasant it would be! There are 2 dear friends
I know of in my beloved country—O for the day when
Makepeace might just cease to be Makepeace and "go
in"!

A great good wh. an Englishman who has seen men
and cities gets by coming hither, is that he rubs a deal
of Cockney arrogance off, and finds men and women
above all as good as our own. You learn to sympathise
with a great hearty nation of 26 millions of English-
speakers, not quite ourselves but so like, the difference
is not worth our scorn certainly; nay I'm not sure I don't
think the people are our superiors. There's a rush and
activity of life quite astounding, a splendid recklessness
about money wh. has in it something admirable too.
Dam the money says every man. He's as good as the
richest for that day. If he wants champagne he has
champagne, Mr. Astor can't do more. You get an
equality wh. may shock ever so little at first, but has
something hearty and generous in it. I like the citizen-
ship and general freedom. And in the struggles wh.
every man with whom you talk is pretty sure to have
had, the ups and downs of his life, the trades or pro-
fessions he has been in—he gets a rough and tumble edu-
cation wh. gives a certain piquancy to his talk and company.

There's beautiful affection in this country, immense
tenderness, romantic personal enthusiasm, and a general
kindliness and serviceableness and good nature wh. is
very pleasant and curious to witness for us folks at home,
who are mostly ashamed of our best emotions, and turn

on our heel with a laugh sometimes when we are most
pleased and touched. If a man falls into a difficulty a
score of men are ready to help. The Editor of a newspaper in this little city with 12,000 whites and as many
negroes was shot in a duel—the city subscribed £200 a
year for his orphans. Meagher told me yesterday (a fine
fellow Meagher, manly, modest, brave, funny, handsome,
immensely in earnest and at war with the priests) that
there came a girl to Washington from New York bound
to Louisiana. She asked leave to sleep on board the boat
at Washington, the Captain took her to his own house,
gave her in charge to the Conductor of the Railway at
Acquia Creek, who saw her through the journey to Richmond, and ran off instantly thence to get her a carriage,
and see her luggage packed and herself forwarded to the
Southern Station. And the Queen being abused by an
Englishman at New York, who should be her champion
but this Meagher the rebel—(this is par parenthèse).
Three as fine Irishmen as ever I met, were he and Dillon
and O'Gorman, refugees and flourishing lawyers at New
York now. I tell you it's grand country entirely. The
young blood beating in its pulses warms one, like the
company of young men in England. I don't know what
I wouldn't do if I were 10 years younger—if I were 10
years younger I might sneer to be sure and satirise Jor-
dan because it wasn't like Abanah and Pharpar, rivers of
Damascus. As a refuge for men who can't make their
way at home, it's a great place. What a country where
a labouring man begins with earning a dollar a day.
An Irishman dictating a letter home to his friends in
Ireland, out of Maryland, bade his Master write, "My
dear Phil, Me Masther is the best of Masthers, and I ayt
mayt three toimes a week"—"Three times a week" says
the Master—"you eat it three times a day you rogue and 6

times if you like!" "Hush Master!" says Paddy—"Sure
they wouldn't believe me if I said more than 3 times a
week!" Think of country laborers in England and 10
children and 10 shillings a week! and to be sure let us
set to and bemoan the blacks afterwards, and sign the
Sutherland House Womanifesto!

The happiness of these niggers is quite a curiosity
to witness. The little niggers are trotting and grinning
about the streets, the women are fat and in good case, I
wish you could see that waiter at our hotel with 5 gold
medals in his shirt 2 gold chains and a gold ring.
The African Church on a Sunday I am told is a perfect blaze of pea-green, crimson, ear-rings, lace collars,
satin and velvet which the poor darkies wear. I don't
mean to say that Slavery is right but that if you want
to move your bowels with compassion for human un-
happiness, that sort of aperient is to be found in such
plenty at home, that it's a wonder people won't seek it
there. I don't think it's of long duration though—unless
perhaps in the cotton-growing countries where the whites
can't live and the negroes can. Every person I have
talked to here about it deplores it and owns that it's the
most costly domestic machinery ever devised. In a house
where four servants would do with us (servants whom
we can send about their business too, when they get ill
and past work, like true philanthropists as we are) there
must be a dozen blacks here, and the work not well done.
The hire of a house slave from his owner is 120 dollars—
£25—besides of course his keep, clothing, etc. When he is
old he must be kept well and kindly, and is—the little
niggers wait upon the old effete niggers. The slave-ser-
vants working in the tobacco manufactories can lay up
100 dollars a year. The rule is kindness, the exception
no doubt may be cruelty. The great plenty in this country

ensures everyone enough to eat—and the people here entreat me to go on a plantation, to go about by myself, ask questions how and where I like and see if the black people are happy or not. This to be sure leaves the great question untouched that Slavery is a wrong. But if you could decree the Abolition tomorrow, by the Lord it would be the most awful curse and ruin to the black wh. Fate ever yet sent him. Of course we feel the cruelty of flogging and enslaving a negro—of course they feel here the cruelty of starving an English laborer, or of driving an English child to a mine—Brother, Brother we are kin.

I am doing very well with the lectures—the 2 Presidents came at Washington—I've saved some money £2,000 in this country, and shall probably make half as much more: but O how sick I am of the business!

I bid you a shake of the hand and am yours always, dear Fonblanque,

W. M. THACKERAY.

Thackeray returned from the United States in April, 1853. In the summer of this year he took his children abroad.

*W. M. Thackeray to Mrs. Frederick Elliot and
Miss Perry*

Hotel Bristol,
Place Vendôme,
Wednesday [1853].

Are your travels over? are you back in Chesum Place? Has K. P.[1] taken her poor little holy day and sent her young people on their tour? Ours has been a very small one—to Calais which is very good fun and a great deal more French than Paris; to Spa which was very pleasant too but for the quantity of acquaintances and ½ acquain-

---

[1] Kate Perry.

tances that as père de famille I did not care to make whole acquaintances; to Dusseldorf where we passed a couple of agreeable days among the painters; and then to Aix la Chapelle which disagreed with me as it always does. Here we heard of the death of Mrs. Robert Carmichael-Smyth, my step-father's brother's wife, and thinking the family would be in trouble, and my mother (who was touring too, we did not know where) would be sure to come to Paris, we came on last Friday. But there was no granny for the girls—she is to stay the month out at Heidelberg—the daughters are gone to stay with a cousin of ours Rue Godot, where they are all very jolly together, and I am for a few days "in boy" at the Hotel Bristol; haunted by No. 1 of Mr. Thackeray's new serial [1] which won't leave me alone, which follows me about in all my walks, wakes me up at night, prevents me from hearing what is said at the play, and yet seems farther off than ever. It seems to me as if I had said my say, as if anything I write must be repetition, and that people will say with justice "he has worn himself out, I always told you he would, etc., etc." But 600£ is a great bribe isn't it? Suppose I do wear myself out, and that posterity says so, why shouldn't she? and what care I to appear to future ages (who will be deeply interested in discussing the subject) as other than I really am?

My poor friend A'Becketts death has shocked me. He has left no money and hasn't insured his life—Down from competence and comfort goes a whole family into absolute penury. One boy ½ through the University, and likely to have done well there I believe—another at a public school, daughters with masters, and Mamma with tastes for music and millinery. What is to happen to these people? Had I dropped 3 years ago my poor wife and

[1] *The Newcomes.*

young ones would have been no better off. Yes, we must
do the Forthcoming serial work, and never mind if it
should turn out a failure. We went to see Mrs. Norton
yeterday who has burned her neck severely, while shield-
ing her little grandchild—a little black eyed curly pated
lazzaronykin Brinsley's daughter—That fellow would
be a good character for a book—and his mother too, if
one could but say all one thought—but in England we are
so awfully squeamish—Ah, if one's hands were not tied
there might be some good fun in that forthcoming Serial
—You see I always come back to it—in fact this very sheet
of paper was pulled out for the purpose of writing a
page only somehow it has taken the direction of Chesham Place and will be read I hope to-morrow by my
bonnes sœurs. Are you all in London? Ah me! What
letters I have written in this very room at this table
some 5 years since. It is a nice quiet room—away from
the noisy street. I daresay the Zouaves are playing their
music in the place Vendôme at this very moment. Blow
away trumpets! We saw the men yesterday. They are
magnificent looking warriors that's certain. The town
is getting too handsome for them. I miss my old corners
—my dining-places have disappeared and palaces stand in
their stead: but the Palais Royal looking seedy and deserted consoles me: and one gets a good time among the
pictures at the Louvre, and with the pleasure of the girls.
What shall I do, if any scoundrel of a husband takes away
Anny's kind cheerfulness from me?

I have been twice to the theayter but can't sit out the
plays—the *Dame aux Camellias* I could not bear beyond
the second act: it is too wicked: and so is the *Juif Errant*
—I had intended to go to a screaming farce last night
but came home instead to think about the—Plague take
it! Here is the Forthcoming Serial come up again!

Well, you let me say whatever is in my mind, and you know of some people who are always there. God bless them all says

W. M. T.

W. M. Thackeray to Mrs. Carmichael-Smyth

Saturday
[*Autumn* 1853].

MY DEAREST MAMMY,—I only got last night the last proof sheets of No. 1 of the *Newcomes*: Doyle has been three weeks doing the engravings, and they are not so good as mine now they are done. And I have been delayed by Governesses, and this mg. comes a letter wh. may defer the Roman trip altogether—a proposal from a publisher to edit Horace Walpole's letters wh. is just the sort of work I should like—such as would keep me at home pleasantly employed some evenings and pottering over old volumes (I'm flying from pen to pen to see which will answer best) of old biographies and histories.

When the imaginative work is over, that is the kind of occupation I often propose to myself for my old age. This and the governess business may keep me 3 or 4 days more. But don't please be disquieted on my score. The little trip to Brighton always braces and benefits me. If I dared to have 3 houses at a time I would have taken a lodging there for a fortnight. My good nature has kept me out of a fortnight's work here, for my visitors, the best of people, put me out of my way, and I can't write for them.

The girls especially Minny want a woman always with them. Three hours a day of Miss Collemache isn't enough. There came a Ger-woman the other day: but well enough recommended as times go. But I found I couldn't live with her. There are some people, ever so many, who shut me up or drive me to my own room, and this would be one: and I must send her a congé and look elsewhere. Now that the Roman trip is doubtful, the Governess is not so necessary perhaps.

We had a pleasant little journey to Oxfordshire did the children tell you?—and as for that Brighton it's wonderful how it seems to answer with me. I found myself longing to get to work: and wrote a ballad [1] there, day before yesterday, with quite a juvenile pluck. As for appetite it is quite marvellous how that grows there. I wonder is Kensington unwholesome, or is it only fancy on my part?

Charles has been here hunting all over the house for fancied goods of his. What a strange mania! We have seen the poor Brookfields and the moral I have come to is "Thou shalt not pity thy neighbour's wife." Keep out of his Harem; and it is better for you and him. I send you a line only to tell you that I'm quite well: we shall let the Emperor go through Boulogne before we land there: and then may we have a couple of nice months with my dear old G. P. and Mother.

W. M. T.

Notes on Family History

My sister was thirteen and I was sixteen when we went to Paris one autumn with my Father, and from Paris to Rome where we spent the winter.

It seemed all golden, like the great pictures at Venice, when we landed at Civita Vecchia. I have never been there again, but I dare say it all looks just the same, the blue sky and beggars in the sun, the shadows and the old sloping ruins and arched palaces.

---

[1] "Organ Boy's Lament." The last poem he ever published in *Punch*.

As we got to Rome it was evening, and my father said, "See! there is St. Peter's," and we looked out, and a great dark living sort of dome seemed to hunch up its shoulders, as we drove along under the stars; next a sentry stopped us, and then we rattled through the streets to our hotel in the Condotti. The next morning when I looked out, I saw a bandit and an Italian woman with a red bodice and white sleeves walk by the window, and all the bells were jangling. My father took a lodging in a great Palazzo and hired an old cook called Octavia, and Papa's servant Charles waited upon us, and used to fetch us from the tea parties and friends' houses to whom we went. The two people we liked best in Rome were Mrs. Browning and Mrs. Sartoris. Walter Scott's son-in-law, Mr. Lockhart, was there. I am glad to think that I once saw him. Only once just before he died. It was one early afternoon in the Piazza at Rome. Mrs. Sartoris came out of some doorway near which her carriage was waiting, not drawn to the roadside but standing well out, and the sick man was sitting inside propped up with pillows. She laid her hand upon my arm and said: "That is Lockhart. Fanny and I are going to take him for a drive in the Campagna." He looked very ill, very noble, like a solemn brooding eagle, silent and mysterious. He was wrapped in a cloak and wore some soft travelling cap; I only saw his profile, and the pale, clear-cut features. I stood looking up with a thrill, for the incident, trifling as it was, impressed me. The sick man, the great Campagna waiting for him, the good and loving company, the glorious warmth of land and sky, I shall never forget.

Minnie and I used to write for Papa a great deal at his dictation, and it was here at Rome when we gave a

children's party that he drew us all the funny pretty pictures for *The Rose and the Ring*.   The little children for
whom he first drew the pictures are grown up and married people now and Pen Browning can make pictures
for himself.

My father was very ill in Rome and then we went to
Naples and one evening we were out late in a beautiful
sunset and the next day I awoke with a sore throat and
a headache, and all day long it got worse, and the doctor
came and said it was scarletina, and Minnie jumped up
in the night and gave me water to drink.   Nobody was
such a good nurse as Minnie.

Her little hands always seemed to send pain away—
when her kitten was ill she stroked it quite well, and
once she kept a little fly in a doll's teapot for two days
with rose leaves.   We told her it was dead, but she would
not hear of it, and the second day she took up the lid
to put some sugar crumbs in, and out flew the little fly!

Thackeray in his lecture on "Charity and Humor"
refers to Minnie when he says:

"All children ought to love him [Dickens]; I know two
that do, and read his books ten times for once they peruse
the dismal preachments of their father.

"I know one who when she is happy, reads *Nicholas
Nickleby;* when she is unhappy reads *Nicholas Nickleby;*
when she is tired reads *Nicholas Nickleby;* when she is
in bed reads *Nicholas Nickleby;* when she has nothing
to do reads *Nicholas Nickleby;* and when she has finished the book reads *Nicholas Nickleby* again.

"This candid young critic of ten years of age said, 'I

like Mr. Dickens's books better than your books, Papa,'
and frequently expressed the desire that the latter author
should write a book like one of Mr. Dickens's books.
Who can?"

MINNIE READING NICHOLAS NICKLEBY
Drawn by Thackeray

V

1854—1860

AFTER his return from Rome, Thackeray left 13, Young Street, and moved to 36, Onslow Square. My mother writing of the new house in her Journal says, "It was a pleasant bowery home with green curtains and carpets; our windows looked out upon the elm trees of Onslow Square. We lived for seven years at No. 36, where so many things happened which were beyond me, and where so many things were said which I did not follow. In those days I was more used to look at my father's guests than to speak to them."

W. M. Thackeray to Mrs. Carmichael-Smyth

36, Onslow Square
[1854].

[1] *My dearest Grannie,—Papa says you've been in a fright about my ankle,* but it is very much better, and I manage with the very greatest difficulty to keep the young woman quiet.

Only since the last 4 days I have got into full work again: it was impossible before with the racket of moving, and the hammering and ringing of bells incessantly going on—but now the stream is beginning to flow again and the old mill-wheel to turn.

I have begun a piece of buffoonery for *Punch,* wh. will pay the rent of the Château at Boulogne;[2] and have done

[1] These two first lines are in my mother's handwriting.
[2] A house he had taken for the summer.

a month's number of it already. I didn't get your letter
till late on Saturday, that is it came in at 3, and opening it
to see that all was well I went on with my work till 7
o'clock, and then found too late that you wanted an immediate answer.

I have a party for Miss Thackeray on the 21 wh. I
wish her to be at, and introduce her to some folks who
will be kind [to] her next year: and I am engaged to
dinner up to the 24th., after wh. I shan't accept any more
victuals. But I am in full work and don't mind and
besides must stay in London over the 17th. when if as I
expect Doyle has not done the *Newcome* plates I shall
take them in hand and do them henceforth myself.

Enter Honeywood, Mark, Mrs. Cole, Mr. Sleap the
amanuensis, a man with a bill, a messenger from Mrs.
King about an invitation for the young ladies requiring an
answer. Mr. T. must see all these and give an answer,
and at 2 Mr. T. must take Miss Hughes and the girls
to the Crystal Palace (I shall make Anny go about in a
chair) but Anny and I have done a couple of pages of
Newcomes upstairs already, and now I've only 5 more
notes to write before going out.

O what a row and a racket it is! But it is pleasant
enough. When Anny could walk, we 3 had plenty of
pleasant walks together. She goes on Wednesday 14 to
Mrs. Marshall's music, Wednesday 21 to Mrs. Bates's
music. I think it is possible that Lord Palmerston will
ask me on Saturday to dinner wh. I don't choose to refuse
him again. I was obliged to do so last week being engaged
to Tennant. And he is the man who has Police Magis-
trateships in his gift. O thou schemer and artful dodger!
Monday 25 is the day I ultimately fix for the movement
of these forces.[1] The bed room I shall have, is for *anyone*.

[1] To the house Thackeray had taken for the summer.

There is a very good study for me on the ground floor
off the dining room, another for the girls off the drawing room. The best bed room of course is for my
Mamma and the room next for the Major. I shall put
Sleap the Amanuensis in a lodging in the town (he will
follow after us probably) and bring Charles and Eliza;
and Grey the cook subsequently. It is a big house and
there will be plenty of work for the servants, and An-
nette's valuable services will be absolutely necessary as
aide-cuisine and interpreter. What a comfort I have
devised that little scheme for paying the rent! and can
pay a month of it by a day's work!

Here ends the rigmarole dashed off in a furious hurry.
Aren't there all those other notes to write and aren't I,
always writing or not, my dearest old Mammy's and
G. P.s

W. M. T.

*A Journal written by Anny Thackeray at the age of
seventeen*

For the week ending Sunday 18th. February, 1854.
Being minded to keep a record of those adventures which
I hope are going to happen to me, I begin to-night to
write down my week's doings and I have no doubt this
diary will last just as long as the thirty others that I
have commenced!

Sunday, I in my right of out young lady, presided at
a dinner party which Papa said was exceedingly stupid.
Mr. Millais was there, a tall good-looking Pre-Raphael-
iteish young man with a quantity of wavy hair, and I
listened with great eagerness for all the valuable remarks he was to let drop. Mr. Leech and his wife came

and Peter Cunningham and his, also Mr. Phillips, Mr. Charles Taylor and others.

Grannie sent us a long letter for Valentine's day and I to my great delight got a mysterious Valentine called "The Pervert" with C. de Pryme's name written on the bottom.

Friday, Uncle Arthur, Aunt Shawe and Mr. Fitz-Gerald dined, he was more melancholy than ever and told Papa he wouldn't come again—"that everyone had had enough of Fitz."

Saturday, I paid some of my first visits: Lady Airlie, Mrs. Procter, Mrs. James, Lady Rodd, Mrs. Ford, and Mrs. Frederick Elliot—where I went in a dreadful fright to one of those "teas" they give now before dinner.

Sunday. A great event, Amy's [1] brother Joe came back from the Crimea, with a red beard and lots of money. Joe says he is quite a lion at the Clubs, and Papa wants him to make a lecture.

Monday. Papa reads us his play that they won't have at the Olympic, *The Shorn Lamb,* and we thought it capital fun. The first act was rather long, but the second as good as anything I have ever heard.

Tuesday. We walked out and saw the skating on the Serpentine with Uncle Arthur and Miss Evans. I think Miss Evans is one of the most perfect ladies I know.

In the evening Joe [2] came to dinner, and poor fellow he has brought home an intermittent fever amongst other things from the Crimea, and after dinner I got ready and put on a white gown and a white cloak and went to two

---

[1] Amy Crowe, an adopted daughter of the house. She married our cousin— now Sir Edward Thackeray, V.C., K.C.B. She died June, 1863, and was the mother of Margie and Annie to whom so many of my mother's letters are written.

[2] Sir Joseph Crowe, C.B., K.C.M.G., is best known for his History of Art, in conjunction with Cavalcaselle.

parties. Mrs. Brookfield's, where I fell in love with Miss Geraldine Mildmay and where I saw the Sterlings, also Mrs. Prinsep and Mrs. Cameron, Mr. Maurice and many more. I was very sorry to go away to Mrs. Ford's, which was so stupid and where we only stayed a quarter of an hour. The only thing I cared for there was a lame Crimean.

Wednesday. We dined at Little Holland House, where we met Tom Taylor and had a pretty pleasant party.

Thursday. We didn't do anything remarkable. I ventured rashly into a house in search of Mrs. Cameron, and presently I was met by a severe young lady with a lot of little dogs barking at her heels, who said, with great dignity, "There must be some mistake, I am Miss Gammon!"

Friday. I wrote for Papa and Mr. Morgan John dined with us, full of the theatricals they are getting up for poor Mr. Reach. There came a long letter from Grannie, a sort of leading article abusing the ministry of Lord Palmerston all except Mr. Roebuck.

Joseph Hume died this week; there was a life of him in the *Times.*

Saturday. A dreary foggy day and I stopped at home writing [1] for Papa.

Tuesday. Rain still and mud. We walked round and round the Square, and in and out, and Amy went out with her brother, and Papa and Minny and I dined together off a leggacio di muttone.

Wednesday. I had an invitation from Mrs. Thomson Hankey but Papa could not take me, having a public dinner to attend, at which he made the most beautiful

[1] *The Newcomes.*

impromptu speech, as I have good reason to know, as he delivered it to me from his bed the day before.

Thursday. Madame Marochetti came to dinner with her son, Maurice, such a nice modest lad. The Baroness enflamed me with a desire for early rising, and I accordingly got up at 6 o'clock the next morning and did nothing till breakfast.

Sunday, March 4th. A very dreary day for us. The sky was so bright and blue and my poor Papa lay ill in bed with one of his attacks. In the afternoon Amy and I went to Church at St. Pusey's hard by. There were four children christened, Grace Emma, Anne Caroline, Charles John, and Charles Frederick. I wonder what is going to happen to them, and whether Grace will become Mrs. Charles John, and Anne Caroline, Mrs. Charles Frederick? and whether they will lead calm happy lives and be buried in the little churchyard.

It's rather awful to think that all this nonsense I am writing here, will be alive and full of meaning years after I too am lying in Kensal Green, and I wonder what will be written on these clean white pages of my diary, so silent and blank as to the future, so mournful and full of meaning as to the past, perhaps.

Wednesday. Mr. FitzGerald and Mr. Spedding came to dine, and were as kind and queer and melancholy as men could be. I think the company of these kind old friends did my father more good than a dozen bottles of black dose alias poison.

Thursday, September 30th. We set off for Mr. Leech's and lost our way completely, before we found out his address from the Sterlings in Queen Square. Mrs. Leech's baby is the dearest little maid with dark solemn eyes. Mr. Millais has made a sketch of her. We thought we almost liked his drawing better than Miss Ada her-

self. I wish she hadn't that ridiculous name—Ida! anything would be better. It was so pretty to see those small
little hands of hers ordering and forcing about her severe Aunt Esther as if she were the autocrat of all the
Russias. That makes me wonder how I can put down
all this nonsense when such news has come in this week.
The death of Nicholas, the battle of Eupatoria,[1] and the
birth of an arch-duchess.

What a queer thing it is to think that I care more if
my father's finger aches than if the whole Imperial family be extinguished. That to me everything happens only
to make part of *my* existence. Kings die, armies are
defeated, treaties signed, victories won—all are parts of
this tremendous play. To myself it seems acted for *me,
alone,* and so I suppose it does to every other human
creature.

Perhaps these times appear differently to me, to what
they do to every other mind? Perhaps Minny sees the
trees blue not green, and Amy thinks them red. How
is it that we do not all like the same persons? Mr. Fitz-
Gerald was praising Mrs. ——— the other day who
bothers me and Papa too, beyond expression—simply because she always puts her head on one side. Perhaps Mr.
FitzGerald thinks I carry my head on one side, and
that the tower of Pisa is straight and Nelson's column
leaning to the right. Goodnight, Mr. FitzGerald. Poor
Minny wants to blow the candle out and go to sleep, and
I don't think she can be very much interested in the above
horizontal reflections, inflections I mean, or perhaps
inflictions.

We had a young ladies' tea-party last Tuesday. N. B.
It was rather stupid.

Friday. Went to Mrs. Elliot's where we found those

[1] A Russian defeat in the Crimea.

kind Miss Barings and Henry Philip van Artevelde Taylor, a grand looking man with a high forehead, whom I felt very proud of talking to. I went back to Mrs. Brookfield's and had a long talk with her. I hope I didn't say anything I ought not.

Sunday. Going to St. Luke's we heard the best sermon that was ever preached almost, about Charity, from Charles Kingsley.

On Monday I went to a party at Mrs. Mildmay's and afterwards to Mrs. Ford's where I was introduced to Mrs. Norton. O! what a handsome woman she is. She said, shaking her head: "I have often heard about you. How is your sister? Does she help you to dress and do your hair? I always used to dress *my* sister's hair when I was a girl." I don't think she cared immensely as she turned away before I could answer.

Tuesday I forget, but *Wednesday,* I went to tea at Miss Belle Smith's. Miss Parkes was there and Mrs. Howett, who announced her opinion that women should sit in Parliament.

Sunday 25th March. I went to Church and I forget what happened afterwards. The next day to Mrs. Rees who instead of being in misery and a garret, we found very cheerful and comfortable. We dined at Mrs. Freek's where Mr. Douglas made himself most fascinating and I am sure it was very good fun.

Friday. Mrs. Brookfield and I went out shopping to buy some flowers for me to wear at Lady Palmerston's party and after a great deal of trouble that important business was completed, and Miss Thackeray appeared with an elegant clump of wild roses and may flowers stuck in her dress.

Saturday. A very eventful day. My pleasure was rather marred at first by a scolding from Papa which I quite deserved, as I invariably keep him waiting. I was introduced to more Lords at Lady Palmerston's than I ever had seen in my life before. Lord Somers, Carlisle (Viceroy of Ireland) Tollington Lady Georgina Fullerton who won my heart, Lady Aylesbury and Lady—I have forgotten her name.

Sunday. I am ashamed to say I didn't go to Church, but I made a picture which was so bad, I could scarcely believe I had done it myself.

Tuesday. I got a letter from Mrs. Fanshawe; I think I will copy it out and keep it for ever, in case I am in want of advice.

June 9th, 1855. And now my birthday has come round again and I have been determining to spend my eighteenth better than my seventeenth year, and to be less sentimental, more cheerful and honest and charitable.

W. M. Thackeray to Anny Thackeray

June 9 [1855].

My dearest Nan must have a paternal God bless you to-day—many such please God may I send you. You see every year now as you grow older we shall grow more intimate, at least I hope and think so: and as it is an ascertained fact that I can't live without female friends I shall have a pair at home, in my own women; who'll understand my ways, laugh at my jokes, console me when I'm dismal etc., as is the wont and duty of women in life. Less and less of the Season every year seems to suffice for me now: and I have had almost enough now in ten days: after the twentieth at any rate I will have no more, unless I should give way to a project I have sometimes of uttering a lecture about the United States; which no doubt people would crowd to hear. Several persons

have urged me to do this; and if I had my Secretary [1]
here, who knows what might happen?   But without one
I cannot positively get on : and dawdle through the days
meanwhile, doing nothing.

. . . What shall be my dear Nan's birthday present?
You two can have what you want any day as well as a
birthday. That's why I don't think of such gifts for you.

The edition of the Lectures is nearly all sold and a
new one ordered. People are thinking of other things
now however, and whether we are to have a war or not is
the question over wh. all men look glum, and I am my
darling Nanny's affectionate Father

W. M. T.

Journal (1855)

June 10th. I have been out a good deal with my
father. Once I went to a most splendid reception at Lord
Lansdowne's. The gentlemen all in court dress and the
ladies in their very best. Lord Cardigan, Sir Charles
Napier and Admiral Dundas.

Serena left town after writing me a noble letter and
I felt so ashamed and so wicked that I should have liked
to—I don't know what.

We had a pleasant little trip to Gravesend and Roches-
ter, and coming home my Father had some dinners at
which his daughter presided, I fear with very small
grace. But tant-pis, when I'm older I hope I shall do
it better.

Saturday. I went to Lady Molesworth's and Sunday
we had Mr. Kingsley's brave sermon. And I wish I
could do something better than make good resolutions.

[1] His daughter Anny.

W. M. Thackeray to Miss Perry

36, Rue Godot-de-Mauroy,

Paris.

July 2nd [1855].

MES BONNES SŒURS,—I think it is time you should hear from your elderly relative and as J. may be on her way to her holy days and Miss K. I know is in England, I write my little line to Eaton Place West wishing my very best wishes to all J's. and K's. We have had a pretty busy pleasant time here: except that as in London and everywhere else, there has been a little too much feasting for me, too much Burgundy, too much Bordeaux. Isn't this hot weather feverish enough without these stirrers of the blood? I have cut off 2 dinners for to-day and to-morrow. It is true they would have been very stupid: but it's at those stupid dinners the Claret is most dangerous.

Last Thursday, the 28th. at 7 o'clock in the evening, I wrote the last lines of the poor old *Newcomes* with a very sad heart. And afterwards what do you think I did? Suppose I said my prayers, and humbly prayed God Almighty to bless those I love and who love me, and to help me to see and speak the truth and to do my duty? You wouldn't wonder at that would you? That finis at the end of a book is a solemn word. One need not be Mr. Gibbon of Lausanne to write it. There go 2 years more of my life spent over those pages: I was quite sorry to part with a number of kind people with whom I had been living and talking these 20 months past, and to draw a line so——————on a sheet of paper, beyond which their honest figures couldn't pass, and that melancholy leave taken, I went out to dine by myself and to see a Pantomime over which I fell into a sweet roseate slumber.

The girls were gone to see the great Italian tragedian the Ristori who was acting Mary Stuart that night, but I thought it would be pleasanter to see Clown jump through a window than a Queen have her wicked head chopped off. By the way she is not made wicked in the play. It is Schiller's and she is as pure as Alabaster.

I have been twice or thrice to the Exposition des Bosarts. The English Pictures show very well indeed I think. One night with Maclise the painter, I went to the Château des Fleurs which inspired him with ravishment, and me with mortal melancholy. Crowds were standing round Lais and Phryne dancing the cancan—all sorts of elderly fogies and respectable people. What was Bonneval doing at the Castle of Flowers I should like to know? Venait il en cueiller le monstre—leaving his own languid lily at home? At Lady Ashburton's next day there was the Duchesse d'Istrie at dinner—beautiful splendid a thought aged and stale—she put me in mind of the handsome wicked Château des Fleurs. Mérimée came in—it's very odd, admiring his writing as I do, what an antipathy I have to him. I had a capital breakfast with honest Jules Janin, who lives up in his cinquième quite poor and honest and merry. I went moreover to see the *Demi-monde*. It put me in mind of myself rather —it's a comedy of Beckys and Madame de Cruchecassés and the like. It is wonderfully acted—there is a man— M. Dupuis the Jeune premier, who is quite a pleasure to behold, so easy quiet nonchalant and gentlemanlike is he. And these Mesdames I think have been all my doings. If any of our friends want to hear about them you can say please God bless all friends. We grow old; we work and struggle on with our day's burthens, we groan and we laugh and we scheme for next year—and lo the end comes, doesn't it? This letter is not gay eh! what will you? One is no longer gay at our age, one is content. The girls are very well. Anny is a perfect well-spring of happiness in herself. Thank God. The thought of parting with them for the American expedition disgusts me more and more. Fired with emulation by Dickens's capital speech I have been getting one up—another—but not so good as his though. I wonder whether I shall come back to London by next Wednesday week to speak it? I don't know in the least what I'm going to do, but am yours always my dear kind friends,

W. M. T.

Journal 1855

Wednesday, August the 8th. I wrote about the apartment [1] to-day which gives one a turn. O my dear Papa.

We have been away to Paris and Baden and Hombourg and we came home by the Rhine and Brussels and Dover, but it all feels like a dream. I see our drives driving off farther and farther and the music we heard sounds fainter and fainter.

We had a long pleasant walk to-day (Sunday) with our father, along the Thames to Chiswick, past quaint old Georgian houses, gaily decked with flowers and sunshine, and children playing about and kindly holiday people.

Tuesday, 14th day of August. The days keep dashing on and now it is Tuesday again, and in a few minutes it will be Wednesday, and I am just come home from a not dangerously exciting party at Mr. Robert Bell's.

Mrs. Glass spent the day with us and she gave us some small idea of the splendour of Papa's state in America.

---

[1] Thackeray's second visit to America was impending. He left Oct. 13th, 1855. My mother and her sister went to their grandparents in Paris.

To Hatton, the Chief Baron,[1] as kind as could be and everybody else. Julius photographed us all. The Lord Chief Baron made us each three presents:—

1. A bottle of the very best Eau de Cologne, warranted to make one perfectly lovely.

2. A box of matches, which when you strike a Genie appears who does anything you tell him.

3. A piece of soap, which when you wash yourself heals every disease and makes you perfectly invulnerable.

At least I daresay that is the case, or it would have been, had we all lived once upon a time, and if Papa had been either a king or a poor woodman, and if the Chief Baron was a magician, and Hatton a castle, and if the cruel Fairy—but lo! the clock strikes, and the enchantment vanishes, the Chief Baron fades away into his castle, our Royal Father disappears to his study below, the young Prince isn't born yet, my extraordinary loveliness has disappeared, Minnie's is hidden under the bedclothes, the soap is lying resignedly in the soap-dish, the Eau de Cologne is bubbling in the uncorked bottle, and as for the matches! I am sure if they don't take care, their rage will set themselves and the books on fire, and what will become of the poor Genie then?

Why am I writing about matches and fairy tales when the bells have been ringing for the taking of Sebastopol, the guns are firing from Cremorne?

Sept 21st. Ten more pleasant days are gone and that fatal 13th of October [2] comes nearer and nearer. I found Madame D'Arblay in my father's room yesterday, and that has excited me to go on with my own journal and I am seriously thinking of sending a Pepysina of my own

---

[1] Sir Frederick Pollock, Bart., Chief Baron of the Exchequer.
[2] The day of Thackeray's departure for America.

to Messrs. Bradbury and Evans. Evelyna, she says, was taken from Evelyn.

I am very sorry that I have not written down minutely all that I have seen and heard. Surely Mr. Carlyle is our Dr. Johnson, and I don't think my father is unlike Goldsmith; I am sure that he has as tender a heart though perhaps a better head. Mr. Frederick Tennyson dined here the other day with a Jewish painter, Mr. Solomon Hart. As I had not read Madame D'Arblay then, I don't remember much of their conversation. They talked a good deal about Italy and Italian politics, about Florence and the bad society there, about Lever who puts all his acquaintances into his books—and then they began to speak of bigotry and the domination of the priests.

I have been drawing pictures for Aunt Shawe but I care for too many things ever to do one perfectly. At one minute I'm mad to be an artist, the next I languish for an author's fame, the third, I would be mistress of German, and the fourth practise five hours a day at the pianoforte.

At Mrs. Browning's where we went one day to thank her for some kind enquiries after me—(One day I suddenly fell to the ground fainting, it was horrible) B. R. P.[1] was there talking intellectually. Mrs. Browning said she saw no reason why without illness the mind should ever fail. B. R. P. made a good many good-natured remarks upon the subject, but complained the next day, when we went to see her, that Mrs. Browning did not give evidence enough of a poetic mind. I laughed and said that was why it was so strong when it did appear, that keeping it bottled up like that, it came out with

[1] Bessit Rayner Parkes, afterwards Madame Belloc, the mother of Mrs. Belloc Lowndes and Hilaire Belloc.

much greater force, than if she let her ideas come dribbling out here there and everywhere.

ROBERT BROWNING
Drawn by Anny Thackeray in her Journal (1855)

I think Mrs. Browning the greatest woman I ever knew
in my life. She is very very small, not more than four feet
eight inches I should think. She is brown with dark eyes
and dead brown hair, and she has white teeth and a low
harsh voice, her eyes are bright and full of life, she has

a manner full of charm and kindness. She rarely laughs, but is always cheerful and smiling. She is great upon mysticism and listens with a solemn eager manner to any nonsense people like to tell her upon that subject. Her husband is not unlike her. A dark, short man, slightly but nervously built, with a frank open face, long hair streaked with grey, and a large mouth which he opens widely when he speaks, white teeth, a dark beard and a loud voice with a slight lisp, and the best and kindest heart in the world.

Monday, the 24th. I have been hard at work upon Madame D'Arblay and have nearly finished four volumes since Friday. Reading a book is not the business it used to be in her day, when Queen Charlotte asked Princess Augusta's advice as to whether she should read *Camilla* at once quickly, or wait till they went to Windsor. Fancy anybody waiting till they got to Windsor to begin a novel. Miss Burney is delightful. It's almost as good as if it wasn't true.

Madame D'Arblay is ruining my good intentions of getting up early. I am rarely able to read her in the day time, and then I can't drag myself away at night. I gave her up yesterday for something far less entertaining,— Captain Mark, Maria and Eleanor. The evening, however, was not as bad as I expected. Captain Mark politely requested us all round to favor him with a little music, and then sitting down at the piano himself played a little tune with one finger, at which his daughters laughed good naturedly. I can remember his doing it last time; I think it was the same tune and the same finger.

This morning we rushed into Papa's study; he was sitting in a funny costume writing in his scrap book, and he left off and kissed us and looked at us with his dear kind eyes, and told us to give him a tendero embraccia-

mento. He laughed and said Mr. Hodder had been copying something for him at the British Museum, about Lady
Something who was always called "the Ang Anglais."

MINNY AND HER DOG BROWNY
Drawn by Anny Thackeray in her
Journal (1855)

Whereupon the Hodder,
justly reasoning that the
lady was feminine, altered
it with the greatest presence of mind to an ange
anglaise.

There has been a dismal
parting in the house just
now. Mrs. Bakewell came
to fetch away our little
dog Browny to live with
Mama. Ever since my
Minny's poor little nose
has grown redder and red-
der, and the tears keep dribbling out of her eyes.

As we shut the front door Browny looked up at us so
wistfully, to see if we were coming too.

I think I could almost cry as Minny is doing but I am
sure Mama will like her very much. O! my dear Browny,
shall we ever see you again?

In her *"Notes on Family History"* written in 1894, my
mother describes her life at Paris during Thackeray's
absence.

When my father went away to America for the second
time, we went off to Paris with Mrs. Sartoris. We lived
in a little apartment next Grannie and learnt to play the
piano, and to draw with the Dickenses, and French with
a master, and looked for letters from week to week. They

came with pretty good news, and we led a very pleasant
life.

We used to go to tea at Mrs. Sartoris's who now lived
in Paris, in a beautiful old house in the Rue Royale. She
used to have music there and pink lamps, and beautiful
ladies came, and grand looking gentlemen. Of an evening
she used to sing most wonderfully, and the house seemed
all full of light and music. One day I went to dine with
Mrs. Sartoris, and after dinner she took me to the play.
While the play was acting she said, "Look!" and there in
a box was a lady with coal black hair, and a hard red
face, and a light black silk dress and a cameo brooch.
"That is George Sand, my child," said Mrs. Sartoris. I
was very glad to have seen her once tho' I did not think
she looked very nice, or at all like her beautiful thoughts.

Mrs. Browning was also in Paris this winter, in a
little warm, sunny, shabby, happy apartment, with a wood
fire always burning, and a big sofa, where she sat and
wrote her books out of a tiny inkstand, in her beautiful
delicate handwriting. Mr. Browning would come in and
talk. Pen was a little boy with long curls, and some of
the grand gentlemen from Mrs. Sartoris' used to come in
and sit round the fire.

W. M. Thackeray to Mrs. Carmichael-Smyth

[1855].

In both visits to America I have found the effects of
the air here the same. I have a difficulty in forming the
letters as I write them down on this page—in answering
questions, in finding the most simple words to form the
answers. A gentleman asked me how long I had been
in New York?—I hesitated and then said a week—I had

arrived the day before—I could not gather my thoughts
together readily enough to be able to reply to him—hardly
know what is said, am thinking of something else, nothing
definite, with an irrepressible longing to be in motion.
I sleep 3 hours less than in England, making up however
with a heavy long sleep every 4th. night or so. Talking
yesterday with a very clever man (T. Appleton of Boston), he says the effect upon him on his return from
Europe is the same—There is some electric influence in
the air and sun here wh. we don't experience on our side
of the globe. Under this sun people can't sit still, people
can't ruminate over their dinners, dawdle in their studies
and be lazy and tranquil—they must keep moving, rush
from one activity to another, jump out of sleep and to
their business, have lean eager faces—I want to dash into
the street now. At home after breakfast I want to read
my paper leisurely and then get to my books and work.

The men here read surprisingly, one tells me—a busy
man keeping a great Store in the City—that he does all
his reading in the railway-cars as he comes in and out
from his country residence daily. Fancy an English City
Grocer reading Tennyson and Browning on his way from
Brighton to Bread Street every day! A look over the
Times, a snooze for the rest of the journey wd. be enough
for him. Yesterday as some rain began to fall, I felt
a leaden cap taken off my brain pan and began to speak
calmly and reasonably, and not wish to quit my place.[1]

We are going to a party of 4 to dine with Mr. Dening
Duer, banker—most kind worthy man. We crossed at
the Ferry whence the Liverpool steamers sail (I had my
wishes as I saw one there in the dock)—the pavement is
infernal—disgraceful to a great City: the steam ferry

---

[1] These two paragraphs were printed by my mother in her Biographical Introductions to *The Virginians* and *The English Humourists.*

boat admirably commodious—(everybody has described the steam ferry boats). We drove through a part of Jersey City—a great raw comfortless city it is, and presently through the grounds of Mr. King's country place, wh. are famous for their beauty—A fine thunder storm darkened the place as we passed it and a hurricane blew for a minute—I could only see in the grounds, very lean spindle shanked little trees with their naked branches shivering—about Mr. Duer's house were the same scrubby melancholy bushes. I had been looking at sketches (by an excellent artist, Kensett) in the morning, of New England wood and sea-shore scenery, and the character of them seemed to be scraggy wan melancholy.

I went to see Laurence [1] who is doing very well. It does me good says he, to see an English coat—I understand the home feeling. An English servant maid opened the door at a friend's house yesterday and spoke with her kind modest way.—My man complains sadly that no one will speak a civil word to him—those polite accents wh. we remember in Ireland from the people, are changed here to a brusque sharp nasal defiant tone—not sweet to listen to. Looking for my companion the other day, as we arrived from Boston through a line of several cars— the cars set off in motion down the street. I begged the driver to let me out, and he began through his nose a shrill blast of curses quite curious to hear—he was only squealing the steam off. "Thar! Now! Jomp farrerd," says he not unkindly and I jumped and ran back to the Station.

Saturday 17. Dined with Mr. C. King—son of a Minister to England—A man of fortune once, as some of his brothers still are—then unlucky—Editor of *The*

[1] Samuel Laurence, the artist.

American newspaper—now President of Columbia College, lively amusing bright well-read thorough gentleman of the old school—very few like him. Was at school at Harrow with Peel and Byron—spoke still in admiration of Byron's pluck. Harrow challenged Eton to a match at cricket. Eton wh. had just been playing Westminster refused Harrow, saying that "Eton only played matches with schools of royal foundation."—"I am not good at cricket," said Byron, alluding to his foot; "but if you will get up an eleven to fight an Eton eleven I should like to be one of ours."

Peel, a lazy boy not mingling in games at all, was very good-natured. The boys would crowd round him before going into school begging Peel to do their verses—Greek Iambics or Latin Hexameters, nothing came amiss to him, and he would scribble off copy after copy of verses for the idle or dull ones. He was celebrated as a "shy"—his pleasure was to walk the fields solitary with a pocketfull of nice round stones; and if he saw a bird on a bough, to fire at it; and his skill was such as to bring down one bird in three—he would bring home strings of little birds with him. Byron would have been good-looking but his complexion was tallowy and his black hair had a greasy look.

Novr. 20. N.Y.

This is not very good fun is it? I don't know that it's worth keeping a journal but I think I shall go on—got my dear old Mother's letter and am thankful all are so well and busy. The lectures go better and better; the lecturer very well—God bless all at home, he says, and O but he longs to be there! Haven't been able to write this morning for the visitors pouring in.

W. M. T.

W. M. Thackeray to Mrs. Frederick Elliot

New York
November 27, 1855.

O you kind friend who ask me for nice long letters, you little know how difficult it is to write 'em! Three days ago to Anny I began and wrote 10 lines—never 10 minutes leisure have I had since—the room is never clear of visitors. I have been lecturing every night except 2 in the week, and in the intervals fever and ague. Isn't it good fun? Four attacks this month; and yet mussifully I have never missed a lecture—only a dinner or a breakfast or two wh. would be more pleasant than shuddering in bed but wh. I don't care for losing. What a comfort it was to me to get your letter on Sunday Mrs. J. E.[1]—and to hear your voices again after this long silence.

I have been away for 2 days to Troy on the Udson River and staid with some kind people, English and of the H. droppers too but very good and hearty, at a pretty country house between Troy and Albany— preached to a multitude at the former place, pocketted 200 dollars, agreed to go back again day after Christmas —spending the Anniversary with my English friends, and think that country the prettiest I have seen in the States. The river is like unto a certain Rhine we saw together, Albany is a fair old city with some houses 100 years old. Troy very picturesque, in fact it was a pleasant trip but for the 5 hours journey in the stifling cars where your feet freeze whilst your head throbs with heat. What very small beer is this I am letting run! This gay world of New York I have not seen. I am not a man, I'm a lecturer this time.

[1] Jane Elliot.

Of all the birds in bush or tree though many be more
    gay,
The one I love to hear and see, it surely is a J!
(What matter though its wings may be a somewhat pied
    with grey),
Those plumes are dearer far to me than birds of more
    display,
Than Molesworth splendid as a pea-hen on a sunny
    day—
Than golden pheasant Ailesbury—what other name to
    say?
O happy shall that meeting be (for which my heart will
    pray)
When I (as Alphabets agree) shall once more come
    near J.
O blessed shall the steamer be and fortunate the day
Which sees me safe across the sea and moored beside
    my K.[1]
Quick weary months and flee and flee! Speed dreary
    frost away
Come Spring! and those will seem to me as welcome as
    the May!
Quick William! go and fetch the tea and bread and
    butter tray,
And send—next door to sixty three—and if Mr. B's away,
Our best regards and Mr. T. has come back home to-day.

I see 3 *days* in the rhymes and I don't know what more
repetitions, but isn't friendship only a continuation of
repetitions? and don't we go and see each other though
we have no news? You must know I came home from
visits wh. I must pay thinking I was going to have a chill,
and have been toasting at the fire and written myself out

[1] Kate Perry, Mrs. Elliot's sister.

of it. Let us go out again on the tramp and come back at night well after the lecture please God, and write the girls their letter for tomorrow's steamer. *Wednesday 28. Bon jour Mesdames Adieu Mesdames.*

W. M. Thackeray to Mrs. Frederick Elliot

Buffalo, *Dec.* 28. New York, *New Earsday*
[1856].

A friend who takes charge of me at Philadelphia writes me word, that several letters are there waiting for me—most looking like business letters—one in a female hand wh. he daresays I should like—I wonder whether the female letter is from Chesham Place, London? I should like it to be from there. What have I been doing since I wrote to it last?—having a very good time at Boston. The Bostonians much better pleased and of course far better judges than at New York. At Buffalo they came two nights running, 3,000 of them! They are really surprizingly almost touchingly friendly. Prescott gave me his book—but Ticknor, whose book no one reads, is a cleverer man than Prescott. Both have comfortable old houses, handsome large libraries and famous Burgundy and Claret in their cellars. So has Longfellow at Cambridge, who lives in a noble old house whilom occupied by Washington. I have fallen in love with Bayard Taylor. He was a poor boy almost without shoes 10 years ago, since then he has travelled the whole world over to Europe, Egypt, Nubia, China, Japan, buried a wife whom he married in the last stage of consumption—made 6000£ by his books and lectures—is coming to London in Spring and is one of the most interesting men I have ever seen in my life. Lord, you should have seen the theatres full of people coming to hear yours truly! Providence is as jolly a place as Boston almost. There is always a knot of pleas-

ant folks, fogeyfied, respectable, fond of literature with
whom it is jolly to consort, and I shall remember Lawyer
Ames and a nice old University Library and a half-dozen
fellows with kindness always. From Boston I came 100
miles through a sweet country wondrously peopled to
Greenfield—such a nice village—with such a good fellow for my host here, Hon. G. T. Davis, a man you'd all
delight in. And the people flocked through the snow and
absolutely peopled the railway cars to hear the lecture.
Bon Dieu, what do they mean? It was Xmas Eve when
I was there and in a glass of wine I drank it to friends at
home. I wonder whom I thought of besides my children?
Can you guess? All Xmas Day travelled to Albany and
drove to Mr. Dunlop's house where was the kyndest
welcome and quiet, and a jolly little sleigh drive next
morning through a fairyland of frozen land, river and
city-scape where all the trees were glistening with silver, and all the houses iced with plum-cake snow, and
so, on the 27th from Albany I came on to Buffalo wh. I
reached at midnight—and to-day I have been sleighing
about the grim looking place and seen the darkling lake
and a bow shot across Niagara river, the black firs and
glittering white houses in Canada. But I mustn't write
any more of this letter but keep it for next mail. Next
year I am to begin at Philadelphia and then who knows
whither I go? to New Orleans perhaps—but wherever
I am you know there's always an electric telegraph between me and Cheshogan Place.

New York, *January 1*. A happy new year to all dear
friends says somebody who thinks about them a great
deal. What a blessing to be able to come 500 miles
through the driving snow—warm, snug I was going to
say, and comfortable I shd. have been but for an Irishman

who sate next me and had a cold and used his fingers as we use a pocket handkerchief. 20 years ago that journey wd. have taken a fortnight. Oughtn't I for one to be thankful for railroads, who never could have made all these dollars without 'em? Aren't you bored by my perpetual talk about dollars? Last night 2 hours after my arrival we had a fire in the hotel. Didn't I dash at my desk and sermons? It burned in a cellar but luckily the hour was early, the injines quickly on the spot—sermons, preacher, portmanteaux all were perfectly safe—and I went to sleep so sleepy that I guess I forgot even that little prayer which is said upon my pillow most nights.

Now I have put my holiday clothes on, and am going a-visiting. How will the Baxter house look now that Sally has left it? The marriage was very smart I hear— the bride looked lovely. Except my own gals I tell you I care for no women under 30. Good-bye—write me again long letters you women under 30. Address henceforth care of Messrs. J. G. King's Sons, New York, and they will forward to me. So hail Fred, and God bless J. and J. and K.

W. M. Thackeray to Mrs. Frederick Elliot

Cairo, St. Louis
March 24-26 [1856].

I did not write to you from New Orleans, but a pleasanter thing I heard from *mes bonnes sœurs*. I am just off the *Thomas Small* Steamer. Don't you see how my hand trembles? The boat in her passage up the river throbbed and trembled so that I thought she would shake her cranky sides off her ribs. And the river or the trembling of the boat gave me a fit of my old chill and fever which served *pour passer le temps* and occupied one day

out of the 5. "Look there, Sir!" says a cheerful friend of
mine on the Levee at N. O. as we looked at a hundred
enormous steamers moored there—"There, at the white
mansion do you see? That post was knocked out by a
piece of the boiler of the *John Jones* which burst here,
Sir—here on this spot where we are standing—and the
heads and mangled limbs of the people were scattered
and a mule, by G——, Sir, was cut in two in a dray, and
I saw it lying where you stand now!" The morning I
came away I read that a ferry steamer had taken fire on
the Delaware and 25 persons were killed, that the Alabama steamer on the Red River had bursted her boiler
and afterwards taken fire, the number of the killed not
known—pleasant wasn't it? for a man just setting out
on the river journey—but it's over and we didn't blow up
and we only took fire twice and burned down our upper
cook house and 2 hours ago I was quite sorry to leave the
T. Small. She was very clean and the servants civil and
I had Marryat's novels which kept me in amusement
through Alabama and Mississippi too.

He is a vulgar dog but he makes me laugh and very
few can now. Certainly not yours truly the author
of *V. F.*

Where do you think this is written from?—the place
they say that was Martin Chuzzlewit's Eden, Cairo, at
the confluence of the Ohio and Miss. such a dreary
Heaven abandoned place! but it will be a great city in
6 years spite of overflows and fever and ague. Twelve
hours to-night D. V. will take me to St. Louis and then I
shall feel as if I am on my road home again to see my
children and my *bonnes sœurs.*

Why need I go on making a quack of myself any
more? But if when I come home—after speaking of

Queen Vic. in the very handsomest manner, after making thousands of folks that hated him feel kindly for old George, I am attacked for speaking my mind about George IV (mind I left out the Q. Caroline scandal entirely)—by Jupiter!—It will do me good. I want a fight, I have always told you I can hit harder than any man alive, and I never do—but o! I think a little exercise would do me good! . . . In fine I want to get home more and more every day. To do what? to dawdle about Europe again and write another novel? Who can say for to-morrow? But I want to kiss my dear children and see my *bonnes sœurs* and speak to people whom I *can* speak to. Two months more of the *tréteaux* and mayn't we hope for these things? Yes if winds and waves and Heaven permit. I wonder after being how many whole weeks in London I shall want to be on the move again? God bless you, I keep this little piece for to-morrow and this is the 24th of March and isn't to-morrow my lady's day?

St. Louis.

Although it was my Lady's day I didn't fill the corner:
But each day here and far away I love and bless and
    mourn her.
Upon My Lady's Eve the cars a weary wight did carry
He wakeful looked upon the stars the pinewood and the
    prairie,
And as the weary travel ceased the sun arose in splendour
And sure he looked towards the East where dwells his
    lady tender.
He blessed the East he blessed the mother (methinks
    'twas mid-day yonder).
That saw his gentle Lady born——

And O me! I couldn't finish the rhyme—haven't I had
10 visitors? And isn't it post time now and mustn't I put
up with a kind kind greeting to *mes bonnes sœurs.*

W. M. Thackeray to his Daughters

Mobile, Alabama.
[1856].

A welcome letter of *Feb. 1* reaches me on the 29th.
after such a dreary weary half dozen journeys from
Savannah—to Macon 10 hours 200 miles through pine
flats—3 days there and only 170 dollars for my trouble—
to Columbus 100 miles in 8 hours through pine flats; to
Montgomery 100 miles 7 more hours, and 100 miles more
pine flats, and from Montgomery down the Alabama
River to this place—where I have got into such a nice
hotel, into such a beautiful room, have had such a comfortable warm bath and read over a clean breakfast such
a comfortable letter from my women. I think sometimes
of writing descriptive letters with remarks on the scenery
and illustrations—but I have not the face for that kind of
conversation with my family. The dreariness of this
country, *everywhere,* almost consumes me—there is
nothing to draw—one sketch I made on the river yesterday—o what a dismal scene!

This is what you see day after day—but the stink and
the dirt the foul glasses, the dingy shirts (many of them
with grand diamond brooches making a sunshine in those
shady places) the peeps of flannel, the hands and nails—
o my, who is to draw those? On board the boat a gentleman asked me to drink at night. We go and liquor at
the bar. Next day after dinner I offer *him* a drink.
"Nossir I have dined Sir—we don't drink *after* dinner,
Sir!" Before breakfast there was a fine groggy smell
about the bar though. What I shall never understand is

Mobile. Alabama

A welcome letter of Feb 1. reached me on the 29th after such a dreary weary half dozen journies from Savannah – to Macon 10 hours, 200 miles through pine flats – 3 days there and only 170 dollars for my trouble – to Columbus 100 miles in 8 hours through pine flats; to Montgomery 100 miles 7 more hours, & 100 miles more pine flats, and from Montgomery down the Alabama River to this place – where I have got into such a nice hotel into such a beautiful room, have had such a comfortable warm bath, and read over a clean breakfast such a comfortable letter from my women. I think sometimes of writing descriptive letters with remarks on the Scenery & institutions – but I have not the face for that kind of conversation with my family. The dreariness of this country. everywhere, almost consumes me – there is no thing to draw – one sketch I made on the river yesterday – o what a dismal scene!!

A city.

What you see
before you al dinner

This is what you see day after day - but the stink and the dirt the foul glasses, the dingy shirts (many of them with grand diamond brooches (making a sunshine in those shady places) the peeps of flannel. The hands and nails - O my who is to draw those? On board the boat a gentleman asked me to drink at night. We go and liquor at the bar. Next day after dinner I offer him a drink - "nossir I have dined Sir - wadont drink after dinner Sir. Before breakfast there was a fine groggy smell about the bar though. What I shall never understand is how there were no brigs or boars. As a favor I got a basin & towel for myself - other gentlemen fixed themselves in the barber's shop.

From Wilmington to Charleston | Augusta, Augustato | Savannah to Macon, Columbus, Montgomery.
350 m. | Charleston to Savannah | 200 m. | 100 | 100
| 140 m. 160 m.

General View of the Road for 1000 miles. —

This is far too pretty a view of the country for a thousand miles. The trees are not so tall nor can one give the ragged air W. forwards everything by any scrabble of the pen. Well. I am glad this journey is over so far. To me it is beyond measure stupefying and depressing. In the midst of it though I heard people talking about longing to get home and when they did get home — o mon dieu! It was a swampy sandflat of 100 wooden houses 4 churches and a hotel and a newspaper office — where they stopped and quite pleased to be back at this Elysium. When we emigrate it must be to live at Boston. That is a Xtian place anyhow.

We had beautiful weather on the steamer, and a volume of Marryat's collected novels kept me quite amused. I might as well have seen Hannah make though — This trip will not make us 100£ the richer, 100? no scarce 50. Never mind I did the best. How can I help it that it's pouring with rain so that hundreds will be kept away from hearing me to night? —

Sunday. Another famous letter from my gals and their Granny. But when will this one reach them? Why, it cant leave Boston for 10 days to come. And though I've cautioned Granny yet I know she'll go for to frighten herself. I am very well here, and as for money, how much do you think we cleared by our lecture of last night? no less a sum than three dollars. The night was awful that is the truth, the rain was making such a row on the roof of the hall that I was obliged to uplift my voice

how there were no bugs on board. As a favor I got a basin and towel for myself—other gentlemen fixed themselves in the barber's shop.

This is far too pretty a view of the country for a thousand miles.[1] The trees are not so tall nor can one give the ragged air wh. pervades everything by any scrabble of this pen. Well, I am glad the journey is over so far. To me it is beyond measure stupefying and depressing. In the midst of it though I heard people talking about longing to get home and when they did get home O mon Dieu! It was a swampy sandflat of 100 wooden houses 4 churches and a hotel and a newspaper office—where they skipped out quite pleased to be back at this Elysium. When we emigrate it must be to live at Boston—That is a Xtian place anyhow. We had beautiful weather on the steamer, and a volume of Marryat's collected novels kept me quite amused. I might as well have seen Savannah though—This trip will not make us 100£ the richer, 100? no scarce 50. Never mind I did for the best. How can I help it that it's pouring with rain so, that hundreds will be kept away from hearing me tonight?

Sunday. Another famous letter from my gals and their Granny. But when will this one reach them? Why, it can't leave Boston for 10 days to come. And though I've cautioned Granny yet I know she'll go for to frighten herself. I am very well here, and as for money, how much do you think we cleared by our lecture of last night? no less a sum than three dollars. The night was awful that is the truth, the rain was making such a row on the roof of the hall that I was obliged to uplift my voice and master if possible the roar of the storm—I wonder that 120 people were to be found to venture out on such

[1] See sketch on the preceding page.

a night—The hall cost 50 dollars that was 100 of 'em—
the advertisements 5 dollars, 10 people more—the door
keeper 2 dollars—remain 3 for me, Charles and my
family. But what must it be when 50 poor devils are
dependent upon a theatre, and nobody comes; and they
want money for their dinners and breakfasts? Afraid I
shan't get those other 9000 dollars I want. Well, we
must be longer getting them that's all. Have been to
church and heard a good sermon—saw the parson at my
sermon last night.

March 4. The boat for New Orleans sails in an hour
and I pop my little letter into the post beforehand. Have
I said that I have had famous good health here? better
spirits and appetite than I've had since I've been in the
States. Last night was a famous full house and I hope
we shall have the same at N.O. where at any rate I shall
have 10 jolly days, and then for the West and then for
my old friends of Boston Philadelphia New York—and
then for some older friends yet—O how welcome the end
of May will be and the sight of Liverpool steeples. God
bless my women and my dearest old Mother & G. P.—
and Miss Anny I insist on your having some money—and
that's a famous letter about the *Cricket on the Hearth*
and I am my dearest Children's loving father always.

Journal (1856)

Friday, 3rd April. We went to meet Papa this evening
at King's Cross Station, waited half an hour in dimness
and desolation, till ring a ring a ring, up go the lamps, a
hundred people start out of the earth, in drubs the train
with its two yellow eyes flurrying along the line, out pour
the passengers and we were just getting frightened, when

yes there he is. And so thank God for bringing him home again. Grannie had a better day than yesterday. Papa has done her good already. I have finished up my little medicine bottle and feel quite a dozen spoonfuls better.

Good Friday. A very dreary sad day but I think it has given me a lesson I shall never forget, and since then, what a jolly time we have had, thanks be for that. I hope I may be better in this new three shilling diary I have treated myself to! I hope I may have as pleasant things to write about in it, as in this one. Even the unpleasant things I did not write down have had a certain charm, and now as the past months are all vanishing away, they seem to glimmer brighter and brighter, and the notes to sound more beautiful as they recede. I daresay nobody could exactly see the drift of my remarks, but as I am making them to myself, I don't mind, so long as I understand them myself.

We had a great dinner on *Easter Sunday.* Albert Smith, Mr. Mayhew, Mr. Lever at last, Sturgises and Synges.

Thursday, the 20th I believe of April. We went to tea at Mr. Monckton Milnes'. Miss Wynn was there looking like a Queen and as I was talking to her a little old gentleman [1] with a decoration came up and said "You too—you go wid de papa, you travels wizz 'im?" "That would never do," says Miss Wynn, for I hardly understood what he said, and was awfully pozed when a little later Papa introduced me to him as a young lady who had read his history of the Popes, and didn't know if he were Catholic or Protestant! "So: you have read my bookes? In German? Heé hé?" "No, in English. I only

[1] Von Ranke the historian.

wish I could read them in German." "Ah! whiche tranz-
latione? the Scott—eh? eh?" I had read them, it's true,
about 8 years ago, and had entirely forgotten all about
them and when he asked me how many volumes and what
edition, I boldly said four and nervously talked about
Rome, without stopping for an instant to let him ask any
more questions.

Dean of Westminster in neat black silk stockings, and
Professor Thompson [1] who came with us from Mrs.
Macaulay's, where we went to pick up Papa in the
carriage. Professor Thompson, tall and good looking.
Papa said, "Here my dears, this is Professor Thompson,
a much greater man than your father, let me tell you,"
and Professor Thompson was too polite, I suppose, to con-
tradict this assertion. He went to Cambridge the same
year as Papa.

We also were made acquainted with Mr. Elwin for
the first time. He wears a hat very much on the back of
his head, and is perfectly tremendous in enthusiasm for
Professor Thompson. "You're not half appreciative,"
Minny says he said, "not half; you should hear my wife
and me." And when we asked him if Papa had told him
about *The Virginians,* he cried out, "Ah noble! noble!"
Well, it's pleasant to have people praise Professor
Thompson, and they may go on for a great many years
more. That is what I do not wish the lectures to do.
Papa is going away again on Monday, and it's horrible
saying goodbye once a month to him. [2]

To-day I was groaning over my Algebra when Amy
shrieked out, "Look! Look! Look!" and a beautiful

---

[1] Afterwards Master of Trinity.
[2] After his return from America Thackeray gave his lectures on *The Four
Georges* in England.

little open carriage drove across the retina of my far-sighted eye, and who but Papa inside (looking rather too big for it we thought) who had just bought it at the Panthéon, and instantly took a drive in his bargain.

W. M. Thackeray to his Daughters

Barry's British Hotel
Queen Street, Edinburgh
[1856].

MY DEAR LITTLE GURGLES,—Your dear Papa arrived last night at 9.30 and commissions me to tell you that he slept satisfactorily both in bed and about half the way down: losing the romantic scenery along the line and only waking up at the border to demm the railway man

who asked for his ticket. Your father is already a good deal engaged to dinner: and his faithful servant James says that there is a very good subscription list for the lectures—but your Papa suspects that there will be more praise than money at this town.

The inn is very comfortable and the city splendid—the

houses grand—the streets broad and spacious, beyond anything in London, only there's nobody in 'em. This is the grand St. with 2 inhabitants.

I think this is all your Papa's news. His cough he hopes is a little better, and he writes this while waiting for Dr. Brown [1] who is going to lionise him about the town—He did a little of his novel [2] this morning and he kisses his 2 darling gals with all his heart, and he sends his best regards to Miss Trulock and hopes you had a pleasant evening at Mrs. Bayne's. And so God bless you young women, prays

W. M. T.

W. M. Thackeray to his Daughters

November 21st [1856].

Yesterday I dined at the Artillery Mess with Col. Hamley—very agreeable Artillery officers from the Crimea—one a pompous good natured old fogey with dyed hair, who showed us a gold snuff box he had taken from a French General at Waterloo—another a very pleasant heavy Dragoon Colonel MacMahon, also Crimean—saw him at the Review a few days since roaring at the head of his men.

Was to be off to Glasgow this morning & got as far as the station just in time to remember I had forgotten the lecture, came back and read the paper in peace & quiet—think I shall be very glad when the 22 December is over & I have done wagging my jaws for a while—shall have enough to live next year without touching a penny of the Good for Nothing money—so much the better for you girls.

Am not in love with Miss Block any more since Mrs.

[1] Dr. John Brown, author of *Rab and his Friends*.
[2] *The Virginians.*

Brown told me she is here under a rubbing Doctor, and is rubbed every day for 2 hours with lard—of course she has a female rubber—but still . . .

Well this is Thursday now—I have been to Glasgow, lectured to 2000 people, come back again, taken a dose of dear delightful calomel and a dose this morning—for you see I am in a dreadful fright lest my attacks should come on; and go to Glasgow again tomorrow & lecture every night next week. So you need none of you spare yourselves anything—not carriages horses fires comforts of any sort—when for 2 hours talking we can have 50£ —Mind this.

I have been reading Walter Scott's Life all day and how at 60 odd he sat down to pay off a debt of 1300£ with his pen. What a courage! At Glasgow I went & took tea with Mrs. Blackburn who is painting with wonderful skill and beauty now—and she showed me a new invention which I think will spare poor Eyre all the trouble with my plates. And what more have I to say? Why that's all for the night I think. Please G. P. give the girls any money they want. I still think you might all take a fine day and X from Havre to Southampton, and so we might all dine in O. Square on Xmas day. I am answering letters every day about the lectures.

Friday morning. Nov. 22, 1856. And now I am going to Glasgow. It is a pretty drive and it would have been prettier if, etc. etc. not that I should have seen much of you, and you would have been a clog sometimes and no mistake. Last night we began the second series, very good audience considering. Afterwards I was obliged to go to a supper—of ladies and gentlemen. We had songs after supper, it was very odd and old fashioned and kind and huge tumblers were brought in, in wh. every man made himself a glass of whiskey toddy. Mine did me a great deal of good for I was tired after my day's work and dosing and this morning I woke up as fresh as possible. Have been spending it in writing lots of letters as usual—and now I send my benediction to my daughters and my humble duty to my parents and will go pay some visits. So farewell my dears.

W. M. T.

Journal (1856)

June 8. As I am very sleepy I only want to say two words before I go to bed on the last day of my eighteenth year. Goodbye, farewell, days!—you are dashing off much quicker than I expected, and I want to write down how happy this Paris winter has been. June has come again, and Papa and the old life, and another year of my life has gone by just as usual, except that I hope I really am a little older and wiser, though I haven't kept one of those resolutions I wrote down on my last birthday.

I won't write any more to-night; what's the use with this badly cut pen?

June 16. Came home from Shere with Tishy and find my Minnie has been ill. Had a very pleasant exerciseful time there, and three helps of beef for dinner.

June 25th. Has been a very pleasant day at Sydenham. Mr. Morris invited us three to fruit, flowers and testimonials on a long gay table. The Palace in the moonlight with the bright stars twinkling through the panes was mysterious and jolly. The gentlemen whooped foolishly and talked very loud, and the drive home in the open was delicious. Minnie has been telling me how cross I am getting sometimes. Twenty isn't a great deal, but things seem to pierce through and through my brain somehow, to get inside my head and remain there jangling. I wonder if it is having nothing to do all day pottering about with no particular object? It is no use writing novels, they are so stupid, it's no use drawing little pictures, what's the good of them? Reading Algebra is no use, I can't understand it. It's the same with Astronomy, and I mingle them all up together. I often think how pleasant it would be to have no brains, only good honest well-defined bodily labour.

I had one of my nightmares last night, sleeping and then presently waking up in a wretchedness impossible to describe. All my nerves in a state of tension; any fancy gripping hold of me and getting perfect dominion, *i.e.* that I can't turn in bed—that my heart is going to beat too quickly, tap, tap. It is only by determining to lie still with all my might and to go to sleep again, that this sort of state of annoyance with a tremendous jangling goes off.

To Anny Thackeray from Mrs. Dickens

Tavistock House
December 1st, 1856.

MY DEAR ANNIE,—Hoping that a long notice of our Christmas Theatricals may have the better chance of finding you disengaged at that Season, I send you the bill and hope we shall have the pleasure of seeing you, Mr. Thackeray and Minnie on the night to which it refers. I give my invitation this informal shape in order that I may assure you that it will give Mr. Dickens great pleasure to have you among the audience at a new play, with which he and all concerned have been taking great pains; also that I may ask you to favour me with as early an answer as is convenient, and that I may beg you to be here as near *half past seven* on the night as you can.

Yours very sincerely,

CATHERINE DICKENS.

TAVISTOCK HOUSE THEATRE.

Under the Management of Mr. Charles Dickens.

ON TWELFTH NIGHT, TUESDAY, JANUARY 6TH, 1857,

AT A QUARTER BEFORE 8 O'CLOCK WILL BE PRESENTED

AN ENTIRELY NEW

ROMANTIC DRAMA IN THREE ACTS BY
MR. WILKIE COLLINS

CALLED

THE FROZEN DEEP

The Machinery and Properties by Mr. Ireland of the Theatre Royal Adelphi.

The dresses by Messrs. Nathan of Tichborne Street, Haymarket.

Perruquier—Mr. Wilson of the Strand.

W. M. Thackeray to his Daughters

. . . There came along with this,[1] such a beautiful play bill in black and red ink—an entirely new Romantic Drama called the FROZEN DEEP with scenery by Telpin and Stanfield (Stanfd. in large capitals). The prologue by Mr. John Forster (that will be fine)—the characters by the old set, the ladies by Miss Helen, Miss Kate, Miss Hogarth, Miss Mary, Mrs. Wills, Miss

[1] Mrs. Dickens's invitation.

Martha to be followed by the farce in 2 acts called *Uncle John*. God save the Queen; carriages may be ordered at half past eleven.

It pains me to call you home,[1] but you can't live always away from your father. The arrangements must be made now or later, another maid as I opine, and a lady as companion for Granny. I wish she could be convinced that her illness is not much. . . . I have had fits of the fiercest depression—eh bien? With blue pill and Quinine, please Heaven the disease is to be put an end to. And so goodbye my dears says Papa. Mind my address is

> *Monday 8,*
> > 9 Bradford, Talbot Hotel.
> *Thursday 11*
> > Liverpool.   Care of A. Radcliffe, Esq.
> > > Northumberland Terrace, Everton.

Journal (1857)

January 25th. I can remember writing such an enormous quantity of melancholy these last two years in my journal, that it's quite a relief at last to say what fun we have been having. We came home yesterday at half-past five in the morning, from Minnie's first ball at Mount Felix. I wore a white silk gown and lilac flowers in my hair. Minnie had a green wreath and plenty of partners. I had only thirteen. Waltzing is Oh! so delightful and I danced with a cousin of Mr. Synge's who pleased me absurdly by a compliment as to my dancing. Minnie looked very nice indeed, just as a girl should look. I am so glad that this has been such a good beginning for her. It is much more wholesome to be undignified and happy than to know the world and be sullen.

[1] His children were staying with Mrs. Carmichael-Smyth.

I have come home thinking twenty-one is not such a tremendous age after all.

W. M. Thackeray to his Daughters

White Swan, Halifax
Friday, 1857.

MY BELOVED (ANGELS),—Although I am still at Halifax, instead of going to Sheffield, yet I am greatly better, have just eaten 2 wings of a fowl for dinner, and wished the poor bird had 4, and have no doubt after the prodigious discipline I have undergone that I shall be able to get through the rest of the campaign without trouble. Min's letter arrived from Leeds his morning—so that was as good as another letter from home. I have been reading Mahon with great comfort—am quite brisk and gay in my spirits though a trifle weak though for reasons wh. my blushes forbid me to mention, I am not quite good for a public lecture tonight.

Never mind—Tomorrow will begin again. We won't lose heart for a little check or two. I think the Dr. I have had here is about the best of them all. His name is Garlick, and I like him both in cookery and as a medical man. God bless my women. Write a famous account of me to Granny, and so good night says Papa.

W. M. Thackeray to his Daughters.

Royal Hotel, Sheffield
[1857]
*Chewesday—*17 of *Feb.*

This comes rather late for Valentine's Day. It is copied from 6 mugs in my sitting room at the horrible Inn at Halifax. This is a byootiful Inn. I have the gayest parlour looking over three cheerful smoky streets

My beloved

White Swan
Halifax
Friday.

Although I am still at Halifax instead of going
to Sheffield, yet I am greatly better have just eaten 2
wings of a fowl for dinner and wished the poor burd
had 4, and have no doubt after the prodigious discepline
I have undergone that I shall be able to get through the
rest of the campaign without trouble. Minis letter arrives
from Leeds this morning — so that was as good as another
letter from home. I have been reading Mahon with great
comfort — am quite brisk and gay in my spirits, though a
trifle weak, and though for reasons w? my blushes forbid
me to mention I wamnot quite good for a public lecture
to night. Never mind. Tomorrow will begin again. We
wont lose heart for a little check or two. I think the D?

Royal Hotel Sheffield
Chewsday. 17 Feb.

This comes rather late for

Valentines day. It is copied

from 6 mugs in my sitting

room at the horrible inn at

Halifax. This is a byootiful

Inn. I have the gayest parlour

looking over three smoky cheerful streets — a clean

snug bed room. a snug sleep. a pleasant book to

—a clean snug bedroom—a snug sleep—a pleasant book to read—Colonel and Mrs. Forrest came to tea last night after the lecture that's why I didn't write to the girls. I liked them both, she pretty and blonde, he very gentlemanlike. The people for the most part didn't understand a word of the lecture. Old Fogy President of Institution introduced me and insisted upon toddling into the room with me on his arm. What, is Mr. Thackeray infirm? asks Mrs. F. of her husband. It was Old Fogy who was infirm. I had a very pleasant calm day at Fryston, and yesterday for dinner here ate a pheasant, one of a brace which old Mr. Milnes insisted on sending to my daughters, though I told him I wasn't going home. The last time I was at F. in the year 41, Mrs. Milnes gave me a ribbon and a little étui, a something for my children—they were little trots of small size then—and she has been in Kingdom Come these 10 years I believe.

I wish those horrible newspapers would leave my health out. Some day the wolf will really come and no one will be frightened. Keep off Wolf for a few months! I want to put my lambs in comfortable shelter.

I am in the 4 vol. of Mahon. It amuses me. I have read Cockburn's *Memorials,* very pleasant too. It is delightful weather and the skeei is blyew through the smoke. Poor old Brookfield was born here my ♡ feels very soft towards him. Do you smell anything in this ink? It was thick, and I filled the bottle with brandy and soda-water. I have nothing to tell my dawlings but that I am very well busy and cheerful. I go to Leeds lecture, and come back tonight to York. I like the quarters I am in. So you may go on directing to this Royal Hotel till Saturday. I mean you may send by Friday night's post. I am glad you liked the drive to Q, never mind the 2/6.

Write to Granny and tell her how cheerfully your
dear father writes and God bless my women says Papa.

W. M. Thackeray to his Daughters

Sunday *March* 8 [1857].

MY LOAVES,—It was very comfortable having nothing
to do; and a good dinner and a good sleep also refreshed
your dear Papa. The Scotch expedition is a failure as
regards money, but pleasant enough otherwise—and this
confounded election too will deprive me of ever so much
more. Never mind: we shall only be a little longer
getting the 20,000.

At Dundee I found and read *Pendennis* & thought it
dreadfully stupid—Here I found and read 2 numbers of
Newcomes and thought them—O for shame you con-
ceited creature!—well—I can't help it. If I think it's
bad I say so with just as much candour—and the desire
of pease came into my mind—pease, repoge, and honest
labour not this quackery wh. I'm about now. Let us
NOT go into parliament: let us retire and take that
atelier and work and write honestly and humbly. The
frontispiece of *Pendennis* is verily always going on in
my mind.

Here are yours of yesterday just come in. I don't
think there would be any good in going over just now to
my dear old Mother—the coming away gives her more
pain than the meeting gives her pleasure. You see what
you do when you marry.—What slaves you become.
Well? and what immense happiness you enjoy I daresay
with the right man. These folks' pleasure has no doubt
been very greatly increased during 40 years by their
living together—the bottom of the Cup is rather bitter.
So may other dregs be.

That last was getting to be a very stupid sentence

Cause why? There is somebody sitting in the room. It is Professor Ferrier father of the pretty girl I wrote you about and whom I don't like quite so much on 2d thoughts —but those good people at Glasgow are quite as nice and kind. I had a quiet evening on Friday with them, after a delightful ride through lovely country from Dundee, by Perth, Stirling, to Glasgow. And tomorrow it is Glasgow again, & Glasgow on Friday, and Dundee Wednesday—care of Mr. Chalmers Bookseller—but I don't care about your writing unless there is something particular to say, as I shall be 3 miles away from Dundee at the house of Sir J. Ogilvy wherever that may be.

And so with a benediction on my gals their Papa puts a cigar into his mouth, and goes out to take a little walk in Church time. Mind and go to Chesham Place to-morrow night & say I got a letter from there on Saturday only, and give my best love to all there including poor J. O. B.[1]

W. M. Thackeray to his Daughters

Keir-Dunblane
Monday Apr. 26 [1857].

MY DEAREST WOMEN,—These last few days I have wished for you for the first time since I left home for I've been staying in a most beautiful house and country and have such a prospect before my eyes now as wd. do yours good to look at.

Mountains as handsome as our Swiss mountains with a little snow on some of 'em; and beautiful rocks and dark pines and larches bursting out into green, and on the prettiest of the rocks in an immense great plain cov-ered with 1000 villages, there's Stirling Castle looking

[1] Mrs. Brookfield.

as grand as may be, and placed there for the very purpose of making a landscape.

Then the Park is full of birds singing and sheep and the most jolly little lambs—Minny would give 2.ᵈ to see the little lambs and I would give 3.ᵈ to see my young muttons. And I went to a Scotch Church yesterday and heard 5 psalms sung, and a sermon, and an elder of the congregation ordained, and Stirling of Keir who is my host, says he hopes I'll bring you here but I've my doubts, and James says the place looks like a Paradise after Glasgow; and I'm going to Greenock a lecturing, and shall be glad when I see old England again.

On Saturday is the Royal Academy dinner, and on Sunday I have a party at home, so I shan't have the pleasure of snoring after dinner in your company till Monday evening.

Tell the Cook that there will be 8 gentlemen to dinner on Sunday, and I would like a clear soup, fish, 2 entries, and sweets and Macaroni for second course—a nice dinner—and something plain for dessert afterwds. Isn't this an amusing letter? It's one of 10 I'm writing—I can't afford to amuse you but I can always love my dearest women. God bless you.

W. M. T.

Journal (1857)

July 8th. Home at four o'clock this morning from Woolwich Ball. Very pretty, but somehow it wasn't quite up to my ideal. Sun rose and Minnie went to sleep in the carriage coming home. Should like to go to a ball three times a week.

Tuesday night. Mr. Cardwell, M.P., is getting into bed I should think. Papa came home beaten [1] but in

---

[1] Thackeray stood for Oxford City; in the Biographical Introduction to *The Virginians* my mother quotes from her journal this description of the election.

capital spirits and we are very happy again now, but the
first news that Papa wasn't elected wasn't at all agreeable.

Thackeray 1005
Cardwell 1070

About five o'clock Amy and I thought we would walk
off and try and get some news of how the election was
going in town.   We met Mr. Helps on the way, who came
part of the road with us; he said that though Papa denies
it he really does speak very well.   I can't help being glad
on the whole that he didn't get these grapes.   When we
reached the news-shop we asked for the evening paper,
only one *Express;* and a scornful young shopman dived
into the sheet when Amy asked him the state of the poll,
and instantly informed us it wasn't decided.   We took
the paper into the Park to read, and there was Cardwell
calmly ahead with 857 votes and poor Thackeray coming
after.   I gave a great jump of disgust and flung the paper
away, and as we came home through the drizzling rain
we felt dreadfully inclined to cry.   Grey had got another
newspaper when we got home with even worse news.
This protracted agony was dreadful and gave me a sensation of toothache in the mind.   It was the greatest relief
to have it out at last in the shape of a telegram, and now
Papa has come home so cheerful and well that it has left
off being a sorrow at all, only a little trial.   He has been
telling us of a fat auctioneer who would call him Thackeray; he says if the poll had been put off a single day
more he would have been obliged to kick him.   He says
he will never go canvassing again, it's too disgustingly
humiliating.   "Are you Mr. Neat's friend?   Master's
h'out, but he said I was to say he would vote for yeou."
Papa himself is a Cardwellite he says, only of course

he couldn't well say so—my politics are filial politics and
so goodnight.

We have been having a very delightful month at
Brighton learning to ride and being really very happy.
That is what Papa and I were talking about just now,
happiness I mean; and indeed when one comes to think
of it apart from religion, life and happiness are utterly
incomprehensible.

. . . If one were to die tomorrow how dreadfully idle
and vain and selfish one's past life will have been. I
don't steal or lie or get into passions, it would be too much
trouble, I live a lazy luxurious comfortable idle life
without courage or energy. I say to myself I cannot
understand religion; therefore I leave it alone and read
novels on a Sunday because I do not think it wrong,
while Brother Tompkins at the Oratory is starving and
thrashing himself because he thinks it right.

August 21st. It is a very hot day and Papa has invited
ever so many Americans to dinner, besides Punch.

The drawing room looks very brilliant from the square,
but the party doesn't sound as if it was being very
amusing.

I think we have had quite as good fun as the distinguished company upstairs, picnicking in the dining room
amongst undulating scenery of chairs, cushions and
tables, and eating up some horrid tough mutton.

We thought the drawing room got larger and larger
at every fresh move: when the table was pushed into the
back drawing room we were enchanted, when the arm-
chairs went rolling in we stood admiring, and when the
dining room table from downstairs travelled up on the
shoulders of Mr. Gunter's men, we said it was exactly
like the Waterloo Gallery and so it was.

Mr. Bayard Taylor is here, "der ein Hero ist." A

gallant bearded man with a handsome face. He is very like Francis I, so we think, and we like him even better. Ah! America if your sons are all gallant gentlemen like this one, if your daughters simple ladies like his sisters, I wonder—what profound remark shall I make now?

W. M. Thackeray to Mrs. Carmichael Smyth

[1858]

I must send my dear old Mother and G. P. a line of Xmas greeting, and tell them how well and happy the young ones are whom I left a couple of hours ago at Walton, in the midst of such lavish splendours and magnificence as I have never seen the like of in the finest houses here—all wh. splendours, Christmas trees loaded with presents, fountains of Champagne and Hock, drives in coaches and four & I don't know what more, are lavished upon 8 or nine young girls and 2 or 3 gentlemen —One of them was busy all day concocting the speech wh. he is to let off in an hour or two at the City of London Tavern in behalf of the Commercial Travellers school. Anny to whom I dictated the speech remembers all the points, and the very words deuce a one of wh. I recall verbally. I should not be sorry to fail, for then people won't ask me again and I shall be rid of a very severe tax wh. is laid on men in prominent positions.

We are to have more holiday making at the Pollock's, and I can't resist for I can't bear that the girls should lose any pleasure, and meanwhile how is No. IV [1] to be got out? Well, other folks have their drawbacks and their encumbrances—let us bear ours without too much grumbling.

[1] *The Virginians.*

Your heart would have melted over a little boy [1] of 2 last night trotting round the Xmas tree crying out "O Crissamy Tee Crissamy Tee!" He looked like a little cherub just peeping into heaven: & he didn't like even to take away his own share of toys from the general splendour—O dear—I should like very much to stop at home alone for 3 days and get on with that No. IV! It was kind of the Sturgis' to ask Amy and as much is made of her as of any one—and very well she looks too, and so does Miss Anny who has got thinner & is a comfort to look at, especially to her father & to your son my dear old Mother.

God bless both of you he says, and now let us rehearse that speech.

Journal (1859)

March 3rd. Awoke very tired and drowsy and read Tales from Spenser's *Faery Queen,* and considered that I too might be a Knight to a certain degree and that I was certainly wasting my time in the Castle of Indolence at that very moment. It was Miss Agnes Strickland who had suggested a new phase of existence to me the night before.

Rotten Row with Amy in the afternoon. Somebody on a white pony came up to us. It was Arthur Prinsep looking like a little Knight out of Spenser with violets in his button hole. "Where are you going to-night?" "Nowhere, I beg to say, though we have several invitations." Then he talked about Mrs. Senior and rode away. Everything delightfully glittering and life-full, ladies horses, spring sunshine. In Kensington the white horse caught us up again. "I like your violets very much," said I, and of course they were instantly presented to me.

[1] Howard Sturgis.

"Do come to lunch," cries the youth. But I shake my head. "Do come on Sunday. What a wonderful season this is," and off he rides. Amy and I walk home along the roads and we moralize over violets.

March 6th. Read Meteorology from 12 to 1. Went to dine at Mr. Sterling's, sat next Mr. Reeve. Mrs. Norton was there, wonderfully kind and stunningly handsome with a golden "salve" on her forehead.

March 8th. Mrs. Brookfield to dinner, Mr. Harcourt, Mr. Massey, Mr. Moseley. I talked to Mr. Moseley, and Mr. Harcourt said aggravating things about women as usual. It's absurd to be annoyed as it's only a joke but it's very riling. O ye heavens! look at him and then look at me! Why am I to be contemptible all my days long?— Why is he to be so much more worth in his own, in everybody else's estimation? Why has he got work and leisure and strength and height and a thousand more advantages which I can't get at, not if I try till I burst like the frog in the fable? Why am I ridiculous when I spar at him with foolish little thrusts? I'm sure my brains are as good as his. I could feel this last night while I was listening to his talk with Mr. Brookfield.

March 21st. To Mrs. Carlyle's where we found Lady Stanley looking very jolly who told us how she had lived for two years on mutton and rice. "Love to your father," says she, "Come along Maude," and off they go. Mrs. Carlyle was speaking enthusiastically of *Adam Bede.* She has written some of her enthusiasm off to George Eliot and had grateful messages in reply. Mr. Carlyle quite declines reading the book, and when Mrs. Carlyle hoped it might be sent to her, he said, "What should George Eliot send it to you for?" "Why shouldn't he, as he sent me his first book?" says she. "You are just like all weemen," (Mr. Carlyle always calls them weemen).

"You are always forming unreasonable expectations," growls he, and at that moment ring at the bell and in comes the maid with a brown paper parcel containing the book!

March 22nd. Felt miserable and sick of the world in general. Picked up a kind cheery Papa at the Reform Club. To the Bishop of London's where I talked to Mrs. Twistleton. I told her I had asked Mrs. Carlyle who was her greatest friend and that Mrs. Carlyle had said Mrs. Twistleton, at which she looked delighted. Mrs. Clough was there too and after all my liking for her and correspondence she mistook Minny for me. Dean of St. Paul's [1] asked, "Do you know who the lady behind you is?" so I replied "Mrs. Grote." "My dear Mrs. Grote," he cried, "Heaven forbid! It's Miss Agnes Strickland in black velvet with a bead berthe," and then turned his courteous old back upon her. Came home without Papa who went on to Lady Derby's.

Friday. In the Park saw Mrs. Norton careering along between two young men. One of them, B. Norton, in an astounding hat shaped like a very hideous Etruscan vase. I had a pink gown and blue shawl, and was ashamed of being recognised in such a garb, so we dodged about on the grass and let Mrs. Norton go by.

Anny Thackeray to her cousin Emmy Irvine

36, Onslow Square.

Minny says that if the Angel Gabriel came to fetch me I should say, "Just wait a minute till I have finished this note," and in the meantime with all this scribbling I have kept you waiting ever so many days.

[1] Dean Milman.

Papa gave us a letter to read this morning; it is from Edward Thackeray's colonel recommending him for a V.C. Colonel Smith says he is one of the bravest of his Engineers, and after all, as Papa says, bravery is the best thing in the world and makes everyone more friendly and enthusiastic than cleverness, or wisdom, or learning, or rank or whatnot, and so it is no wonder if we all feel proud to have a V.C. come into the family.

We have got some people coming to dinner tomorrow, one Sir Edwin Landseer, who has sent us a little dog picture. Another is Dr. Sandwith, an exceeding stiff and disagreeable young man, who was locked up in Kars, and performed prodigies of valour, and is, I believe, covered with Victoria Crosses, but all the same not in the least pleasant to sit next at dinner.

I dined the other day at the grandest dinner I ever went to, the Duke of Argyll's on Campden Hill, but the Duchess was so kind, that it wasn't near as alarming as I expected. Archdeacon Sinclair was on the other side of me at dinner, and you are announced when you go in, by a Highlander in a kilt, who suddenly steps forward, bare-kneed strap shoes and all, and says, "Mr. and Miss Tackey" in an imposing voice at the door.

Journal (1859)

September. We went to Folkstone and very jolly it turned out to be, except that when we got out of the train we found we were at Dover! We had a pleasant little sitting-room on the ground floor. Freshness, the Pier, the bathing-machines. Breakfast in the public room, Hythe every day, and drives back at night under the stars. Papa was in a bad way most of the time with the end of *The*

Virginians, and came and went and left us perforce a good deal to our own devices.

After six weeks we crossed over to Boulogne. All night in the train to Tours was delightfully ghostly, swift, fresh, and then came the solemn old city asleep. Then the South luxuriant to begin with, then vine-clad and garlanded, then arid, dreary, covered and muffled with dust. When we got to the shores of the Mediterranean we began to breathe again. Then came Milan, where we saw the wounded French soldiers crawling in the sun, Magenta [1] with the bullet marks still on the lamp posts and houses, and Como where they are illuminating and where I began to be unwell. Through the Via Mala next day to Chur, where we stopped at last and my illness declared itself.

Then as soon as I was better to Paris, where we picked up Grannie and G. P. Twenty one days have gone since we reached home, during which the *Cornhill* [2] has been put together. Papa delightfully well and in good spirits, two new members of the establishment Theo and Hetty.[3]

W. M. Thackeray to Mrs. Carmichael-Smyth

Chur
Saturday 1 *October* [1859].

MY DEAR OLD GRANNY,—We have not been in Paradise the last week, but please God, Anny's difficulties are nearly over. There is good however out of all these mishaps, Min has been a famous nurse for her sister and has borne her hard times very well: and if she repents of having had her own way, somewhat in opposition to her Papa's, I shall not be sorry for the circumstance.

---

[1] Battle of Magenta, June 4, 1859.
[2] The first number of the *Cornhill Magazine* was published January 1, 1860, with Thackeray as editor.
[3] A pair of ponies.

We could not have had a prettier prison than this dear little old town: nor I am sure a more patient prisoner. If I could but have had pluck enough to do some work, I might have turned the imprisonment to some account; but I tried and hadn't the heart that's the truth—though I recollect having to work when poor Nan had the same complaint as a baby twenty years ago, and it was necessary to find a guinea for the Doctor. If I can work for 3 years now, I shall have put back my patrimony and a little over—after 30 years of ups and downs. I made a calculation the other day of receipts in the last 20 years and can only sum up about 32000£ of moneys actually received, for which I have values and disbursement of 13000£ so that I haven't spent at the rate of more than 1000£ a year for 20 years. The profits of the lectures figure as the greatest of the receipts 9500£—*Virginians* 6 —*Vanity Fair* only 2. 3 years more, please the Fates, and the girls will then have the 8 or 10000 a piece that I want for them: and we mustn't say a word against filthy lucre, for I see the use and comfort of it every day more and more. What a blessing not to mind about bills![1] The expenses of this journey for the first 18 days were prodeegious; and who cares? I, for my part, should have liked no journey at all, or no farther than Homburg and Baden, but the young folks willed otherwise, or seemed to will—and I like them to have their holyday. All along the road they have worked the prices up to be pretty like England—the inn at Milan where they charged us 12 francs for rooms 8 years ago, they make you pay 25 now, and so on and so on—I wonder what your resolves have come to by this time, and whether you stay on in England, or have gone back to Paris, or will

[1] This passage was quoted by my mother in her Biographical Introduction to *Philip*.

try Bath or Brighton? I have been living at Bath for the last ten days in Miss Austen's novels which have helped me to carry through a deal of dreary time—they and the *Times* newspaper which the landlord of this out of the way Inn luckily takes in for the English who *don't* come. How dismal I should have been without the *Times* newspaper! Well, I have been dismal enough with it: but my dear Nan is better please God; and her Papa's spirits rise accordingly. Now let us go and get some money from the Banker's, and tomorrow D.V. let us be on our way home to work and printer's devils. I have dreamed constantly that the number wasn't ready, and here was the end of the month: it shows how the care weighs upon one: but Law bless us, who hasn't cares at 50 of some shape or other? As I think about the poor Corkrans and their cares, I am ashamed of my own good fortune. Here's my paper full. Goodbye my dear G. P. and my dear old Mother.

W. M. T.

VI

1860—1863

IT was in the *Cornhill Magazine* of May, 1860, that my
mother's first article was published. How it came to be
written is told in the following letter to George M.
Smith, in answer to his question, "At what age did you
begin to write?"

1900.

"I feel much flattered you should ask such a question.
I had written several novels and a tragedy by the age of
fifteen, but then my father forbade me to waste my time
any more scribbling, and desired me to read *other*
people's books.

"I never wrote any more except one short fairy tale,
until one day my father said he had got a very nice subject for me, and that he thought I might now begin to
write again.

"That was 'Little Scholars' which he christened for
me, and of which he corrected the stops and the spelling,
and which you published to my still pride and rapture."

George Smith in his own *Reminiscences* writes of the
essay and says, "Thackeray sent it to me with a letter containing the following passage: 'And in the meantime
comes a contribution called "Little Scholars," which I
send you, and which moistened my paternal spectacles.
It is the article I talked of sending to *Blackwood;* but
why should *Cornhill* lose such a sweet paper because it

was my dear girl who wrote it?   Papas, however, are bad
judges—you decide whether we shall have it or not!' "

W. M. Thackeray to Mrs. Carmichael-Smyth

Palace Green, Kensington, W.
July 5 [1862].

My dearest old Mother gets the budget from the girls
and the history of our doings.   On Thursday at 6.15 p.m.
after working all day I wrote Finis to *Philip:* rather a
lame ending.   Yesterday I spent all day in great delecta-
tion and rest of mind making a very bad drawing.
Young Walker who is 20 does twice as well: and at 20
you know we all thought I was a genius at drawing.   O
the mistakes people make about themselves!   Then at 5
we drive down in our pretty new carriage to the Aumale
Fête at Twickenham, where I daresay the Dukes and
Duchesses would have admired my new lavender gloves
(price 2/s) very much—only I forgot 'em and left them
in my great coat pocket, never mind it was a beautiful
fête and I am all the better this morning, because I could
only get a crust to eat and a scrap of galantine—and did
the girls tell you how I had no dinner the day before
having to take them to the *Barbiere* (a new opera by Mr.
Rossini)—and where I had a most refreshing sleep in
the back of the box.   And this is our life: and now there
is a little lull after a constant care and occupation.   No
by the way, not yet, quite.   Mr. Smith says "Do, pray
write a Roundabout paper" and that, you see, is churning
in my brain whilst I am writing off a scrap to my dear
old Mother.   Mesdemoiselles . . . were not ready for
prayers, so I was parson, and I can tell you one person of
the congregation was very thankful for our preservation
and all the blessings of this life which have fallen to us.
Think of the beginning of the story of the Little Sister

in the Shabby genteel story twenty years ago, and the
wife ill and the Publisher refusing me 15£ who owes me
£13.10. and the *Times,* to which I apply for a little more
than 5 guineas for a week's work, refusing to give me
more—and all that money difficulty ended. God be
praised and an old gentleman sitting in his own house
like the hero at the end of a story. The actual increase
of health and comfort since we got into the Palazzo is
quite curious. I am certainly much better in body—I
think the novel-writing vein is used up though and you
may be sure some kind critics will say as much for me
before long.

Anny's style is admirable and Smith and Elder are in
raptures about it. But she is very modest and I am mis-
trustful too. I am sure I shan't love her a bit better for
being successful.

Here comes Mr. Langley [1] with the proofs which must
be read and there is a good morning's work over them.
And then that Roundabout Paper—a plague on it—But
it will be 60 or 70£.

"Mr. Langley, where is the Cicero? in 2 volumes
quarto. I want a quotation out of it?" Mr. Langley
maunders about the room helplessly. He won't find it:
I shall: and he will be persuaded that he found it, and
that I cannot possibly get on without him. I wonder
shall we make out the Petersburg journey? I have a
fancy for it, because it will pay for itself in a couple of
papers that will be as easy to write as letters and won't
wear and tear the brains. Then we must do some more
work. I think the story which I began 20 years ago and
then, and then——

Did you read about poor Bucklo when he got the fever
at Damascus crying out, "O my book, my book!" I don't

[1] Thackeray's amanuensis.

care enough about mine to be disquieted, when that day comes. Shall I live to do the big history? Who knows? But I think I shall like to work on it if the time is left me. God bless you, dear old Mother, I don't write to you by post, but I am writing through the printer all day long and the song is always Ego, Ego, God bless us all— and now come Mr. Langley and let us go through those proofs and all the blunders.[1]

W. M. T.

"Little Scholars" was followed two years later (1862) by a novel, *The Story of Elizabeth,* which came out as a serial in the *Cornhill Magazine.* In April of the following year it appeared in book form with illustrations by Frederick Walker. The success of *Elizabeth* was immediate, and although published anonymously, the book was at once recognised as a work of originality and genius. When the authorship was made known my mother's reputation as a writer was assured.

Rhoda Broughton has written of the impression the novel made upon her: "Vividly comes back to me the memory of my astonished delight when *The Story of Elizabeth* burst in its wonderful novelty and spring-like quality on my consciousness, written, as I was told, by a girl hardly older than myself!"

Anne Thackeray to George M. Smith

Palace Green
[*August* 1863].

DEAR MR. SMITH,—Thank you for your note and for letting me see *Elizabeth* in her beautiful new clothes.[2]

---

[1] Passages from this letter were quoted by my mother in her Biographical Introduction to *Philip.*

[2] A new edition of *The Story of Elizabeth* had just been published by Messrs. Smith and Elder.

I am quite proud of such a type and take it as a personal compliment.

I am also very much pleased because two different heroes have asked me confidentially if I was not thinking of their *affairs* when I wrote the story!

Yours sincerely,
ANNE THACKERAY.

Journal (1863)

Feb. 9. Elizabeth continues to be a success. It's quite a little fortune and more that is coming to me. My good fortune, I don't know why, makes me feel ashamed.

. . . We have been to Mentmore [1] for a week, and were immensely amused and well treated. We made some new friends. We lived upon damask and paté de foie gras. Cavendishes, Harding Russell, Fitzjames Stephen, Miss Probyns, Curries, Lady Augusta Bruce, every one of them pleasant to know.

To Rhoda Broughton we owe another recollection of the book. She writes of Thackeray's delight in his daughter's success. "Do you remember Mrs. Kemble telling Henry James of a luncheon party, where she met Thackeray and your mother? It was just after the publication of *Elizabeth* and Mrs. Kemble said to Thackeray that people were beginning to say that Anny stood next to him as a writer, and he replied with emotion: 'Yes, it tears my guts out!' "

[1] A contemporary of my mother's wrote in September 1918: "It was at Folkestone in 1861 that I saw so much of the Thackerays. Anny Thackeray was then writing *The Story of Elizabeth* and was very splendid in every way. She also stayed at Mentmore when I was there, but she was always a personage and I was a mere girl."

Notes on Family History

Papa took up my diary for 1864 and said: "Next year begins with a Friday." And I, little thinking, replied: "Papa, I assure you Friday is our lucky day. Indeed it will be a happy year."

I remember now, only I can't bear to think of it, that all last year he was never well; he said: "Life at this purchase is not worth having. If it were not for you children, I should be quite ready to go."

One day not long ago, I came into the dining room and he was sitting looking at the fire. I do not remember ever to have seen him looking like that before, and he said: "I have been thinking, in fact, that it will be a very dismal life for you when I am gone. If I live, I hope I have ten years' more work in me. It is absurd to expect a man to give up his work at 50." He said too: "When I drop there is to be no life written of me; *mind this* and consider it as my last testament and desire."

To-day I do not remember many things he has said. I can see him passing his hand through his hair, laughing, pouring out his tea from his little silver teapot. I can see him looking at his face in the glass and saying, "I am sure I look well enough, don't I?"

Thackeray died suddenly on the morning of Christmas Eve, 1863.

Mrs. Carmichael-Smyth.
From a sketch by
Anny Thackeray

JOURNAL

VII

1864—1867

Journal (1864)

THIS sad year began at Freshwater. It was bitter weather. Minny and I were at Mrs. Cameron's cottage. She was goodness in person. Alfred Tennyson used to come and see us in his cloak. Hardinge Cameron would ask us to go for walks and try to interest Minny in painting.

From Freshwater we went to the Ritchies at Henbury. Grannie came and joined us there. Terrible religious discussions: Grannie's religious views were always very intense and she took our different habits of thought passionately to heart. It used to make us miserable to make her so unhappy. Minny would be made downright ill, and I used to get half distracted.

At last Grannie went away to London looking very ill. (I can still see her as she looked at Henbury, a noble and magnificent figure like one of Michael Angelo's sibyls, only with a far gentler and more beautiful expression.) [1]

February 22nd. Had a good cry under a tree among the crows. For a walk with Minny along the road; all the trees looked like people we knew. Birds circling over the fields.

March 2nd. From Henbury we went back to Freshwater, and then to Warnford, to Mrs. Sartoris. Warnford was a great house in a great park; a wide river ran

---

[1] A note added by A. I. R. to her journal in 1895.

across the meadows with drift wood, bare ash trees and willows everywhere.

The drawing-room was a lofty room, lights burning, yellow curtains, tall cabinets, a high chimney piece and the fire smouldering on the hearth. Mrs. Sartoris singing Gordigiani's passionate complaint.

Everything harmonious and bright, except that my heart ached and ached. Minny sat leaning her head against the chimney. Grief amidst carving and splendours—it puts me in mind of Mendelssohn's *Wedding March*.

Mrs. Sartoris in her own room, sitting at an open window with a stone terrace. China and tapestry on the walls within, without the old court. The rooks fly round and round, there are green hills beyond the fields; one seems stifled and closed in on every side, and I feel as if some day the hills will come rolling down and overwhelm the house.

There is a fountain on the terrace, and brick steps wet with rain lead down to the lawn. The rooks are flying in the air ever so high. I hate them. One little bird trilling freshly in the rain. He makes me feel more idle and more sad. Let's improve our minds and read something. Saw advertisement of the sale at home, as they all sat reading in the lamp-lit room.

We have been making up our minds to go. A sweet lovely day, walked out with May.[1] As we were walking on the terrace, with the fields and the meadows all bathed in evening light, suddenly looking up we saw the little new moon up in the sky.

May asked for a bit of silver to turn in her pocket. Mrs. Sartoris replied: "Certainly, child, if you ask her for anything." I said: "There seems nothing left to ask

[1] Mrs. Evans-Gordon.

for any more." Mrs. Sartoris answered: "Ask for peace."

In April Minny and I took a cottage at Putney while everything was being settled, coyprights, houses, lawyers' business. Mr. and Mrs. Prescott were at Clarence House close by. They had a lovely old garden, and a kind big house filled with boys, girls, sick and sorry people, and we went there constantly.

I am sitting under the trees, in our little garden, a big bumble bee buzzing and a lovely throstle singing. Minny said: "Annie, while we are bodies, it is no use pretending we are spirits."

Mr. George Smith wrote to us that Papa's bust was to be put up in Westminster Abbey.

In August we were at Arromanches in Normandy. On St. Michael's Day, September 29th, Minny and I came from Normandy to our little house in Onslow Gardens. It wasn't nearly so sad as we feared. It was like coming home again.

To Mrs. Fanshawe

16, Onslow Gardens
[1864].

The first word to you from this new life. We are very peaceful, we two together, a little lonely as you may think. It is like living at an Inn and does not feel as if it were home exactly, but when we look at Papa's picture upon the wall, and sit at his table, and see things which were his, then it becomes a strange bit of wreck saved out of the past.

We have been here a month, and Grannie is coming this week, and that will take away a little of the loneliness.

. . . I have a study I like very much, though other people think it gloomy, and we have a pretty square grey-

walled drawing-room with chintz and china. We find
the dining-room a hole, but the bed-rooms are airy, and
there's a bath and everything we want.

We have had to buy one or two things for the house,
among them a dining-room table. I was amused to go
off with Fanny into the city to find one. It's a little bit
of a thing but round, and strangely enough we happened
upon a shop where Papa used to go, and where we found
our own old table from Onslow Square, but it would have
been too big.

The other day we were at Cambridge and found Papa's
name written in the old college books, among many more
of the old familiar names. It was like getting nearer to
Papa to see his youth with our own eyes. We passed his
rooms without knowing them. A kind sick clergyman
who was there remembered him in Mr. FitzGerald's
room quite well, and again drawing pictures at a water
party.

. . . It is a gusty grey Sunday; out of the window there
is a green square and then unfinished houses and scaffold-
ing. This house was Hobson's choice.

Journal (1864)

November 10th. Grannie suddenly to our great pleasure came back to stay. She liked the house and settled
down with us.

Mrs. Carlyle used to come and fetch me for drives all
this winter.

November 26th. I went for a little walk with Grannie.
She said she had changed her mind about many things,
especially about religious things, and that she could now
sympathize far more than she had once done, with what
my father used to think and say.

December 17th. Our last peaceful evening together. Grannie sat in her corner by the fire. She began talking of the past, of her life in India, and of Papa's father coming to see her on his white horse. Then she got up saying she must go to her rest, and she kissed us and blessed us. A moment after she left the room, Fanny came running to call us—she had passed away.

Journal (1865)

Wrote and worked very hard at *The Village on the Cliff,* which I was beginning to write at this time.

George Eliot sent me word she liked my Clarence article.

Early in the year to Waltham Cross to stay at the Trollopes'. It was a sweet old prim chill house wrapped in snow.

The Merivales were staying there too. I remember so well saying to Rose Merivale how *terrible* this pain of parting was and would it ever cease? She said: "Life is over so quickly, so very quickly," and now I feel how true that is.

I can also remember in the bitter cold dark morning hearing Mr. Trollope called at four o'clock. He told me he gave his man half a crown every time he (Mr. Trollope) *didn't* get up! "The labourer is worthy of his hire," said Mr. Trollope in his deep cheerful lispy voice.

June 10th. To the National Gallery with Mr. Millais. Met Sir Charles Eastlake there. Millais shook his fist at the Raphael Madonna.

To Walter Senior

We send you our love and hope you are both hungry and sleepy, and we do wish you were here. It is the funniest place in the world. Last night Mrs. Cameron invited us to tea to meet Mr. Jowett and his four young men. We went and found them looking at photographs in a bedroom, rather shy apparently, with Charlie Cameron's little combs and brushes all lying about. We then went on to the Prinseps' next door, the four young men each carrying a candle, and Mrs. Cameron's three maids in little knitted waistcoats carrying a huge box of photographs. There we all sat round a table and looked at the pictures, while the young men each had a tumbler of brandy and water.

We have a nice little drawing-room opening on a garden, and a nice little dining-room opening on a garden too. We have shocking bad dinners, and are obliged to have eggs and bacon to make up for almost every meal.

. . . Everybody is either a genius or a poet or a painter or peculiar in some way; poor Miss Stephen says is there *nobody* commonplace? We drove in to meet her the day before yesterday and found three cousins with whom she had come. They are at the Hotel, but rather bored and bewildered . . .

Mrs. Cameron sits up till two o'clock in the morning over her soaking photographs, Jowett's lamp also burns from a casement, and the four young men are intently studying at another. I have not quite begun my holiday, for I had promised to finish two little articles for Mr. Smith, but it is very different writing with a pencil on a down top, with the sea and a lark twiddling most beautifully overhead, to a two-pair front in London.

We are going on all sorts of little expeditions to castles in the air, which are such very small ones that perhaps they won't turn into smoke.

I cannot tell you how much we enjoy it all; of a morning the sun comes blazing so cheerfully and the sea sparkles, and there is a far-away hill all green, and a cottage which takes away one's breath it looks so pretty in the morning mists. Then come eggs and bacon. Then we go to the down top. Then we lunch off eggs and bacon. Then we have tea and look out of window, then we pay little visits, then we dine off eggs and bacon, and of an evening Minny and Emmy, robed in picturesque Indian shawls, sit by the fire, and Miss Stephen and I stroll about in the moon-light.

To-night we are going to tea at the Tennysons' to meet these dreadful young men again. They give whoops and make us jump, and have each been presented with two photographs by Mrs. Cameron, besides the tumblers of brandy and water. The only other young man here is our cousin, who is a misogynist, and when he sees us coming he rushes away across a field, or if we call he leaves the room. . . .

Mr. Prinsep wears a long veil and a high coned hat and quantities of coats. Minny goes and reads Froude to him.

. . . We have had two misadventures since we came. The first, that we tried to walk from Yarmouth and lost our way, the second, that being rested next morning, we thought we would change the furniture in the room, and Minny carried a coal scuttle into the garden by way of clearing the coast and at that moment just as she was flourishing it round, Jowett and his four young men went by, and I believe that is why they yell at us when they see us coming. Goodbye, dear Walter, give them all our love and get well soon.

To George M. Smith

Freshwater
[*Easter* 1865].

It is so heavenly lilac down here. There are nothing but poets and painters everywhere, and it is all gold and delicious up over the downs.

Do you think you could let me have a day or two more to finish my review for the *Cornhill Magazine?* Never mind if it is not convenient; perhaps Mr. Enoch would send me word. I refuse to receive any more letters from you.

Thank you for the proofs. I am quite sure about Mrs. Cameron's photographs. She paddles in cold water till two o'clock every morning. Jowett is our next door neighbour. Miss Stephen is staying with us. Mr. Allingham drops in to tea.

. . . Mrs. Cameron says: "Why does not Mrs. Smith come to be *photographed?* I hear she is *Beautiful*. Bid her come and she shall be made *Immortal*."

To J. E. Millais

Freshwater
[1865].

. . . I thought of you one day last week when we took a walk with Tennyson and came to some cliffs with a sweep of land and the sea; and I almost expected to see poor Boadicea up on the cliff, with her passionate eyes.[1] I heard Mr. Watts and Mr. Prinsep looking for her somewhere else, but I am sure mine was on the cliff.

[1] Millais' picture: "The Romans leaving Britain."

Mr. Watts has been painting Hallam and Lionel Tennyson. We hear him when we wake, playing his fiddle in the early morning. They are all so kind to us that we do not know how to be grateful enough. We have had all sorts of stray folks. Jowett and the Dean of Christ Church, and cousins without number.

It has been very pleasant and sunshiny, and we feel as if we should like to live on here in lodgings all the rest of our lives.

Last night "King Alfred" read out *Maud*. It was like harmonious thunder and lightning. . . .

Journal (1866)

January. Writing *The Village on the Cliff*.

To the House of Commons to hear Gladstone's great speech on redistribution of seats. We stood in a cellar under the floor of the House, and all I could see was the two soles of Gladstone's feet above my head while I heard his wonderful voice coming down like a flood through the ventilator.

June 9th. Picnic for my birthday, very great success. Mrs. Sartoris, Leighton, Val Prinsep, Julia Jackson, Leslie Stephen, Herman Merivale, etc., etc. Luncheon at the Inn, tea under great trees, carts to the station, Mrs. Sartoris singing.

September. To Caen for my book to see a Normandy farm.

October. Back to London. Leslie Stephen came and asked Minny to marry him. I was finishing *The Village on the Cliff* when she came up to tell me.

Two days after Minny's engagement, Tennyson came and I asked him to help me with the last paragraph of my book *The Village on the Cliff*. I was overwrought, and I could see the characters of my story walking in the air very much smaller than life, like a bright-coloured magic lantern. I have heard of this odd impression from others since then.

"When I was writing *The Village on the Cliff*, I was very nervous about it, and quite at an end of my ideas and resources, when one day came the first proofs of the lovely drawings by Frederick Walker. They were so completely everything that I had ever hoped or imagined, that the sight of them gave me a fresh start, and I have always thought that *he* wrote the book not I, for the figures were to me almost miraculous realisations of what I tried to imagine the people might become. As a curious instance of a sort of brain wave, I had a nightmare one night, and saw the figure of Reine, very bright, coming *down* upon me, and when the little letter piece came next month there was the identical figure I had dreamed of, with a basket, descending; no longer a nervous terror, but a delightful reality. I have always thought M. le Maire playing the cornet was the keystone of the little story. My sister and I walked through a fog one evening to the studio, and he showed it to us on the block.

. . . The day before my sister married, Frederick Walker came to see us and said he should like to give her a drawing for a wedding present and at her request, then and there he sat down and made a most charming delicate little pencil sketch of our little adopted niece, a child then—now a woman and married and to whose husband I have given the little picture." [1]

[1] Written by my mother for the *Life of Frederick Walker*. My thanks are due to Messrs. Macmillan and Co. for permission to print these passages.

VIII

1867—1875

MY mother writes in her journal, "On the 18th of June 1867 Leslie and Minny were married."

After the marriage Minny and her husband returned to Onslow Gardens. Leslie Stephen and his wife and sister-in-law shared the same home until Minny's death in 1875.

At the time of her engagement Minny had written to Mrs. Fanshawe, "I hope never to be separated from Anny, except perhaps during my wedding tour. I am sure she will have no reason to regret this change in our lives."

The following description of Minny, written by her sister-in-law Caroline Stephen, gives a vivid picture. "She had a singular and indescribable social charm—a humourous wayward and changeful grace, which captivated not only for the moment but for life. She was, beyond any one I have known, quaintly picturesque, tender and true. She could never have been put into intellectual harness, but there was a rare sureness and delicacy in her critical intuitions, whether as to personal or literary qualities. Her own pen, though sparingly used, had a felicity worthy of her parentage, but what comes back most vividly in one's memory of her is the half playful motherliness of her household ways, which was both amusing and pathetic in the youngest and most fragile of the little family party."

To George M. Smith

16, Onslow Gardens
[*July* 1867].

What a delightful and astounding surprise to come home, and find your note and the third Edition.[1] Thank you, and I believe it is somehow your doing!

I have had such a pleasant trip, and such happy letters from my bride and bridegroom who are scrambling about, Minnie on and Leslie walking beside the mule, which has to have steps cut for it as if it were a member of the Alpine Club. . . .

Give my best love to dear Mrs. Smith; tell her the Paris Exhibition is charming, and the fashions hideous.

To George M. Smith
(*On returning some borrowed stamps*)

16, Onslow Gardens
1867.

From the Lady High Executioner :—

> Six dozen heads
> To clear the score,
> To come again
> I'd borrow more.

Journal (1868)

January 2. To stay with Mrs. Prescott at Clarence. The *ghost* of one of the old days—wind—snow, Leslie walked over to see me. Mrs. Prescott playing Marcello in the twilight, and the paralytic man beating time. Colonel Hamley standing by the fireplace, "I never quite understand Kinglake. It is in fact impossible to understand

---

[1] *The Village on the Cliff*. First Edition, February, 1867. Second Edition, March. Third Edition, July.

anybody—oneself least of all. I believe other people know one a great deal better than one knows oneself. I try to write a diary but it all seems sham."

This year my book *Five Old Friends* published.

To George M. Smith

Warsash
[1869].

Thank you so much, for much too much, for such a stupid little sketch. It ought to have been finished in one number. I see it doesn't do to write about things one likes very much, for one has such a pleasant notion of them in one's mind that one proses on and on. I wish Miss Vanborough [1] would get on—I shall take her to Rome with me. It is odd and sad to go back to one's heroine of fifteen years ago. And after this I shall take to writing memoirs.

I am here till the 10th; there are people building the house all round us, while we sit still in the middle of the room. I seem to have newly discovered that Mrs. Sartoris is *extraordinarily* clever; if she had been a man instead of a woman I don't know what she would not have done. She has been reading such a lovely novel of George Sand's to me. O if one could but write like that!

We take a walk among golden leaved trees, we dine, we wander through the ladders back to the half lighted drawing-room. It is very even, rather a grandiose sort of life, with books and singing instead of people and bustle. No towns, no sound; Mr. Sartoris is away haranguing his constituents.

I am very much excited about this little dream of Mrs. Tennyson's and mine, of a sort of living club for single women. I think it would cheer up some of the forlorn

[1] The heroine of *Old Kensington*.

ones very much to have nice little apartments and a cook's shop on the ground floor.[1]

In April, 1869, my mother travelled to Rome with Lady de Rothschild and her daughters, to stay with the Storys.

To her Sister

Palazzo Barberini
Rome
[*April* 1869].

. . . It's a great deal bigger, grander, *Romer* than we remember it even. Every doorway and window and arch is noble, and seems glad to see me, and to say how is Minny?

I came all night from Florence—I don't know why exactly, but it seemed convenient. There was a grubby old priest and a little French woman in the carriage, with whom I made friends. All the big cities rolled past, Perugia, and paintings and academies and ever so many more, and at last in the morning the priest said: "There is St. Peter's," and there it was. The Storys didn't expect me exactly, and the little French lady begged me to come with her and to leave my luggage to her servant. She was a very vulgar kind little lady and when I wanted to pay for the carriage, said: "Ce n'est pas gentil," but we all opened our eyes when we stopped at a palace [Barberini] a great deal grander than Windsor Castle, with sun rippling all down the marble steps.

The Storys were almost kinder and gladder to see me than I can tell you. I had breakfast directly, the instant I arrived, in the boys' schoolroom, with the sun in it.

Then I had my bath, delicious spranking water, and now I have looked out of window and seen Rome and a Dominican.

---

[1] My mother always took a great interest in philanthropic schemes: all through her life she did much work in poor districts and schools.

. . . There was a brilliant little assemblage last night. I wore my white poplin. How I do wish my hair grew in thick natural plaits and scrolls alternated with elegant rows of curls like the Italian and American ladies!

We have been to St. John Lateran—the monks in white, the grand ladies followed by footmen, the people confessing, the violet priests chanting. At one of the high altars sits a cardinal administering absolution for the most terrible crimes that can only be forgiven at Easter and Christmas, and people sit round in a row to watch the expression of the criminals' faces. I took the spectators for the criminals, and was rather surprised to see quite young ladies in fashionable bonnets among them.

It's bitter, bitter cold to-day, and yet last night the sun set in such a gorgeous stream that it looked like weeks and years of fine weather. I had forgotten the sunsets. We were down in the Corso when it began and all the crowds of people were lighted up with a curious lurid light like the night of the great fire at Covent Garden. Then we drove up on the Pincio and saw fiery seas and bays.

There go the guns and bells. I don't know what for. I must go out on the balcony to see.

To her Sister

Palazzo Barberini
Rome
[1869].

Yesterday was like one of the days one remembers, but the thing is one *doesn't* remember it!

I meant to get up early to write to you, but I didn't wake till I don't know what o'clock, and there are no noises in these Italian palaces.

When I was dressed, I breakfasted with Mr. Story,

who railed at philanthropy and observances, and said that as for a sense of duty, it was only an imaginary thing, and duty meant doing as one really liked best. I never know what to think—when I see people like him and Leslie, who speak the truth and work hard and keep faith to their neighbours, talking in this sort of way. . . .

The room I inhabit opens straight into the old nursery where the Storys have taken to live of late. A canary hangs in the window—just think what a view it has— and there is a wood fire and a little square table laid in a corner of the room, where Mr. Story breakfasts. The other breakfasts travel about on little trays, and I some- times take one little breakfast at eight, and then appear again quite natural at ten-thirty and take another with Mr. Story. Can you fancy him and me talking the above horrible talk, and the canary shrilling, and Stephano and old Rosa pottering about with tea-pots and bread and butter?

Yesterday morning Sir William Alexander and I went to see the "Cenci" together, and like all the pictures which I didn't want to see, I have found the poor little thing quite different from what I expected. She looks at one with an appealing face (not the least like the pic- tures who only smirk at one in nightcaps). It's just a tremulous sort of look, a little bit like you, darling, it's *horridly* touching; and Sir William and I turned away quite overcome with emotion. No, but *really* I think you would have felt quite fond and sorry for her too. . . .

I find one of the odd effects of Rome is to set one longing, I don't know for what exactly. The beautiful things and sights excite one, and it is not warm enough to soothe one at the same time. I keep wondering where all the great men and women can be gone to, and whether the Huxleys and Spencers are really the statues and con-

querors of these days? In the Capitol we came into a
sunshiny marble room with two rows of busts. They were
Aristides and Hippocrates and Solon and I don't know
who. They looked exactly like Dr. Hunt and Huxley
and Mr. Spottiswoode.

Last night there was another party; ever so many people
came. Little old Sir William Alexander and I settled to
go again and see pictures, and I met one charming lady,
a sister of Mrs. Pell's, who quite won my heart. Also the
beautiful Miss Wadsworth, whom I don't admire at all,
and Hatty Hosmer quite grey and hung round with
sequins. But I want painted people and marble hearts
just now, and don't seem to care to devote myself to all
these grandly dressed strangers. I find myself wishing
that the peerage of the United Kingdom could be swept
away at one swoop. Lords are like meteors here in Rome,
and still more Dowager ladies and their daughters. Lord
Taunton came to luncheon yesterday. He's charming.
Mrs. Dexter came to meet him. She had had him to
dinner in America thirty-five years before; a dinner seems
so much more after thirty-five years, doesn't it?

After luncheon what Mrs. Story calls "Julia's Trump
Card," Lady Dunmore, called. She called, and called
and called for such a long time, that I thought all the
bright afternoon would be over, but it wasn't, and we
went and fetched Mr. Story at his studio, and took a
drive, and then went to see Odo Russell and Lady Emily
in blue, on a sofa with a newborn infant. Lady Emily
is like the twins, and Odo Russell is diplomatic in large
trousers, and little pointed toes.

He was telling us all about the old palace in which he
lives, and how whenever a member of the family dies,
it is a tradition that all the curtains, and hangings and
pictures and furniture should be swept away into vast

store-rooms upstairs, where the things moulder and
moulder, tapestries and wonderful drawings and stamped
leathers. It's like the parable to hear of these people
piling up and piling up. They never go and see their
treasures, and only laughed at Mr. Russell for wanting
to explore.

Did I tell you of my delightful expedition? I went
off early and joined the Wards and Normans at the Vat-
ican. The statues were all smiling and nodding in those
beautiful halls full of sunshine. It is like scales fallen
from my eyes. Do you remember how we did not care
for them? Now quite naturally as I look, I love. It
isn't sham make up feeling, it's as if a new delightful sense
came to me, which I didn't know I possessed. And I
am sure you would feel just the same.

The statues stand alive, serene, with noble heads bent,
and shining torsos; they drag a trail of glory with them,
and I think I have been to Olympus and feasted with
Gods.

Except the statues, all the things I tell you aren't the
things I specially like, which are just the odds and ends
which I forget again as I drive by. There was the King
of Naples yesterday, there was an onion shop—there was
a little marble seat in the corner of a palace where we
sat—a dab of blue through a door—and a girl whirling
her arm.

. . . Edie and I went into San Lorenzo (which is in
Browning's poem). The sun was streaming in, there
were gilt trestles and a cloth where a coffin had been all
night, and candles and flowers and two old men pottering
about clearing away, and a blear-eyed young man whose
business it was to sleep by the corpses. Coming into the
church from the rolling street, all chattering and twinkling and flowering, it seemed so strange and melancholy.

The Storys say nobody ever wrote such good letters as you and Leslie. He has, just think, dedicated a poem to me in the *Graffite!* and said he nearly dedicated an Alpine one to Leslie but thought he would think it absurd.

To Mrs. Tennyson

South Cottage
Kingston
[1870].

We like our little cottage, by which the river flows peacefully, and where roses and strawberries come out of their own accord, to my great surprise, for I somehow only expect things to come out in shops.

It is the house Millais' mother once lived in, and some strange grotesque early works of his still hang on the walls. The sun sets just opposite the dining room windows, and the water and the dark trees and the brick red solemn sky of an evening put me so in mind of his pictures—Sir Isumbras crossing the Ferry, and the Vale of Rest.

. . . I go to London when I can. Last night I dined out and met De Lesseps, who said that Sarah Bernhardt first suggested the Suez Canal to him and that they can trace the march of the Egyptians, and that the Israelites crossed close by their present works. Lord Broughton and Mrs. Norton were also there. She looked like a beautiful slow sphinx.

To J. F. Stephen [1] (in India)

[*September* 1870].

I am all packed up, and for the last hour I have been struggling through a snow-storm of bills, letters, MSS., and putting things straight before I leave this kind green

[1] Afterwards Sir James Stephen, Bart., K.C.S.I.

funny fat sleepy Snowdenham. They are all asleep in the house, and the moon has streamed herself off, and I am very sorry to go, though I shall enjoy my excursion very much, if all keeps well with the dear folks here.

. . . What a strange tumultuous week this has been; the very silence of this place has brought the din more clearly to our ears, and we seem to have almost seen those poor doomed armies sweeping by.

When we heard the astounding news of the capitulation[1] we were in Guildford. Carry and your mother were waiting for me at the street corner, and when I told them (someone had just told me) Carry ran off in her blue shawl up the street for a paper, and your mother and I sat in the carriage and wondered about everything. We thought most likely you had just heard it too, and all the way home, driving through the sweet evening with sunsetting clouds, we talked war, and the extraordinary chances that seem to come to sum up the past.

To think of that dead old Napoleon filling the world *now* with blood and sorrow, "Fire and blood and tears," as the *Times* has it. What a history in a fortnight, since I last wrote to you, and while the nectarines on the old wall have been sweetening.

I shall never forget the double impressions of utter stillness and peace here, and the vivid blaze of horror and battle there, of which the accounts reach us day by day. Hayward goes off to the station for the *Times,* and your mother sits reading it in her chair by the open window all the morning, and all the evening,—I cannot help myself—I go on and on reading column after column. One can think of nothing else.

I was French on Saturday, but since their insane flourishing and hurrahing, and embracing on Sunday, I began

[1] Sedan.

to think that a despot's was the only rule they were fit
for. You will read of their all *keeping* the guard at the
bridges, and fraternising over the republic—and stabbing
the picture. It is all so utterly silly.

. . . I wish you could see how well Minny is looking,
thanks to this country air. We were secretly much relieved when Leslie came back safe from Switzerland, for
even to be imprisoned as a spy is disagreeable. He has returned very brown and well, and *most* elegantly dressed!

Journal (1870)

September 10th. I went north to the Lakes, to Edinburgh and from there to the Lows' at Clatto. *October 1st.*
I returned home. Dr. John Brown came to see me off
at the station, and brought me a basket of fruit and a
silver fruit knife. As the train started, two people in the
carriage said, "Well, we have seen everything we wanted
to see in Edinburgh except Dr. John Brown." I said,
"Why that was Dr. John Brown—won't you have some
of his fruit?" To my dismay, they took the beautiful
peach in the centre of the basket, leaving me only the
humbler plums. So much for affability!

To Mrs. Tennyson

16, Onslow Gardens
[*October* 1870].

. . . I was just going to write to you, when your note
came, to ask if you would join in a little conspiracy to
give Mr. Carlyle a small token, like the seal he sent to
Goethe?

I have written to Lady Ashburton and to Lady Stanley,
his faithful friends. Lady Airlie suggests a clock. I

have asked her and Mrs. Froude, about twelve ladies in all, and we think the clock should cost twelve pounds.

I long to see you again, and I send you all my true love.

The token was duly purchased, and on February the 27th [1] my mother writes in her journal: "We met at Lady Stanley's and gave Carlyle the clock."

In *Chapters from Some Memoirs* she has described the scene:—"The small presentation took place on Carlyle's birthday, a dismal winter's day. The streets were shrouded in greenish vapours, and the houses looked no less dreary within than the streets through which we had come. Somewhat chilled and depressed, we all assembled in Lady Stanley's great drawing-room in Dover Street where the fog had also penetrated, and presently from the further end of the room, advancing through shifting darkness, came Carlyle.

"There was a moment's pause—no one moved; he stood in the middle of the room without speaking. No doubt the philosopher, as well as his disciples, felt the influence of the atmosphere. Lady Stanley went to meet him. 'Here is a little birthday present we want you to accept from us all, Mr. Carlyle,' said she, quickly pushing up before him a small table upon which stood the clock ticking, all ready for his acceptance. Then came another silence broken by a knell sadly sounding in our ears. "Eh, what have I to do with Time any more?' he said.

"It was a melancholy moment. Nobody could speak. The unfortunate prompter of the scheme felt her heart sinking into her shoes. Had she but had the wit to answer him cheerfully, to assure him that anyhow time had

---

[1] This extract from my mother's diary and the quotation from her memoirs are inserted here to complete the story of Carlyle and his clock.

a great deal to do with him, the little ceremony might
have been less of a fiasco than it assuredly was. And yet
I think afterwards the old man must have been pleased
and liked to think he had been remembered."

In the Carlyle Museum, Cheyne Row, Chelsea, the
following "paper of signatures" which accompanied the
clock is still to be seen:—

   "To Mr. Carlyle from his affectionate friends 27
February 1871.

H. M. Stanley of Alderly.	Anne Thackeray.
Juliet Pollock.	Louisa Ashburton.
A. Blanche Airlie.	Emily Tennyson.
Anne Simeon Farrer.	Mary Rubina Stephen.
M. O. W. Oliphant.	Henrietta Froude.
Frances Mary Blunt.	Harriet Marian Stephen.
Maude Alethea Stanley.	A nameless friend." [1]

Journal (1870)

October 25th. To see Madame Marochetti, now in
humble lodgings in Alfred Place, having left her beautiful house for the Germans. Madame de la Haute in the
same lodging, also having been obliged to leave her home
and park. Madame de Saade and her girls there too.
Madame de Saade still commenting and keeping up her
rôle of family mouth-piece.

It was really moving to see them all so poor, so ruined
and so undaunted. I had last seen Madame Marochetti
in her Château Neulan-les-Muriers. Real ladies, well-

---

[1] One last guinea was needed to make up the sum for the purchase of the
clock. The "nameless friend" was my mother. In a letter to Mrs. Oliphant in
July my mother writes: "Minny met Mr. Carlyle the other day; he still talks
about his clock and the paper of signatures."

bred, high thinking and just the same as ever. A lesson to all middle class ladies.

To J. F. Stephen (in India)

16, Onslow Gardens
November, but I can't remember where in it.
[1870].

I did so like your last letter. It was like a real any-time talk with you, and every word you said I could understand and sympathise with so entirely. Before you get this we shall have seen the lady you thought about at Metz. Poor Metz! I think Bazaine is the man I most dislike and detest in it all. How awful and vivid and branding it is on one's mind, or is it turning us all to sharks? I hear of people shot and maimed, and I hardly care, and yet it's all through everything. Yester-day, when I bought a penny paper, and read of certain peace, of a congress, and of every hopeful blessing, a load lifted from my mind—but in the *Times* of today there is nothing more of this, only worse and worse news.

God help us and give us enough of the spirit to still angry passions, and put an end to war for ever.

To J. F. Stephen (in India)

16, Onslow Gardens
[*December* 1870].

Received of the Honble. Fitzjames Stephen one, two, three letters, with many many thanks.

A. I. THACKERAY.

This is a receipt, dearest Fitzy—and a little bit of paper to say a big thank you for the most delightful letters— one written in Council—one a little scrap—one an answer to what I had written to you about my mother. They

come in so kind and unchanging, like handshakes across
the sea. When will it be the real hand instead of the letters, and yet one is content to think that what one loses, is
so great a gain to others.

Minny is saying that she is happy to say that since
Leslie's marriage, she thinks he has got to enjoy his food
more than he used. Enter Leslie who denies it. Now
they are talking about *our* niece.[1] What new relation am
I to you?

. . . Now I am starting off for a walk in the snow
from a sense of duty, for it's impossible to get warm in-
doors. I am going to see a poor little refugee lady with
a husband fighting before Paris. Paris is farther than
India nowadays. Pray God help them. It makes one's
heart sing to read of Aubouchères as I did last night.

Who says, "Women who tacitly encourage fighting are
the real mitrailleuses"? and that if *all* women set their
faces against war, it would do more than all the peace
conventions. It comes over one with a sort of shock to
think of the horrible tortures we civilized nations inflict.
We who shudder at thumb-screws and religious perse-
cutions, and yet think nothing of two countries going to
war for the name of a province and the uniform of its
militia. It is awful awful awful, and please God a day of
peace will come at last, of real peace, not breathing time.

To J. F. Stephen (in India)

16, Onslow Gardens
[1870].

It's so cold I can hardly hold my pen—a blue three
o'clock frost with a muffin—why do muffin bells always
tinkle in the frost?

One doesn't know yet what news there is to-day. I

---

[1] Minny's infant daughter.

suppose you as well as we, have read the telegram of the great battle, and I daresay you are thinking about it at this instant just as we are, God help them.

I was so touched by the poor preacher who prayed that he might pray only for a little success before the end —just enough to raise the French from the hopeless sorrow in which they were overwhelmed. When I heard Mr. —— and Mr. —— shouting out for war the other night, I felt I could have knocked their stupid heads together. War is so different from fighting, and shouting from either.

I saw the Sterlings yesterday, who were telling me how their Quaker friends had gone straight off at their own expense to the peasantry. I have been writing a foolish little appeal for the French wounded.

In the spring of 1871 my mother went to Paris to see her cousin Charlotte Ritchie, whose home was there. The Germans were still occupying the north of France, and the "Commune" had begun before my mother came away.

Journal (1871)

March 18th. To Paris with Alice Probyn. Came from Le Havre. Saw the German helmets gleaming in the villages—blossoms on the fruit trees and the snow lying on the ground everywhere. The fortresses and outlying fortifications all round Paris terribly grim. Charlotte and Félicie's welcome to us all dim and grey— everyone in black—empty streets. Drove to Versailles next day. German notices on the walls. To St. Cloud, burnt, utterly destroyed—sunshine—people singing. Frenchmen to me—"Ecoutez les! Ils chantent avec leur pays en ruines."

March 17th. Awakened by the cannon of Belleville. News of a Revolution—murder of the generals. *People acting* in the streets as they described it all to one another. Woman comes up: "Vous êtes Anglaise. Fuyez, fuyez!"

March 21st. Drove up Rue Pigalle, saw a barricade. Dined with D'Eychtals in the evening. Met M. Bercier, and heard of arrests.

March 22nd. To Madame Mohl's in the sunshine, met hurrying crowds of figures who looked as if they had come straight out of the French Revolution. Massacre in Place Vendôme. Charlotte and I were out together; we rushed across fire of the guns to escape. We took refuge in the Church of St. Roch; Rue St. Roch crowded with people turning out to fight, others running away, while others stood joking in their balconies.

Determined to leave Paris. Railway in the hands of the Blues (Order). Reds advancing. Our train moved out of the station just as the fighting between the Blues and Reds began. Charlotte refused to come. We got home by Newhaven. At Rouen the Germans all asking us, "Was ist geschehen in Paris?" Home, calm silence, no guns—most horribly frightened now it was all over. To bed quite done up.

March 25th. To Aston Clinton, travelled down with Joachim. Everyone coming up and asking me about Paris.

March 25th. The news of the burning of Paris. Burning sunset. I telegraphed to Charlotte through the Rothschilds.

To J. F. Stephen

16, Onslow Gardens
[1871].

This is a race against time and the postman, and I seem to have so much to say to you, and so little time in which to say it! Our clocks are badly set, I mean living clocks, and some go slower than time, and I am sure that is what makes me unpunctual!

. . . The other day I met dear old Mr. Carlyle walking along, and I rushed after him to talk to him about his *Life of Sterling.* You must have sent a brain wave, for oddly enough we had all just read the book and were full of it, when your letter came saying you too had been reading it. I wonder have you ever come across my father's review of it in the *Times?* Some day I should like you to know Julia Sterling—Sterling's daughter—I'm sure you would like her.

. . . I have been wearing the silver bangles in my hair where they look very nice indeed but I cannot get rid of my cold and in consequence have to keep myself to mild entertainments and high dresses. To-night I am going to dine at the Douglas Galtons.' On Wednesday Leslie and I dined at Mr. Newton's, and met Ruskin.

To Richmond Ritchie

Aldworth [1]

[1872].

. . . Minny says, "O Anny, how one does like one's own child," and when Leslie comes home tired, dusty, overworked, I hear the clump clump of footsteps running upstairs to the nursery. We are thinking of a new house; I am to have the ground floor for my own, which I shall like very much, and then Laura [2] will have a whole suite of apartments if she chooses, and Leslie will be up at the top of all with a skylight and a special ventilator for his pipe.

[1] The Tennysons' house in Surrey.
[2] Daughter of Leslie and Minny Stephen.

I only came here for a breath of fresh air. This is such a lovely view, almost too lovely for my special taste. I like a cock and a hen and a kitchen garden, and some lilies and lavender, quite as well as these great dream worlds and cloud-capped lands. To me they are like the sonnet, "Farewell, thou art too dear for my possessing," and I can never *appropriate* a horizon, as one does a haycock, or a bunch of river weeds, or the branches of a tree.

To her Sister

Lion-sur-Mer
Calvados
[*August* 1872].

I am writing on the sands. "Look at that little boy, Aunt Anny," says Francis. "I think he's going to bathe. No! he's standing on his head. The people don't much mind how they go here. I shouldn't think they'd mind much if they were naked, do you, Aunt Anny?"

My own dear. How lonely you must be. I am so glad Molly [1] is coming to you, and *do* get the boys. You can't think how much nicer they are than grown-up men.

[1] Molly Alderson, now Lady Humphrey.

Here comes such a darling little girl, not a bit bigger than this, walking quite alone down to the sea. Happily a lady rose dripping out of the ocean to receive her.

To her Sister

Lion-sur-Mer
[*August* 1872].

What shall my letter be about to-day, darling? It's still fine—still nice—still exactly the same. I go and write all the morning in a little room behind my bedroom, where nobody has found me out yet, except Félicie who rushed away.

We had a grand bathing early this morning. It was such fun to see the children rushing across the sands screaming with laughter, in funny little trousers and jackets, Margaret, Margy, Dolcie and Anny. Then they went into the sea, and the waves rushed over them, and the little ones screamed, and Blanche and Charlotte and I shrieked to the bathing men to bring them out. But the children all declared it was delightful, once they were out.

. . . Blanche and Frank and I had a day of events yesterday. First we got up at six o'clock, then we went to Caen and walked about and saw all the churches; and then after that, we took the train and went to Bayeux. It was so pretty and silent, and the old tapestry and the old cathedral just as usual and the little omnibus was starting for Arromanches, and oh! I was so glad I wasn't going in it. And then when we got back to Caen, we each ate two little cakes, and got a little carriage, and drove back here. Presently as the moon rose, our wheel went crash into the road, and we sat and patiently waited in a ditch, while the coachman stuck it on again. I gave him a hairpin at last for he had nothing else, and the nail was broken.

. . . You will be amused to hear there has been a grand feast at Madame Bertin's. Both the curés came, the fat one and the thin one. The fat one was too tired to eat much. The dinner was solemn and splendid, a turbot crowned with flowers, a chicken buried in sauce and truffles, a wreathed leg of mutton, tarts, cakes. After dinner seven glasses were put in a semi-circle before Monsieur le Curé de Lion, for him to fill up with champagne and serve round to each guest.

I am sorry to say that Madame Bertin, the heroine of the feast, in her turquoise cap and purple silk, suddenly jumped up and left the room. I fear it was my presence! I went with the children to-day to try and mollify her. She was friendly, but as we left the room said, "Those poor children! to have no one to see to them, to have to walk home quite alone!"

Last night the sea was silver clear, the moon and the stars shone, and we watched the fishermen pushing down a boat through the moonlight, and then three great lines of surf came rolling in, as the boat glided from the shore. A poor woman with a baby stood crying, because she did not want her "homme" to go—"A ben! c'est vrai, qu'on donne la vie pour garder la vie."

In March, 1873, my mother and the Stephens moved to 8, Southwell Gardens, and she writes in her *Notes on Family History:* "Good-bye, dear old house. You have sheltered, warmed and comforted us. We were having a tea party, I remember, when the vans came to move us and our cups were carried right away out of the drawing-room."

In a letter to Hallam Tennyson, my mother describes the new house: "Here is a first letter from our new home, dear Hallam. If this is to be my home and my future life, I consider life scarcely worth having. Two gas-men in one room, a carpenter in another, tap, screw, grind, vile bell, creaks. It's like a horrid dream and I don't know why we have so jumbled everything. Having now grumbled I confess this is much nicer (inside) than the other little old house; my room has a sort of imposing jail-like appearance, but a young man with chintz is coming to enliven it for me this morning."

My mother's novel, *Old Kensington,* which had been appearing in the *Cornhill Magazine* from April, 1872, to April, 1873, was published in the spring of this year and went through five editions. The illustrations for the book were drawn by George Leslie.

To Richmond Ritchie

[1873].

Scene—a cup of tea, George Eliot in a beautiful black satin dressing-gown by the fire, snow outside and German paper-books on the table, a green lamp and paper cutter.

The shrine was so serene and kind that this authoress felt like a wretch for having refused to worship there before. She looked very noble and gentle, with two steady little eyes. You must go and see her. I am sure she will be a friend just as I felt her yesterday, not a personal friend exactly, but a sort of good impulse, trying to see truly, not to be afraid, and to do good to other people.

She said it was much better in life to face the very worst, and build one's cottage in a valley so as not to fall away, and that the very worst was this, that people are living with a power of work and of help in them, which they scarcely estimate. That we know by ourselves how very much other people influence our happiness and feelings, and that we ought to remember that we have the same effect upon them. That we can remember in our own lives how different they might have been if others, even good people, had only conducted themselves differently.

This part I'm glad to say I couldn't follow, nor could I remember at the moment a single instance of any single person's misconduct. She said too we ought to be satisfied with immediate consequences, and respect our work. . . .

[The remainder of this letter cannot be found.]

Journal (1873)

February 18th. To Northbank with Mrs. Procter to see George Eliot, such a disjointed visit. Each talking their best and neither listening to the other.

March 15th. Walk in the rain with Carlyle. Splash! Splash! Dined with the Leslies at Stratford Place. Eventful dinner. Sir John told me about Angelica Kauffman and showed me her ceiling—thought of writing story.

Life is like writing a story—people and ideas come and go—and I try to make a plot of which the materials won't work out.

October 4th. The Morleys to luncheon and Mr. Browning. We had a talk; he said, "Everybody knows what they ought to do. It's all nonsense about asking advice." Also he affirmed, "As far as my own experience goes, I can see that all is right for me—I can't answer for anyone else—and that is all one can say."

November 28th. To see Mr. Carlyle who said, "A cheese-mite might as well attempt to understand a cow and the great universe of grass beyond it, as we human mites might expect to understand our making and our Maker's secrets."

December 1st. To Miss Landseer's—I am writing an article on Landseer for the *Cornhill.*

Delicious morning; thank God for sunshine and peace and the fruits of the earth.

Journal (1874)

January 1st. I have just looked for a text for the new year. It is the draught of fishes. If I could only attain to a dozen sprats!

Reproach myself for being morbid. What is to be done? *Neatness,* and as little thinking as possible!

January 14th. To a delightful Ball, music, light, all radiant. Even frivolity may be a divine Goddess after all.

January 24th. To Aldermaston—Herbert Spencer, Mr. and Mrs. Reeve, Lord Aberdare, Miss Francis. Beautiful stars at night with a mysterious call in them. Miss Francis said, "I should like to write the unsuccessful singer's story."

January 30th. Began to write *Angelica Kauffman.* I must give myself four or five hours off every day or I shall break down and be utterly useless.

February 10th. Read *Fumée.* Tourgenieff's novels frighten me, they are so like myself.

March 17th. Dined with Mr. Knowles. Met Cardinal Manning with his ring and his ascetic nose—Bishop of Gloucester and Mr. Arnold there—never to be forgotten dinner.

March 20th. To Paris with Mary Anne, a mad but delightful extravagance.

April 5th. Ritchies, Cayleys dined with us; sat next General Badeau at dinner who asked me if one could do best without people or books? One doesn't want a library of people, but one could live without any books at all. They are only people after all in a different shape.

Millais, Browning, Joachim at the Lehmanns' party. Millais: "Ah! I saw her listening to you, Joachim." I: "Mr. Joachim teaches us to listen just as you teach us to look and Mr. Browning to think." Millais: "O! It is all the same thing."

Mr. Lehmann: "Don't believe him, don't believe him, Miss Thackeray."

April 29th. Dined Lady M. Feilding. Interesting talk with Lord Lyttelton, and still more so with Dr. Liebreich, about the necessity of varying one's occupation.

May 4th. Breakfast with Gladstone. Dr. Tyndall there, invited him to Switzerland. Dr. Tyndall very Irish. "He shall give his Angels charge over you—I will go with you." Mr. Gladstone's tidy, tidy study. Mrs. Gladstone's dress unhooked, he stepped up and hooked it for her.

Whitsuntide at Paris. Pinkie and Leslie with me at Bélard's Hotel. Stevenson lunched with us there, tossing back his hair.

To Richmond Ritchie

Blois
Yesterday [1874].

All the old women have got their white caps on; the east wind has made every weather-cock shine. I can't think how to tell you what a lovely old place it is, sunny-streaked up and down, stones flung into *now* from St. Louis's days, others rising into carved staircases and gabions and gargoyles. This isn't a description—I wish it were—it isn't white or crisp enough, or high enough. There are broad flights and flights of steps going right up into the air, with the Bishop at the top and the Cathedral Service, and then this wonderful old garden and terrace and castle, and the ghosts of Guise and Henry III looking on through a doorway, and Catherine de Medici in her sunny bedroom opening up loggias, and old roofs and birds and gardens. It is much more educated and sumptuous than other old towns.

Gaston d'Orleans knocked down half the old castle and stuck in a hideous Versailles-like caserne. He fortunately died just in time to save a beautiful sort of marble bird-cage staircase, up which we went with a guide who said: "Hushsh—quand je parle, silence!" We are going to Tours tomorrow; Ella [1] has planned it all most beautifully; we lunch at an old castle, five o'clock tea at another, and little Peere fresh from his lessons knows all the dates as we go along.

We went out church seeing quite early this morning; a small pastry cook's boy tripped into St. Roch, where a poor little child's funeral service was being chanted; the pastry cook boy had a tray on his head and a key in his hand, and he unlocked a grating, and then he neatly took his wares out of the tray, and popped them down in a side chapel. I couldn't think at first what it could be that he was leaving there, and I am ashamed to say I asked him. He looked horrified and said, "Pain bénit," and ran away.

Ella was at Chambord when I got there first, and I

[1] Mrs. Williams-Freeman.

straggled up a hill to a little quiet terrace with a plain below, and the boom of the vespers above, and then into the vespers where Ella found me, and took me off to see wonders.

We have dined at the table d'hôte; a general covered with orders came in with a blind brother officer on his arm. They looked very sad, both of them, but it was the same general, I *hope,* that we saw this morning flashing through the streets, with some other gorgeous pincushions on horseback.

To Emily Ritchie

Blois
[1874].

How often I have wished for you these last three days; old castles, hot corners, black sweet shadows, lilacs, and the fruit trees all *smoking* with scent, and flinging with blossom, and rivers crawling and ghosts all beautifully dressed, dancing up and flitting along the paved marble galleries. Ella and I settled that it was like going to a wonderful play, with all the scenery before one's eyes, and somehow one knew all the story of the play beforehand. Then we acted it ourselves and conjured up the figures, Catherine de Medici and her prayer book, and scent bottles and her three sons, and the Huguenots and the King's mistress close by, and the tapestries on the wall, and the mouldy old beds and tables, and then oddly enough all the present coming sailing in and jumbling up with the ghosts. Madame Say buying one castle full of sunshine from the ruined family, our friend Madame Picard installed in another, the Chaussée d'Antin and the Bois de Boulogne comfortably established among the dead courts, like the bees in the lion's carcase.

Chenonceaux is a lovely old place that Catherine

wrenched from Diana as soon as Henry II died: and at Chaumont[1] the portress sat alone crying in a sunny courtyard; the lady was dead, and "ce bon M. le Marquis" and his brothers and sisters had had to sell the property.

One of the absent brothers interested me very much. He had chosen to live in Diana's own room, he painted shockingly, and had stuck up all sorts of artistic things on the wall. His name is Monsieur Georges, and he has never married. The woman cried most of all about him; and couldn't imagine how I guessed he was a painter and of romantic disposition.

To Hallam Tennyson

8, Southwell Gardens
[1874].

I have just sent off a little article to the *Pall Mall Gazette*. It was a horrid corvée to begin with, and only the thought of Mrs. Cameron's indignant apparition this morning spurred me on to it. But I finished in a little thrill, thinking of the day I first read the *Idylls of the King* and of this, which is, that people may say what they like about modern thought, (and I know there is an utterly astounding and complicated Something gathering, which is quite too strong and direct for people like me, who were brought up in narrower times, to grasp or understand,) but what I do feel is, that neither the awful truth from science, nor the melodies and raptures and roses of Swinburne, nor the vivisoulections of *Contemporaries* and *Fortnightly Reviews* need put away the clear clanging of King Arthur's sword or Colonel Newcome's old cavalry sabre, and those Excaliburs, I thank

---

[1] Catherine de Medici's own gloomy castle, which she never desired to see again after the death of Henri II. Catherine gave Chaumont to Diana in exchange for Chenonceaux.

God our fathers have always held. That is the only sentence I *didn't* write in my article, but I can't help finishing it off to you.

To Richmond Ritchie

8, Southwell Gardens
[1874].

. . . We met Salvini that night we came home. Minnie sat next him; he has a vault-like brow, and stood on a balcony and said, "Ora, che la rrrreconocenza, etc., etc." I sat next Mr. Browning at dinner. He described a Greek poem, and suddenly seized my chair and twirled it right round, inspired by the thought of a blind father recognising his daughter's hand; he did it beautifully, but with too much action.

To Richmond Ritchie

Cornwall
July 12th [1874].

Did the wind ever blow your window-pane into the room? The white gulls were going through all sorts of incantations yesterday, and I suppose this is the result. This is a most stormy peaceful time, the most conversational blank vacuity—although we talk on unceasingly.

The elements are our one excitement. You walk through a great blowing wind into a mist, and across a moor with brown cropping cows and a horn blowing out of the sea, with rocks flinging out quite black, and all sorts of currents and waves streaming in from the horizon, and then you come to a most detestable little object called Bude, with a dripping man on horseback riding down the street, and then you are quite wet through and come home in a little thing called a Jingle: and then you go out again next day into another sort of wind, capricious without any rain.

It blew us up hill to a place where a great delicious Italian valley suddenly enclosed us, and after a picnic of whirling viands and papers and sprinkling soda-water bottles, Edward went to fish in a stream, and we struggled on with the Jingle to the top of the hill. An old Saxon cliff, high up among the gulls, with a lovely peaceful crumbling church [1] in a sheltered hollow, and a wall of sudden blue sea and sky and downs, old gates and stone stiles, graves softly rolling into grass, and an old grey rectory. I am sure it was Ophelia's churchyard. It was unexpected and all delicious with ivy and a scent of fragrant herbs—and after our long windy toil everything became sunset, and some day you must see it. Mervyns-hoe is *not* the name of the place. Perhaps if I stay on another year or two here, I shall regain my memory, as well as my other faculties.

To Hallam Tennyson

Venice
[1874].

I wonder if you are driving Minny along the lane at this minute, while I am listening to the whirr of St. Mark's great clock, the humming of voices, the blowing of the trumpet, which seems to tell everybody everything they ought to do. It tells the sun to rise, the soldiers to go to bed.

The scene has changed now to the little apartment (where the ink happens to be) that Mrs. Ritchie [2] has taken, with its grass blinds looking on the sea, and its shuttered windows looking towards the little street at the back. And how the bells are clanging and how impossible it is to write except just to bore our poor friends

[1] The church of Hawker, the Cornish poet, at Morwenstow on the Cliff.
[2] Her future mother-in-law.

with long elaborate accounts of things, that lose all their wonder by being named in wrong words.

Mrs. Ritchie and Chattie are gone to church, a little child is talking Italian outside, all the footsteps are coming and going. I think you are at church too, and Mr. Isaacson has just begun his sermon, because it is an hour earlier with you than with us, and if he were an Italian he would just be finishing it. I heard one last Sunday in Milan Cathedral; the preacher was fulminating against the "heretici," the women had taken off their shoes to listen more attentively, and everything went up and down and the incense burnt and Italy throbbed, when rather to my despair Mr. Mundella, the member, said, "Miss Thackeray, do you remember our meeting at Brixton? etc. etc."

To Margie and Annie Thackeray [1]

Venice
[1874].

I have just come home from a romantic float in a gondola with Pinkie. We started off into the great dark canal with silver ghosts of islands and towers and a moon, and we looked up at the sky, and the gondolier said, "Music, Madama, shall I sing?" So Pinkie said, "Sing," and then he sang us a song, about a lovely blond and "amor, amor" in a loud croaking voice, and between each verse he rocked the gondola very violently.

Then we shimmered out over the moonlight, and the gondolier began to sing another song, (he told us ladies asked for it). It was the "Echo Song," and it came answering back to us over the stars and water, and then a great lighted-up ship in the distance began to hoot and get ready to steam away, and the clock struck eleven and

[1] My mother's adopted nieces who were then small children.

the gondolier sang on, and Pinkie said, "Horrid wretch, I wish you would tell him to leave off," but he only sang louder and louder and everything grew more and more beautiful. To stop him, we asked him to take us under the Bridge of Sighs, and it was so frightening—all dark black and whispering. Our gondola and another whistled quietly past each other under the bridge, and we heard voices singing in the distance and our gondolier took up the chorus and began to row away; and when we came back to the bridge he said, "Now pay for the music, Madama, and we can go home." After that we said goodnight to Pinkie and Charlotte and Nelly, and left them locked up in their little house by their beautiful peasant girl, and now there is a mosquito humming round my room, but Richmond has given me a wonderful box of pastils, that keep them in good temper and prevent them from biting, and so goodnight, my darlings.

From your loving you know Who.

Guess whom I saw before I came away? Miss Yonge! She is very handsome; something like Blanchie [1] only older, with grey hair; and she gets £1,500 a year for her copyrights where I get £150. So you see how right you were to entreat me into writing like Miss Yonge. I am going to read the *Castle Builders,* when I have time, and I am finishing the last fairy tale I ever mean to do.

To her Sister

Perugia
[1874].

This is like a beautiful dream. I am looking at an abyss and a great high dandified exquisite old city, and through the gates the milky oxen go crawling up the hill

[1] Mrs. Warre-Cornish.

with men in long cloaks and swinging lanterns. There
are arches so high up that one's hat tumbles off if one
looks at them and there is the wide wide grey and olive
view. There are little orange trees along the high road,
and narrow streets with sheets of country at the end, and
these high Renaissance tip-toe sort of houses and arches
and dragons and kings and palmers.

We met Sidney Colvin here, who stepped out like a
Mediæval Saint up on the terrace. Gussie and Richmond are going to Rome to-morrow, and we all drive
together to Assisi, and then Pinkie and I are going back
to my circular ticket by a little round. I suppose we
shall sleep at Bologna to-morrow. We are very sorry to
part. We have all been in a most absurd state of rapture,
and next time, unless you come, I shall come alone with
Mary Anne and gush less, and write descriptions for a
book.

To Hallam Tennyson

8, Southwell Gardens
[*November,* 1874].

How do you do, dear Hallam? Various little objects
will come from me to say this to you, also a photograph
from Venice which however has not yet arrived.

It is but an idiotic object that is writing to you, swathed
in veils from the village of Santa Margarita, where I
carefully prepared for future influenza! They (the
veils) were bought in a little sunny sort of parlour with
a monk and a priest at the glass door, and a blue bay just
beyond, and a boat waiting to convey us to a castle on a
hill, and a lovely maiden cooking Italian dishes and an
old woman up in a tree gathering figs for us, and all the
Spezia hills leaping up like fish out of the water.

After this, is it in human nature not to shudder at the

contrast of Wimpole Street, a policeman, and a feeble
effort to find one's way to Weymouth Street in a damp
sort of an afternoon fog? But to-day the sky looks a most
inspiring blue, and Minny and Leslie (he came to meet
me at the train with a hansom that night I came back)
were so glad to see me, and Laura gave such darling little
capers, that it would be inhuman nature to grumble
really.

One very romantic and exciting thing we have done—
the first night of *Hamlet*. Irving was Hamlet, and made
us feel the part could have been played in no other way.
All the reporters were there with their note-books, and
all the house cheered and shouted, and Mr. Aidé sat
behind us and made himself very agreeable, and the
Pollock family floated before our eyes.

We were going away, when old Mrs. Bateman called
us to go behind the scenes. Minny and I stood behind a
drapery, and saw the duel scene, and heard the audience
roaring and roaring, and it seemed as if all the atmosphere of *Hamlet* were round about us. Then up came
Irving looking very handsome and pale, and quite natural, as a man must be who's just been being anything
so real, and he thanked us so warmly when we said how
we admired it. Then someone called to him, "Go, go,
they are calling for you," and he threw down his cloak
and ran off and came back again, paler than ever, to finish
his sentence. I believe it is all your Father's suggestion
to him that night at Richmond.

To Richmond Ritchie

Brighton
[*November*, 1874].

. . . Brighton is very nice and cheering and homish
after my empty Palazzo for three weeks. I came down—

so funnily—with Hamlet [1] in a sombrero, a staff in his hand and a wrapper on his arm. All the ticket collectors and porters knew him, and flew for his luggage, to which he pointed as if it had been the grave of Ophelia.

Irving was very melancholy, and talked mysterious allusions to his wife. He says he envies painters so, who can see the works of those who went before, while poor actors can only look at each other.

To Richmond Ritchie

Paris
[1875].

. . . Mr. Payn writes sternly for the revise for my story, and I must not write any more now.

David Morice beams and comes to luncheon; Charlotte goes her own way, and so do we all, but thank God, though we go our own ways, we can still somehow keep one bit by which we all travel along together, that bit which belongs to us all. I don't think people need ever be afraid of living, or failing, or anything at all, for our lives are much wiser than we are.

This calm has been so good for me, and sometimes I feel for a few minutes quite bored and young and blank, just as I used to do, and so delightfully sleepy.

. . . Yesterday I went to call at a most horrible literary stuffy sham Faubourg St. Germain salon. Madame Blaze de Bury was exactly like a character in Tourgenieff and welcomed an Alexis Alexandrovitch, and gave him tea with shrieks of surprise and rapture, and then asked me with a scream of delight, how I wrote such charming books? These are the questions which are so impossible to answer.

[1] Irving, who was acting Hamlet.

To Leslie Stephen

Paris
[1875].

I think I shall write you to-day, instead of to my Minny. . . . I went to Madame Mohl's last night after dining at Charlotte's with Douglas Freshfield, who is a cheering apparition and who is coming to take me to the pictures this morning.

At Madame Mohl's we found Madame Bodichon and a circle of ladies and gentlemen, and a little round sort of flapping man who talked most beautifully. This was Renan. I like him so much better than I expected, because I see though it's partly put on, yet it is instinctive real feeling which makes him sentimental. He gives lectures on Hebrew, and old Mr. Mohl gives lectures on Arabic and Persian, and another slightly younger Professor who gave lectures on Latin and Greek. They seemed to me like a set of old grammars walking about. But Renan is like a very fat ill-bound grammar and dictionary all put up together. His shirt buttons did not do Madame Renan credit (she is also extremely broad and smiling), and Renan said that everything belonging to sentiment, art, feeling, belief, etc., requires participation, but the things belonging to science are content to stand alone without anybody else. He said that nobody ever persecuted to prove a thing that was provable, such as a problem of Euclid, but only to prove a thing that was unprovable such as religion or dogma, and then they all began to praise Herbert Spencer like mad. It's much nicer there than at Madame Blaze de Bury, with her shrieks and heraldic fuss. I drove home in a coupé along the river, and looked at the stars and wished that Annie and Margie were grown up and could come to parties with me. Young Mr. Bélard, who was taking a sentimental stroll up and down the Rue du Dauphin, stepped up and paid my cab, and I returned to my alcove with a book of dear Sainte-Beuve's. He is much too short, and just makes one interested and then leaves off. How he does hiss at everybody, Rigault, Constant and Lamennais and all of them.

I have been trying to think about cynicism; it is only dwelling on what is not, instead of thinking of what *is* in people. I am sure faults and bad feeling are only "lacunes" and good—facts.

To Mrs. Douglas Freshfield

Paris
[1875].

It seems such a long time since I have had a talk with you (writing isn't quite talking, nor is it thinking, there ought to be some word for it).

My solitary flight has been delightful, and my nerves can't believe that they are me. I can write a note without an effort and read a book again, and Helen Colvin has quite touched me by the letter she sent after she went away.

. . . We went to the play the other night with a moon and shooting stars, and Mr. Aslee in attendance with an opera hat, two little golden sugar tongs and a box of the most delicious iced fruit, that we ate in the intervals of the seventh, eighth, ninth and tenth commandments. All the grand ladies of Paris were in the theatre, sitting about in boxes, with shoulders and diamonds and frizzed heads. Madame de Gallifet, Madame de Pourtalès. They look like thin slim pale Maxses, and the play was wonderful, condensed and powerful like a *gun* being let off. It is called *Julie,* and Madame Favart dies at the end in remorse and pink satin.

. . . This is written upon some special paper I have bought for my new story, so as to keep it distinct from *Angelica,* who went off suddenly to Australia with her feet foremost, and the proofs all wrong and the end *first! ! !* I cannot ·think what will happen, and I am so thankful Australia is such a long way off, and that Trollope doesn't read novels, and that George Grettan is in England.

To Richmond Ritchie

Hotel des Alpes
Interlaken
August 11th [1875].

All Cambridge seems to be about. There is Henry Butcher sitting under a tree waiting for his luggage, in one of Leslie's shirts. Mr. and Miss Browning were not at the station. Mr. Balfour is somewhere. We met Professor Tyndall, D.C.L., in the road, smilingly escorting some ladies of rank. Laura and Leslie on the box, Minny, Gennie, myself inside. We were coming down from clouds and echoes to this beehive, flowing with fountains, and with green benches beside the bubbling waters. Willy and Mr. Drury walked in one day at Rosenlaui, wet through and through, and walked off very dry and cheerful next morning. Have you done your work? Have you been comfortable? Leslie goes back to-morrow and we shall wait for a fortnight.

. . . I have been trying to do my work but I have not done one word; however I think I have seized on two little will-o-the-wisps. I do envy George Sand and George Eliot so when they strike up and begin to tune their instruments, especially George Sand, who seems to me to boom an echo all through her prefaces, and sweep one into her stupid books so that it doesn't matter how stupid they are.

To Richmond Ritchie

Hotel des Alpes
Interlaken
August [1875].

This is a Federal pen; the young lady at the shop strongly recommended it. All the stars are rushing in a stream between the Mountain and my window, the music is over, and so is the Tyrolese concert. I didn't go to it, for Leslie carried me off to-day for a long agonizing delightful toil up a pine wood, through strawberries, tree stems, lake dreams, mountain ranges, to a châlet somewhere high up beyond a raven's haunt, where some Americans on donkeys who had arrived before us were resting on a bench, and where we suddenly saw the great white Monk and Monte Rosa through dappled clouds, as we sat on a little balcony and ate bread and honey, and looked over the valleys.

This is next morning now; how I wish one could send all that one sees to you and to all other poor hard-worked people who really want it! I should like to send you a pine tree, a bunch of wild strawberries, and a valley of sloping, nodding flowers with thousands of glittering spiders' webs, the high up snows and far below lakes and yesterday's yellow evening, dying rather sadly behind the pine ridge and the misty Stockhorn.

We sat on a little bench yesterday looking down at the lake and two lines from a steamer, which rippled on and on, and then a raven came and croaked, and then just as we were going home and considered ourselves exhausted, the American on his donkey came up, and we felt obliged to follow, and Leslie counted his money in something *like* a parlour.

When we got down again, Interlaken was all chinese-lanterned, and stepping out in veils and table d'hôte attire, and not near so tired as we were, and then the music came sleepily in at the open window, and now the "Valse des Adieux" is changed into Sunday bells and a cock crow and a jödel. . . .

We have a very nice gentle doctor travelling with us. He is ill, bald, and has left his family at Freshwater, and yesterday as we went along, while Leslie discovered short cuts and pointed out mysterious little dents and points in the mountains, Dr. Liveing was darting among the brushwood after twistyfolium and stingfingeriensis which he put carefully away in his little box. How nice it would be if one could send one's eyes and one's soul up mountains, and wait on some mossy bank down below. A donkey seems to be a sort of compromise.

Now we are sitting in a little artificial temple, half sham rocks and half real creepers. Through one window there is a fountain, through another there is a glass globe to reflect all the little apparatuses, through another there is a little Russian boy and Einspanners and birds and rain impending, and Sunday godless in hats, and Sunday orthodox going off to church in bonnets, and Leslie gazing at Laura, and Louise saying, "Ach, Miss Tackry, now write a nice book all about all de tings." The little Russian boy is enormously fat and has been adopted by a romantic Princess who lavishes her affections upon him, and he is squeaking and squeaking in the most horrible way to attract our attention, and that horrid Louise is . . .

Here comes the Doctor, and the *Saturday Review* and a little boy with raspberries. Now Leslie is saying very deliberately that I and the Dr. shall go up to-morrow on a donkey to the Schynigeplatte, and he will go down to Grindelwald and order rooms, and Gennie and Minny are going in an einspanner, and how it is all settled I don't quite know.

oneself, for lives that might have run alongside of one's own, there must ever be anguish, but for those older and more tired, whose days have been spent out, if I had my way I should scarcely put on black. I didn't think so once. There was a great field full of lambs yesterday and chestnut trees in bud, which put me more in mind of Minny than all the gloom that ever was massed together.

To Mrs. Oliphant

8, Southwell Gardens
[1876].

I have not yet finished, for as I was crying my heart's bitterness away over your dear dear beautiful words, Leslie came in and I gave him your letter to read. How sweet of you to bring home back again round about us, and give it all back for a little bit—to take a day out of old days that were truly at peace—instead of this strained peace that is beyond us still, though some day it won't be any more. . . .

It seems so strange only to have signs of all our happy past, and yours has been a real sign and God bless you and thank you.

To Richmond Ritchie

Brighton
[1876].

I am sure you will like to know that the sun began to shine and the dog to bark and the kettle to boil and the children to go down by the sea this afternoon and Leslie found Mr. Morley, and Laura has two red cheeks, and Annie and Margie are sitting in the window, and I have got the second volume of Heine from Mr. Morley, and the lodgings are still unutterably fusty, but the window is fresh, and the sea was delicious to-day tossing with little sudden fishing boats, and the fat old landlady cooks very nicely, and Louise is in a good temper, and I am so glad yesterday is over, for to-day is so much nicer.

. . . I *should* like to write something about George Sand.[1] I wish I had sent the letter I wrote her once (which I burnt) so as to have crossed pens with her once.

To Richmond Ritchie

8, Southwell Gardens
[1876].

. . . Mrs. Oliphant and Mrs. Trollope walked in this afternoon most beautifully dressed. Then I went out and I took the train to Clapham, and there I met Tom Taylor who walked with me to Jeanie's.[2] Seeing her did me good, for it was all sunset and gentle, and I sat by her bed in the window. She has a grey room full of azaleas, and all her hair shines and her face looks like an angel's, and little Harry Hughes was deep in an arm-chair reading *Vanity Fair*. All the green was breaking from the branches and the sky was fresh and crisp and indifferent. Coming back in the train there was a little old lady who kept jumping up and down to look at the dome of the oil cloth manufactory and the tower of the water works. It seemed almost too much interest at that age.

To Richmond Ritchie

8, Southwell Gardens
[1876].

. . . I have been spending a very lazy day reading the life of Godwin by the fire. I wasn't very well and I thought I would keep warm and quiet and all these people have amused me. Sometimes for a little bit I forget myself as I read, but never for very long. I was

[1] George Sand died at Nohant, June 8, 1876.
[2] Mrs. Nassau Senior.

very glad when Job [1] came in and called me back to all
the things and people that are not in books . . . When
I am alone I don't know where I go; all the things grow
vague. We went to Kate Perry's in a hansom and found
Julian Sturgis there. Kate remembered Mrs. Shelley
very well, and Job told a little story of Mrs. Opie bursting
into tears and rushing away from a dinner-table at
Rogers.'

I am in such a rage with Mrs. Inchbald for her cruel
letter to Godwin when his wife died, that I don't feel that
I could ever write one word about her. She said to him
that she never knew Mrs. Godwin at all intimately and
had avoided doing so from self-respect, as she did not
wish to make friends with a person who etc., etc., or something to that effect. How could she write like that upon
the day of her death?

. . . They have sent me Charles Dickens from the
library. I can tell you how curiously people's different
atmospheres strike me. I find all my childhood in
Dickens, and then Macaulay is my young ladyhood, and
as for my grown-upness, since that is personal and not
founded entirely on other people, it is in living beings and
not in books.

. . . What suddenly cheered me up just now was
thinking what prizes I have drawn in Life, what dear,
dear prizes. No one ever had such a life as mine, or such
love in it, each after its own kind, and this I do feel in
my heart.

To Richmond Ritchie

June 3 [1876].

It was just as nice as ever, only rather nicer, to see
your writing lying on the little round table in the draw-

[1] Mrs. Brookfield.

ing-room quite calm in the centre of this very whirling day. Bristol, Clevedon, where haven't we been? I found my poor wasted old aunt sitting with her cats in her dreary room. It's a terrible thing to see. . . . It's distracting to think of such a waste of life and generous feeling, and power of affection. She is exactly like Lady Sarah Francis in *Old Kensington,* only much more dreary.

But this isn't what I wanted to tell you about, but the terrace at Clevedon Court,[1] with a fountain dropping into a marble basin, a sight of all the summer in the valley, all the silver in the sea, and the old grey ivy gables.

It only lasted about ten minutes, then the sun came out after the rain and we all went into the garden, and the trees bloomed again, and the lights flowed down the steep daisy slope, and then the fly came, to carry us off. I had a letter from Mrs. Elton this morning, prompted by Job, of course, to ask us there. Papa had always talked about Clevedon, and Job had always told us about it, and I own I had a fancy to go there. So off we started and found Sir Arthur Elton the most gentle and humorous person, who was affectingly kind to us, and a distinguished-looking lady with beautiful little children, like roses picked off the porch—and this wonder of sweetness outside, and inside oak panels, ancestors and oriels.

. . . I finished my story roughly to-day, and am so ashamed of it that I am sending it straight off by the same post as this. I have still a little bit to do in the middle, and then I shall get at last to Susanna who has been waiting and waiting. Paris and the Red Republicans will come in very well, and the seaside and a great deal of wind. How do you think

[1] Clevedon Court was the original of Castlewood in *Esmond.*

Susanna by the Sea-side
a new novel
by the author of
The Village on the Cliff

would do?

To Richmond Ritchie

Low Bank
Coniston
[1876].

This is our address. It is extremely damp but with clear lovely things and scents and tints. The hills are not very high, but they are just like the clouds drifting by the lake, and there are two sloping golden fields to the boat-house, with two little calves browsing. There are syringa bushes everywhere, and streams of buttercups flowing down to the real water which is reticulated with a sort of silver net-work.

We were rather tired when we got here, and then Leslie went to the Victor Marshalls; while I could only go to sleep on the sofa. It would have made Minny so happy to be here, and every little flower and cloud and tint seems to ache for her. . . .

We have to row across the lake to the village. We didn't mean to go to Mr. Ruskin's, but we found our-selves at his door and three maids just like Pilgrim's Progress maidens said Mr. Ruskin only saw people by appointment, and I didn't want to go in, but left my address and said it would be very kind of him to come and see me, and then Laura set off running straight down into the lake and I had to rush after her, and then Leslie rowed us back.

To George M. Smith

Low Bank
Coniston
July [18-6].

Yesterday Mr. Barrow came in with a tray and a letter in your handwriting, a kind, kind, long handshake it seems to me, and I shall think so every time I put on my too-beautiful, exquisitely fitting gloves.[1] I immediately called on Mr. Ruskin proudly, for my fingers were through last time I went, and they are the most perfect fit, and I am so touched and pleased and thank you, dear Mr. Smith.

I wish you could see our lovely lake, and that you could come to lunch this minute—Laura is with her little rake in the hayfield, and there is a Jane Eyre kitchen out of the parlour, with a dear old woman and Timothy her son who are cooking our mutton. Everything is sunning and scorching and melting outside, and we are living in this little farm among slopes and chestnut trees and with a view like a dream.

. . . I am beginning to like it now—at first it only made me long for the holidays that are not ours any more—I do hope Leslie will be better in a few more days. I am getting anxious about him for he doesn't rally one bit, he can't walk without being overtired, and mopes about so that it makes one's heart ache to see. Sometimes he cheers up a little and Victor Marshall is so good to him, but then he goes back again. Laura is the one thing he really clings to.

How are you all and how is my dear Lizzie? She would be amused by Mr. Ruskin's lovely little æsthetic encampment here. They are all in fits of delight over *scraps,* not the lake and the mountains, but a gooseberry,

[1] A gift from Mr. Smith.

or a feather off a chicken's head or something of that sort. But I do like them so, and he is a kind gentle dear old fellow and sometimes he talks quite beautifully. There is Mr. Severn who floats off bareheaded in a small sailing yacht, and we have a sort of punt and the Marshalls a life-boat, and of a sunset it is quite lovely.

Ruskin has beautiful old bibles, and missals and above all such nice strawberries at his house. He says if you can draw a strawberry you can draw anything.

In May, 1877, my parents became engaged to be married. My mother writes of her engagement to Richmond Ritchie in the following letter.

To Andrew Hichens

[1877].

It is very nice to get a friend's good will and wish and may yours bring us in as good fortune as ours brought to you. How happy your marriage did make my sister and me!

If it were not Richmond, I should be afraid to take such a life's gift, but he knows his own mind so clearly, that this blessing of affection seemed to have lightened the darkness in which I have been living, and now at last I feel as if it were ungrateful indeed if we did not take the happiness which has come like a sort of miracle. Please give my love to the dear people all round you.

On Thursday, the second of August, 1877, my father and mother were married at Kensington church.

Howard Sturgis, writing of my father, says: "Richmond Ritchie possessed one of the surest and most brilliant minds I have ever known. He had begun to think, and to think for himself, long before most men are quite sure what thought means. In Cambridge days his contemporaries looked forward to seeing his name blazing

among the immortals, and I have never been able to get
over a certain sense of waste at the harnessing of such a
Pegasus—though the vehicle he was condemned to draw
was nothing less than the huge juggernaut car of England's Indian dependency. We are constantly exhorted
'to hitch our waggon to a star' and perhaps if more stars
of his magnitude were hitched to the official waggons
they might run more smoothly.

". . . No wife ever respected her husband more whole-
heartedly than Anne Ritchie; his nature supplied the
prop on which hers could spread itself most happily to
the sun."

Shortly before his marriage my father had entered the
India Office. As private secretary to the successive Par-
liamentary Under-Secretaries of State, 1883–1891, he
gained a remarkable reputation for insight into the vast
and tangled problems of Indian administration. From
1895 to 1902 he was private secretary to the Secretary of
State for India, Lord George Hamilton. In 1902 he was
appointed Secretary to the Political and Secret Depart-
ment of the India Office, and on the retirement of Sir
Arthur Godley, in 1909, succeeded him as Permanent
Under-Secretary of State for India, which post he held
until his death in 1912. He received the C.B. in 1898
and the K. C. B. in 1907.

Journal (1878)

In May, 1878, Richmond and I settled into our own
house, 27, Young Street, Kensington Square. It was the
prettiest old house with a long garden at the back and
an ancient medlar tree with a hole in it. There was also
a lovely tall acacia tree. In those days before Kensington

Court was built, there were other gardens full of birds
and trees, and beyond the tall spire of the church.

Journal (1879)

January 10th. Dined at Mr. Aidé's. Met Rhoda
Broughton, who began her friendship with Richmond
most characteristically. He was sitting next to her on
the opposite side of the table to me, and when I introduced him she paid him no attention.

He: "I believe we are being introduced."

She: "How very disagreeable."

May 23rd. We went for a little tour in Holland.
Delightful arrival. Walk through Antwerp—Cathedral
—Pictures—drive.

May 25th. Cathedral—mass—Rubens' great Descent.
In the afternoon to the Zoo with Pen Browning.

May 26th. To Rotterdam by Dordrecht.

May 27th. To the Gallery, Frans Hals—Bol—Van
der Helst.

May 28th. To the Hague. The railway journey was
delightful with a sight of a hundred spotless interiors and
then 10,000 windmills and cows. A walk in this Versailles-like town.

In the afternoon to Scheveningen with the fleet coming
in and the miracle of the fishes.

May 29th. Haarlem. Couldn't sleep for delightful
sights! Franz Hals,—wrote to Millais—they are such
kindred spirits.

To Amsterdam in the evening—passed fields of flowers.

June 1st. To the Stadt House. Once more looked
at Rembrandts. Found the Trevelyans there. George
Trevelyan said, "Look at that wall and the faces during

the Spanish Inquisition, and at *that* wall and the comfortable burghers after the horror was removed."

June 4th. Brussels. More pictures. *6th June*. Crossed home.

To Mrs. Tennyson

Rotterdam
May 27 [1879].

I was dreaming of you all last night, and I feel as if I must tell you how I think of you, and send you my faithful love. Richmond told me the sad peaceful news [1] as we were starting. Your sorrows and your realities seem only to make me know more and more how much I owe you, and how much of my life seems to belong to you and yours.

We have had such a happy journey while you have all been in sorrow, but I know you will sympathise in this too. It has done me immense good for I was really ill when I came away, and I seem to have left my languor and sickness at Dover.

We have been at Calais, and at Antwerp hearing the organs and seeing the Rubenses. The fine Rubenses are like sunshine and make one's heart jump, but there are only two or three that one really cares for.

Pen Browning was at Antwerp nodding to the inhabitants. We came here to-day. We are going on to the Hague to-morrow to make friends with Rembrandt.

I can't imagine a quainter and more vivid place to come to for a short time than Holland.

The absurd women here wear *bonnets* with artificial flowers over their caps and gold blinkers and rams' horns. It has the craziest look.

[1] The death of Mrs. Charles Tennyson Turner.

To her Husband

May 24 [1880].

I am still thrrrrrrilling over a conversation I had yesterday with Charles Lewes. Lionel Tennyson was here; he declared that his hair stood on end as he listened. Charles Lewes said he wished to tell me all about the wedding.[1] He gave her away and looks upon Mr. Cross as an elder brother.

I asked him if she had consulted him, and he said no, not consulted, but that she had told him a few weeks ago. She confided in Paget, who approved and told her that it wouldn't make any difference in her influence. Here I couldn't stand it, and said of course it would, but it was better to be genuine than to have influence, and that I didn't suppose she imagined herself inspired, though her clique did. It rather shocked him, and he mumbled a good deal. Young Lewes is generous about the marriage. He says he owes everything to her, his Gertrude included, and that his Father had no grain of jealousy in him, and only would have wished her happy, and that she was of such a delicate fastidious nature that she couldn't be satisfied with anything but an ideal tête-à-tête. George Eliot told him if she hadn't been human with feelings and failings like other people, how could she have written her books.

He talked about his own mother in confidence, but his eyes all filled up with tears over George Eliot, and altogether it was the strangest page of life I ever skimmed over. She is an honest woman, and goes in with all her might for what she is about.

She did not confide in Herbert Spencer. They have taken a beautiful house in Cheyne Walk.

[1] George Eliot's marriage to Mr. Cross.

In 1881 my mother's book *Miss Williamson's Divagations* was published, and to this year also belongs her *Life of Madame de Sevigné,* written for Mrs. Oliphant's edition of Foreign Classics.

To her sister-in-law, Emily Ritchie (in India)

27, Young Street
Kensington
[1881].

. . . Everybody is asking me to dinner and begging for copies.[1] They did not think there was so much life left in me!

Madame de Sevigné has gone to Mr. Blackwood. *Miss Williamson* is a success, but of course the other is what I really care about. Mrs. Procter is triumphant I have made such a sensation.

I am so glad that you have met Mr. Lyall.[2] He is one of my enthusiasms, which are very far between now. His sister, Mrs. Holland, is one of the most charming people we have ever known, and knows everything about Madame de Sevigné. Bernard Holland is his nephew and very often comes to dine of a Sunday, and Mr. Herbert Paul of a Saturday. We hardly see anyone else except five o'clock tea ladies.

To Emily Ritchie (in India)

27, Young Street
[*February* 1881].

I have just come from a happy hour over Petitot's miniatures at the South Kensington Museum. Having sent off my Mme. de Sevigné's MSS, I went to treat myself with a dilettante sight of all my friends' portraits.

---

[1] *Miss Williamson's Divagations.*
[2] Afterwards the Right Honourable Sir Alfred Lyall, G.C.I.E., K.C.B.

They are just like real people only more silent, more courteous, more unchanging.

. . . I haven't written to you since George Eliot died, and now dear old Carlyle is gone. Fred Myers asked me last night which I put highest. Of course to my generation, Carlyle is a far more powerful influence. George Eliot seems more to me like an expression and interpretation than an actual influence. Scribner sent to ask me to write about her, but I didn't feel up to it, and Fred Myers is to do it.

It is absurd, but I do feel George Eliot's death very much. There is nothing to be sorry for—all is at peace for her, poor soul, but it haunts one somehow. She was buried in a great storm of wind and rain or I think I should have gone to the funeral.

To Emily Ritchie (in India)

March 8th [1881].

. . . Think of my taking Billy [1] yesterday to see little Tom Carlyle.[2] The little Carlyle baby is very like his Great-uncle. He gave a grunt like him, and Billy opened his eyes and laughed and looked like his Grandfather for a moment. It was the oddest, most affecting moment to me. There were the two babies in the dear old room, and old me looking on at the new, like a shadow in the past. It was strange indeed, and I am sure you will sympathise.

. . . The armies of buds are out on every twig. The wind is east, the dust is dry, and yet there is a feeling of intense coming life. Everything out of doors looks so alive that it is quite strange to see no little green leaves

[1] Her son aged one year.
[2] Grandson of Alexander Carlyle, a brother of Thomas Carlyle, who farmed at Craigenputtock when Carlyle and his wife lived there.

and twigs bursting out on the furniture and wicker
blinds!

Journal (1882)

Early in the year Mrs. Darwin asked us to go and stay
at Down, and so anxious was I to go, that I mistook the
day, and went just a week *before* they asked us!

We drove to the door, the butler hospitably said, "Mr.
and Mrs. Darwin are sure to wish you to remain, pray
don't go," and Mrs. and Mr. Darwin came out and called
us in, and Mr. Darwin said, "You're as welcome as can
be, and you must forgive me for laughing. I can't for
the life of me help laughing."

There never was a more charming visit, nor a more
delightful host and hostess. He told us about his travels

Hester wishes to go out again

with Admiral FitzRoy, he told us about birds, he told us about fishes, he told us about the tortoises in the Island of Ascension, hatched from the eggs in the sand, and starting off and plunging into the sea, and, "by Jove," says he, "the little tortoises, without compass or experience, sail straight by the nearest way to Algiers. It's perfectly wonderful." Then he announced he should go to rest. "These ladies," he said, "are good enough to carry me off and read me to sleep when they think I'm getting over excited."

At breakfast he appeared, having breakfasted, and sat in an arm-chair and talked about Madame de Sevigné. He said when they were all young, they knew her letters so well that they nicknamed their friends by the names of her characters, the obliging Haqueville and so on.

We walked in the garden, and he showed us his worms which had just been turned out of the study, after a course of French horn.

After we came home, there arrived a present for the children from him, a long sliding board to be leant against the stairs, and up and down which the children slid with delight.

The day we should have really gone he was taken with his fatal illness. These two happy days were the last bright flash of that glorious life.

To Mrs. Gerald Ritchie [1] (in India)

27, Young Street
[1882].

. . . Yesterday I went with Richmond to the London Library, and while I was waiting an old clerk came up and said, "I haven't seen you for a long time, Ma'am. I used to serve your father. Why, I can see him now stand-

[1] Margie Thackeray, now Mrs. Gerald Ritchie.

ing there and asking for his books. It is now some years since he died." "It is twenty years," I said, and there my father was somehow for me, just as though twenty years were nothing, and it is your whole life.

I don't know why, but this gives me a feeling of the nothing of time, of the everything of God's love made manifest in those we love.

To Mrs. Legard (who had sent two poems by her granddaughter Mary Cholmondeley to be criticised)

27, Young Street
[1883].

I have been so much interested in the poems, especially the "Little Child." Perhaps the second one is more like other people's, but they are both very tenderly written, and the longer poem seems altogether true and heartfelt and real. I remember my father criticising my first article, and telling me to "clinch it tighter," and also that I had used the word *little* too often, and it seems to me this criticism would also apply to your granddaughter's work. Just the beginning of the "Little Child" strikes me as too diffuse, as if three verses would be better than four. I wonder whether in that sort of stunned state people actually *watch?* it seems to me as if they knew what is happening, and look on but don't look at.

Do ask her to send me some more some day, and do tell her to go on writing.

To Mary Cholmondeley

27, Young Street
[1883].

I have been reading your story, which is very striking and well written, but wouldn't it be improved by a little chastening?

I remember when I was your age my father told me and it really was a pang to me, to cut out all the *jolly's* and all the slang, and I think your hero would really seem more romantic and handsome if he didn't talk quite so colloquially. . . . You won't think me quite horrid, I know, for wanting you to take all this trouble, and if you would then send the packet back to me, I would try at all events sending it to Mr. Locker.

To Emily Ritchie (in India)

[*May* 1883].

Tonight we went off to Mrs. Oliphant's to tea, cream Scotch bread, and she was so kind. I see a great deal of her.

I have been reading her article [1] which is capital. The only thing I don't agree with her about is her estimate of Carlyle and his notes. She calls them "silly"; to me it seems so inexpressibly affecting that he, the old grumbling cynic, should have been so overpowered by love and remorse, that he takes the whole world into his confidence, and I can't help feeling as if in some mysterious way his work wasn't over, and that a thousand people will be happier for knowing how unhappy those two "noble souls" were, and what Bogies they had to fight.

. . . I am feeling fairly well again, and a little less like the wolf's grandmother. The children were so dear yesterday and Madame Goldschmidt [2] came, and is another of the divine old women by whom we are surrounded. They at least remain to us.

Goodnight, my dear *young* woman.

[1] Article on "The Letters of Jane Welsh Carlyle prepared for publication by Thomas Carlyle."
[2] Jenny Lind.

To Rhoda Broughton

4, Holford Street
Hampstead
[*July 9, 1883*].

We were very much disappointed, and so were your friends and admirers who were hoping to meet you, one especially, Mrs. Williams-Freeman from Paris, who is a very old friend of mine—but it could not be helped—and I for one, always feel it a jar when people ignore natural feeling,[1] and I never can get over it in them.

The one person who will have rejoiced is young Mr. Drummond, whom we had asked to meet you, and who was in despair at having to go off to Oxford.

The following messages were confided to me spontaneously:

Charlie Brookfield
Cecil Spring-Rice } Love.

Frank Dicey
Mr. Morison
Du Maurier } Real regret.
Beerbohm Tree
Gussie Freshfield

Richmond
Ella Freeman
Lady Temple } Much more regret still.
Mr. Warr

Your room was all ready, and a neat dressing-room for your maid, for the Baroness's[2] hospitality is as liberal as it is kind. Goodbye, and oh how I hope some other time you will be able to keep your promise to come and see us all.

[1] Rhoda Broughton had put off her visit owing to the death of a friend.
[2] Lady Mary von Hügel. The von Hügels had lent my parents their house at Hampstead.

To George M. Smith

[1883].

Will you allow me to introduce to you Mrs. Herbert Martin, whose aunt Mrs. Barbauld [1] we all know. I only spiritually know Mrs. Martin through a pretty novel of hers called *Bonnie Lesley,* and as she knows you also spiritually, as most writers do, she is very anxious to see you, or to write to you, and please therefore, for my sake and Mrs. Barbauld's, forgive me for again coming to trouble you.

. . . I am absorbed in Carlyle which does somehow make one forgive a great deal that made one angry. It is overwhelmingly interesting to me, and now I seem to know all the insides of the outsides with which our childhood was passed, though at the same time I almost feel ashamed to know so much. Mrs. Carlyle was always our friend. I remember her telling me once how nearly she had gone mad at one time—No wonder!

To George M. Smith

Lynton,
North Devon
September 1 [1883].

. . . Since I saw you, as I was crossing Lynton moor in a storm, with the children tucked up on my knees, and the wind whirling, I thought of Macbeth's Three Witches, and then it suddenly occurred to me that my new book ought to be called

A Book of Sibyls
by
Mrs. Richmond Ritchie

[1] Mrs. Barbauld died in 1825. My mother gives an account of her life in *A Book of Sibyls.*

and this would obviate the danger of anyone thinking they had already read *Four Old Friends,* and not sending for it in consequence. It would also give a sort of point to my volume, for the Sibyls were certainly authoresses.

I hope you will approve of my change, and will excuse the trouble of rechristening.

. . . We are expecting Richmond next Saturday and a storm tomorrow, so I do hope Lizzie has crossed already, if she was ever able to arrange for her journey to Ethel, and my love to her.

To return to my Sibylline metaphor, I am rather in the condition of the Sibyl myself, coming with my small shreds of literature and large demands.

I am writing with the sea roaring and the white breakers. The Cornishes are in their nest on the hillside, and the Freshfields sliding down the cliff towards the sea. I wish you were coming for a walk over Exmoor with us.

To Mrs. Gerald Ritchie (in India)

[1884].

Can you think of anything but the War?[1] It seems so near and so far that our soldiers seem like companions and friends, though I am thankful I don't know one of them. Did Pinkie[2] tell you that strange little affair in the Abbey? the Bishop of London announcing Gordon's safety from the pulpit, Gladstone in a pew starting to his feet, people all swaying with excitement. Afterwards the *Dean* owning to having told the Bishop, he had heard it from a *Canon,* the Canon had heard it from a couple of choristers, and all the people came bursting into the vestry to know about it, and of course it was only the boys.

[1] General Gordon besieged at Khartoum.
[2] My mother's sister-in-law, Emily Ritchie.

We had an amusing, interesting dinner at the Tennants'. Do you remember Captain Speedy? He came up to Richmond and said, "Are you any relation of some most charming young ladies of your name I knew at Freshwater once. Can you tell me anything of them, are they married?" Then he went on, "And Miss Thackeray, can you tell me about her, whom did she marry?" So Richmond was also able to inform him, and then he crossed the room to me and began asking after you and Annie. I am more Jellyby than ever now, for *Mrs. Dymond* is coming out in March or April, and I had a regular stage-fright last week. I got so frightened, I don't know of what exactly, except that it seems so dull; however cheques are never dull.

To Mrs. Warre-Cornish

36A, Rosary Gardens
1885.

What a kind Beloved you are to think of me so tenderly, and to write such a cordial anti-sciatic anti-bluedevilic prescription. I feel so wonderfully better after to-day's blessed burst of sunshine (which you promised me) that I must send you my love and thanks. Dearest, I'm reduced to much too abject a state of cowardice by sciatica to fly off even to you and your sweet and classic groves, but to-day anything seems possible in time, and there is a moon shining over Rosary Gardens with healing in every beam.

Richmond is smoking a cigar, and I am for the first time for all these weeks *sitting* comfortably in a chair, writing notes like a human being.

To Gerald Ritchie (in India)

Southmead,
Wimbledon Park
[1885].

This page is to tell how I enjoyed getting both your letters, the first in the throes of composition, the second in the less profitable throes of sciatica, which I am joyfully abandoning for the first time.

How we all hope you will keep your palace on the Ganges! Richmond laughed when you described unpacking your golf sticks. He has just come in; he says "Je me rends au bureau . . . par un léger détour,"—He is going to have a game of golf as I needn't tell you, although the fate of India is in the balance.

If I had my way no country should belong to any other country. I would have a republic of the world, and a white-haired administrative President, a sort of wise man like Henry Taylor to refer to in cases of difficulty. I should if war was absolutely necessary, only send people over sixty, or hopelessly ill, or out of their minds to fight, but with my plan there never would be any fighting. This is a dismal sort of joke.

Did I tell you of my meeting with John Bright and how kind he was, and how delightfully he talked of my father?

To her Husband

[1885].

. . . I do feel so lazy, and as if I couldn't settle down to writing. I see I shouldn't at all like a comfortable country life. The only thing which would make a country life endurable would be poverty or an absolute necessity for stirring one's torpors.

A very nice man we went to dine with on Monday sud-

denly asked me, which was most necessary in the country
—a good digestion or an absorbing occupation? He was
a barrister who lived in London. He has bought a farm
here, and brought his children and a wife all over red
plaid ribbons to live in it. He occasionally writes for the
Pall Mall Gazette; he has the occupation and not the
digestion, and is wretched, I believe, but nevertheless
much nicer than many happier men.

To Mrs. Gerald Ritchie (in India)

[1885].

. . . I like to think that death doesn't so much matter,
that one goes on loving and understanding the dead just
as one does the living, and that long after one is gone one
will still be alive in the hearts of those one loves, and
come back at times with a strange sympathy.

How different lives are. My father never lost anyone
by death, except his one little daughter whom he never
could speak of without tears, and when I was thirty-
eight I had lost everyone except you two, Leslie and
Richmond, and now at forty eight I have home and
children and family and blessings innumerable, but I
never leave off thinking of the past.

To George M. Smith

Southmead
Jan. 1st 1886.

As I was going downstairs last night, the front door
burst open with a blast of snowy wind, an icicle man all
over frost and snow stood with a gift in his hand, and as
I carried off the parcel and opened it by the drawing-
room fire we all cried "Oh!" in chorus, when the most
lovely kindest couleur de rosest New Year's token came
out of the packing case.

May *your* New Year be as shining, crystalised, delightful, ornamental and delicious as you have made our opening day.

The children were in bed but not asleep, and Richmond, who had just come home, was warming himself by the nursery fire. I needn't tell you that Hester and Billy instantly sprang from their beds when I appeared the messenger of sweetness and delight. The bonbon tongs had an immense success, the bonbons are an immenser, and Hester says those red ones are "the most deliciousest things she ever ate."

To Emily Ritchie

[January 1886].

It is still so bitter that I want to put off coming for a day or two more, unless indeed it cheers up to-morrow. Blanche came this evening, and although it was my Thursday at home, I spent a long delightful afternoon with Mrs. Kemble, who sends you many messages.

I should not have survived the snow wedding [1] and the confusion and the crowds yesterday, if it had not been for Pen Browning and Henry James, who nobly devoted themselves to extricating me from under the horse's feet, and to finding my deaf and dumb flyman.

Sir Millais was very touching at the top of the staircase, full of gorgeous beings. He was half crying and shaking one's hand nearly off. "These are the things which shorten one's life," he said. "You don't know what she has been to me."

[1] The marriage of Alice Millais to Charles Stuart-Wortley.

To Emily Ritchie

Ramsgate
[*July* 1886].

I have just been reading Edith Sichel's delightful letter to Richmond. She is a living fountain of sparkling ink. She brings it all out in the most delightful abundant way. What a contrast to the reluctant scratches of the worn-out professional.

But thanks to Ramsgate, there is no knowing what revivals may not be in store!

Richmond walked from Deal to Dover yesterday by the cliffs, and I (no less enterprising) walked down to the port and back, to see him off, without an ache. This is the first time I have walked out without any pain at all, and how I did enjoy it. The wind blew, six vulgar delightful steamers started off on their different ways, the sun, the shrimpers, the conjurors, the revivalist all came out on the sands.

I am quite cured of my lameness and delighting in my legs, the most perfect invention that ever was for getting about.

I could swear and declare that one of Phil Norman's pictures of old Inns is here in the town.

To Emily Ritchie

Southmead
[1886].

I went up to see Mrs. Kemble yesterday; there was a lovely Miss Dorothy Deane there who stopped on and on, till at last in despair I arose to go, when Mrs. Kemble said, "Do stay," and to Miss Deane, "My dear, I want you to go."

Among other things Mrs. Kemble spoke of old age and its terrors—then quoted, " 'Courage!' he said and pointed toward the land," and her eyes filled up with gallant tears.

. . . Last night we dined at Leslie and Julia's;[1] there was a lovely little Symonds there, and Stella and Mr. Ford, and Robert Browning and Fred Gibbs. I felt as sad and strange as I always do at first, but I made a push and got happy and joking with Henry James, who devotedly jumped into the cab with us, and drove back halfway to Putney, for the sake of a little more talk.

Robert Browning described his daughter-in-law so warmly and happily; and also a correspondence he had had with little Alfred Browning Stanley Tennyson. Being his Godfather he sent him a present and a letter at Christmas, saying: "You have three names. One is a good name, one is a glorious name, one is an affectionate name," and Alfred wrote back and said, "Thank you for the present, but your name is not only affectionate, it is a little glorious too, like mine."

To her Husband

Aix-les-Bains[2]
[1886].

The Terrace with little tin tables, birds and shimmer. The Lake is so heaven blue and the sky so lake clear, and the vines seem to dance in rings with garlands of green and gold, and the little town glitters all day long in the sunshine.

Your letter comes quite early of a morning and it is so nice to get it. I shall have no end of things to tell you about Aix as soon as I can shake off my heavy head. I went to Mrs. Kemble yesterday and then retired to my couch again, but my head-ache is really going to-day and

[1] Leslie Stephen married Mrs. Herbert Duckworth in 1878.
[2] My mother had been sent to Aix as a cure for sciatica.

I enjoyed my breakfast. Marie the chambermaid brought me a delicious little roll, I should think it must be one of Princess Louise's. She is on the first floor and so is Mrs. Higford-Burr. I see great bouquets like tee-totums all down the passage, which I suppose are tributes to H.R.H.

I am glad I didn't go to Miss Smith's hotel, where Mrs. Kemble is installed. It is like Ramsgate under the trees there, all crowded with bustles and elegancies at little tables. Ramsgate with a difference. I was much pleased with the way the hotel-keeper deeply bowed to me, as I went by in my Paris dress. I found Mrs. Kemble at last, lunching, and she looked sad, but she beamed up and was eighteen all of a sudden. First, however, she blew up the waiter, "Qu'est-ce donc, mon ami?" "It is a puddinge english, Madame." "I *detest* English cookery, and pray why do you speak to me in English and bring me this detestable thing? Is not my French good enough to exempt me from nursery pudding?"

She has a beautiful apartment, a very grand salon with blue silk curtains; and she came like an old dear on purpose to see me.

. . . Dr. Blanc has procured an honorary invitation to the cercle for "Mme. Ritchie, femme de lettres." He has five daughters and a country home to which Madame Blanc is to drive me. He retired to Brighton for six weeks to learn English! Goodbye, there are only twenty-seven days more of my cure left.

To her Husband

Aix-les-Bains
[1886].

. . . Princess Louise sent for me and took me a couple of drives. The Hotel was much interested. One drive was in a little carriage with a lady in waiting on the back seat.

The Princess very handsome, very *quaint* and certainly very charming. "Allons! houp! houp!" she said to the coachman when he got sleepy. She drove me along a dusty road to a little farm where she got out. "They don't know who I am. I often come and see the old woman." We went into a low kitchen where the table was spread for supper. An old woman was stirring potatoes over the fire in the big fire-place. "I'll stir the potatoes," said the Princess. "You can go to your business." "Very well, I'll finish laying the supper," said the old woman.

Then the carts laden with Indian corn passed the windows, and the twilight began to fall, and there was a sound of distant thunder. A little boy came in from the fields carrying a kitten. The Princess left off stirring potatoes, and began to play with the kitten. The old woman lit the lamp, and her son came in and looked at the table hungrily but the Princess took no notice. The lady-in-waiting saw that they wanted to begin supper. The Princess got up to go. "Goodbye—au revoir," she said, nodding.

I thought to myself this is a fairy tale, a real cottage, and a real Princess stirring potatoes and *me* looking on.

To her Husband

Aix-les-Bains
[1886].

. . . I can hardly write for listening to the French people. "Dites-moi, Monsieur, avez-vous vu un livre qui est publié dernièrement, *Lettres à une Inconnue?*" "Non, pas lettres d' une inconnue—Lettres à une Inconnue." "Ah! mon Dieu, ça doit être bien ancien, je ne

connais pas, mais enfin ça ne peut pas être bien inté-
ressant!" "En effet c'est un livre bien fade" . . . Now
they are talking of a remarkable lady who managed Normandy and who received emperors in her mansarde. Now
the young man with the curly moustache is saying that
his grandpapa knew George Sand, and that every ten
years there is a prize of 20,000 francs, which Thiers,
Guizot and his grandpapa had in turn, and that his
grandpapa tried hard to get the prize for her. My
gracious, who can the handsome old man be. George
Sand used to write to him, he says, in a bold, round hand,
and ask for . . .

Here came old Lady Frances prepared for conversation, and then came Lady Somers, who wishes us to go
and see her on Tuesday after you have come, and now
I am going to Dr. Blanc and then to my heiress, such a
nice heiress with a prancing carriage, who is prepared
to be ever so kind. Aïdé was very serious about my
calling, very *earnest*. I went and found a tenor, a bouquet,
a cup of enamelled tea. This kind Miss Fleetwood-
Wilson and her lady-in-waiting are at the Hôtel de
l'Europe, which is quite different from anything else in
Aix, a sort of newsmarket. I do hope they won't all go
away before you come.

Mrs. Higford-Burr and I went for an amusing little
expedition yesterday in the steamer, round the lake to
Haute Combe, where the Kings of Savoy are buried, a
delightful old Cistercian Monastery on the rock. We
wound up a steep hill like pilgrims after leaving the
steamer, two and two, under the pretty oak and plane-
tree avenue, past the beggars and the vineyards, and then
came the monastery, and the brown monk at the door
and the magpie Carthusian just inside the gate, who took
us round a sort of plaster-of-Paris Chapel with cheap

plaster-of-Paris casts of kings and queens and sugar-candy ornaments. The real part was the old priest and the monk and the lovely hill by the lake.

An Anglican clergyman was immensely taken with it all, and came back and bowed a great deal and walked off with a couple of brothers. A nice old monk stepped up to me with such a chaplet. I shall bring it back for you. There was a marvellous plaster-of-Paris lady on board, "The Tinted Venus" for anything I know, who bought another rosary rather to my confusion.

To her Husband

Aix-les-Bains
[1886]

. . . I took the train to Annecy yesterday, and travelled with a nice jolly man and his mother, who kept calling him "mon fils" with such pride, that I tried to bring in "mon fils" too, but I couldn't think how. The jolly man settled all my trains for me, and lent me his Guide Joanne, and I was able to follow Sainte Chantal from convent to convent, and to catch the Annecy steamer too.

The old Annecy is a lovely mediæval town in this style, a castle, arches, rushing water, spires and the ghosts of Jean Jacques and St. Francis exorcising one another.

I took a little carriage and drove from corpse to corpse, and convent to convent. All the nuns are exactly like George Gretton in appearance, and laugh with bright brown eyes. I got into a regular old tumbled-down 1600 quarter, and was lighted down into a black cellar under an old house, escorted by an old woman in rags and a young man in shirt-sleeves who left his workshop. I thought as I went down and down, that it was just possible I might be murdered and buried away, but they had such nice friendly faces, I felt sure they only wanted their fifty centimes. But to my disgust, this wasn't the right place after all; it was to show me the hole where a body had been found. It was only just before the steamer left that I discovered the right place. See my forthcoming immortal work.[1]

. . . Last night I read some more Trollope and a stupid stupid novel by George Sand which she wrote in a week. I wish I could write one by Tuesday when I start home.

To Alfred, Lord Tennyson

Southmead
Dec. 15th [1886].

Thank you so much for my book.[2] Pinkie got hers, and one came for Mrs. Brookfield, and reasonably and unreasonably I went hunting about saying "Where is mine? I want my own," and sure enough in the evening it came, and I began—no not began—I *went on* reading out of the book that I have read and loved all my life, and who knows perhaps, when we are all peacefully together again (and I always think of old days on Freshwater downs as the nearest thing to heaven I ever could imagine), you will still walk ahead and point to the sea and to the sky, and touch things and make them shine for us and flash into our hearts, as you have ever done.

. . . I think the line I like best in the whole book is "Sent the shadow of *Himself, the boundless,* thro' the human soul."

When I think of the past, of the companions so dear, of my father (whom I have now caught up in life,) of the glorious reality of goodness and generosity in which they lived and had their being, the *wings* seem to come

---

[1] *"Sainte Jeanne Françoise de Chantal,"* an article which was republished by my mother in her book *From the Porch.*
[2] *Locksley Hall Sixty Years After.*

to your noble thought, and all that has been, and will still be, grows calm and simple and wide once more.

. . . I am writing also to send you all our *loyal thanks* as you said once, when you telegraphed to Osborne. I, who am a republican, prefer to elect my own Kings and Queens and I need not tell you their names.

My letter is too incoherent almost to send, but I do send it with more love and more thanks, and I'm ever your and dearest Lady Farringford's loving

A. I. R.

To Mrs. Kemble

Southmead
March 24th [1887].

I have it on my mind, that I told you the dream all wrong. It was Joachim, who dreamt that he was in a lovely Claude Lorraine landscape, that Mozart lay under a tree while Raphael stood up in his black velvet cap, and plucked fruit from the tree which he gave Mozart. That was something like a dream and worth repeating to *you*.

Are you more easy, dearest neighbour? I tried to walk up the hill after leaving you, but a whole flood of spring rain came in my way, and now we are in the clouds, but such soft and delicious clouds. . . .

To Emily Ritchie

Southmead
[1887].

. . . Yesterday, feeling a longing for some calm air without any trouble, we started, the children and I, Monsieur Georges and three Stracheys. We got to Putney Bridge for 7*d.*, and got tickets for 2*d.* for each child, and 4*d.* for "adults," and started economically and triumphantly on board the *Wedding Ring* for Kew—"Singulier nom," says M. Georges. Presently after half-an-hour we stuck in the mud, and there we stuck and we stuck and we stuck, and the other steamers went by roaring with laughter, and finally the tide came in and bobbled us to the landing, after nearly three hours. I sternly resisted the children's entreaties to go back by water. It was then past six o'clock, and as we sped along in the train, we actually saw our steamer again stuck in the mud!

There was a glorious deep angry sunset in the west, resulting only in this dusty fusty east wind and uninteresting morning.

Richmond brought such an interesting person home to dine last night, Mr. Middleton, the Slade Professor at Cambridge, who told me to go to the South Kensington Museum and ask to see Ruskin's portfolios. He says they are absolutely perfect in their way, and that people have not said nearly enough of his gifts as an artist. I had a funny little tea-party on Sunday, General Strachey, Sir J. Strachey and Mrs. Shaen, who conversed agreeably, but I have been so stupid these three days that man delighteth me not, nor woman either, only children. Bless them.

To Mrs. G. F. Watts

Aldeburgh
Oct. 7 [1887].

How *am* I to thank you both? They write from home that the picture [1] has come, with such pride and delight that I am quite touched. Richmond is radiant. I feel that you have made me a free citizen of that noble Signorland and I *can't* thank you, so I look gratefully at your two photographs which are on the chimney fronting the sea full of boats and herrings. The sun has actually come

[1] Her portrait given to her by Watts.

out after three weeks, to sympathise with my elation and my gratitude, and thank you with all my heart.

We have been here three weeks and I have lost the headache which persecuted me for three weeks before we came, and I feel as if each whish of the waves washed up one's soul. How I trust your journey will do you as much good. The children are intensely happy with two little friends, less adventurous and not quite in such tatters as themselves, but equally appreciative. Mr. Garret is the host here, or rather the Mayor of Aldeburgh, and Mrs. Garrett-Anderson has the prettiest little cottage that ever was seen. The larks are singing for the fine day, over such lovely gorse and bracken commons, and little robins are hopping all about the hedges, and thank you, thank you from your delighted and affectionate,

A. I. R.

To Emily Ritchie

Aldeburgh
[1887].

I have just had such a funny mysterious little expedition in the dark, first to post a letter, second to find out the omnibus to call at 8.30 to-morrow for Richmond.

A Pickwick inn and bar, a dark stable yard, a Sam Weller with a lantern, and home by the sea walk, with the sailors talking together in the blackness, and then a little home interior, a lamp, the children peacefully at cards, and Estelle stitching—finally my room, my lamp, the fire lighting up the little square den and the sea washing and washing. I was never so near it, and never liked it so well; it is not much farther off than the ivy bank along the terrace at Southmead.

I'm gradually getting calmer and calmer like the lady of Parma, but one doesn't go off in fireworks here as in Scotland. It's been a hideous day; we had the pony carriage and Richmond didn't go golfing this morning, and we got up to a firwood and walked through the pines, and met the pony and drove another bit and walked another bit. It's so like Freshwater, birds and sea and haycocks and ships sailing into the tree tops, I do like it more and more.

. . . Oh, how happy the children are! They have found a live crab and a live starfish, they have made up a scenery of rocks and seaweed in a basin on the floor. What do starfish like to eat? Pray telegraph if you happen to know.

. . . Tomorrow I am going to see my new friend, Mr. Barham the fishmonger. He is so nice, simple, well-bred. He is a gentleman but couldn't get on, and took to a boat, and Mr. FitzGerald helped him to start. I am going there to-day for Mr. Aldis Wright, to see some of the letters E. F. G. used to write to him. It seems such a pity to leave out all that part of Mr. FitzGerald's life from the memoir.

To Mrs. Kemble

Aldeburgh
[1887].

I am more provoked than ever that I could not come and see you before we left. I hear from Pinkie of your abominable intruders,[1]—brutes, pirates,—invective is thrown away upon such wretches. I could have done nothing, but I might at least have sympathised with you, but I can't *bear* to think of what you must have had to go through, and it seems so horrid not to have come to you, dear. Only I am thankful you had Miss Cobbe.[2]

I haven't been well, but this delicious bracing air has done me worlds of good. We are in a charming little

[1] Burglars.
[2] Frances Power Cobbe.

untidy house by the edge of the sea, which washes and
hushes and throbs all day long at our door. The children dance in and out of the ocean (and so do their
clothes.) I potter about and make friends with the
neighbours.

Miss Lynn is a most delightful and accomplished old
lady; she used to play with Mr. FitzGerald on the beach
here as a child, and saw more of him latterly than most
people.

She knows *all* about you and me and old days—it is
so strange to meet a stranger so completely at home with
one's own past life.

A nice woman, Miss Annie Kerrich, his favourite
niece, is also here. She is curiously like E. F. G., as like
as a soft little woman can be, with round eyes, but without
that dimple I always remember.

They tell me that it was not a fact that Mrs. FitzGerald
forced him to marry her. She urged him to break it off,
but he from some sense of honour would go on with it,
and it was more than he could bear. He left some letters
to this niece evidently wishing that the truth should be
known. Miss Lynn said he would never come in to see
her, that he used to sit outside the window till she became
so rheumatic, she said to him, "You really *must* do an act
of charity and come inside, I can no longer sit at the open
window talking," and then he came, and she used to read
to him, and he used to laugh and laugh and be more
delightful than ever.

To Gerald Ritchie (in India)

Aldeburgh
[1887].

Did I ever tell you I have given up meat for two years?
It is inconvenient here, where all the fish rush pell-mell

to the train and take tickets for London straight out of the sea.

But I *have* a fisherman, the dearest of men, who comes to my help. I have just ordered two shillings' worth of poetry for him! He is handsome, charming, a gentleman by birth; he keeps himself by his fish-shop and Mr. Fitz-Gerald gave him his boat. We take little walks together and he carries his shrimps and talks quite enchantingly. I really must make him into a story to the accompaniment of the wind, waves and wild common.

This has been a capital place, very health-giving; I came a wreck and am going back with a new jib boom, new sails and a new rudder.

To Mrs. Gerald Ritchie (in India)

Southmead
[1888].

I have had a most delightful ten days without headache, coming and going just like anybody else. I can't believe it. I have dined at Mr. Gosse's, and been to the New Gallery where Hester's portrait looks charming in the chalk, and I had the pride of leading up the du Mauriers and your Uncle Eyre to see my daughter's picture. Theo's portrait shall appear next and when you bring her home we must get Lisa to take her, "copy her" as Billy calls it.

I had been writing to your Uncle Eyre in vain about the MS. of *Esmond,* which we have given to the Trinity library at Cambridge and of which they wanted the history. He and I wrote the end at Papa's dictation. I was about fifteen and it's so long ago I can hardly remember it, except I do remember writing about Beatrix's silk stockings as she came downstairs to meet Esmond.

At the New Gallery there is a very fine picture of

Burne-Jones' "Perseus and the Dragon" which Mr.
Richmond was looking at, but I couldn't help wishing
he could have had better snakes to paint from. Perseus
and the lady are nobly painted, but the snake is all in
scallops. Mrs. Stillman and Effie were the two prettiest
people there, and so beautifully dressed. Gladstone was
there, very very pale and thin and vigorous, going the
rounds with Charlie Hallé, Mrs. Maxse and Watts who
says: "Humph! *Robert Elsmere* is a polemical work
calculated to influence the age." I began by lunching
with Mrs. Brookfield. When I see her I feel just as I
used to do when I was a little girl, and always felt it such
a treat to go to her; then I get maddened and achy to
think she is to have no rest, no quiet, no peace ever again.
Dear beloved soul, she has got the wrong end of life.
After all, many have a much miserabler life and it's no
use fussing because she won't make herself comfortable
my way instead of her own.

. . . I have got another party this afternoon—Mrs.
Emerson-Forbes, Emerson's daughter, Miss Souvestre,
Mrs. Cunliffe. We are expecting the Chapmans on
Wednesday. I have had such a touching letter this morn-
ing from Mrs. Matt Arnold, I am so glad I wrote to
her, and so farewell.

To Mrs. Gerald Ritchie (in India)

Mount Pleasant
West Malvern
Sept. 13th [1888].

We have had such a golden week since I last wrote.
Our little mouse-trap opens out upon the moor, and the
moon rises and the sun sets on every colour of the rain-
bow, and the cities and cathedrals are scattered about the

plains and the heavens, and the crows come over the crests of the hills and our spirits rise upon the wing.

You will hardly believe that I have been walking and scrambling about and catching trains and coaches all this fortnight to my heart's content.

We must come here when you come back. It is the merriest and most untiring place.

I send you the enclosed letters which will amuse you. It will be somewhat difficult for me to talk over old days with my correspondent, as it was her sister and Richmond's brother who used to meet!

To Mrs. Gerald Ritchie (in India)

Brighton
[1888].

Here is your birthday again, and I send you a hug to-night, with the sea roaring and the children subsided. I read your letter to-day and I could have cried to think you sometimes feel so far away, but one thing you need never feel, that you don't live and talk and *be* here just as much as if you were.

What with headaches and my articles I loathe writing, and yet I do so enjoy getting letters, and I write a great many in my head to you. Real letters are so scrappy and just tell about five minutes, and all the rest one has to guess. However one can guess fortunately and that just makes the whole difference.

. . . It's no use pretending there are no hard things in life along with all its blessings—but as soon as we have docketted one ache it seems to begin to change into some other.

I had a tea-party to-day, Marie Stillman and the dear old Simons and the Black Sheep but now snowy—

There is a most charming little photograph coming out
to you, which Henry Cameron has done of Billy, only
Billy is always laughing and this looks unnaturally grave.
We must take Theo to him when you come home. Lion,
the little dog, cocks up his ears and doesn't breathe when
the camera is opened, and Henry becomes the image of
his mother and even sticks his foot out in the same way,
and Ellen still in that old black bonnet and fusty cocks
of hair comes out of the dark room. But he has taken a
partner and is really getting on.

. . . All Brighton is at lunch; I have had my chicken
(Do you know that I subsist upon fish and chicken, and
have done so for three years?) Billy, I'm sorry to say,
having thrown his spoon across the table into Hester's
face, is left to draw horses by himself, while Hester and
I retire to the school-room, a delightful sunny room with
three windows and a thousand miles of sea.

To Emily Ritchie

[1888].

Your card came, and your delightful last letter, which
seems to me very comforting about Blanche. One can't
hope for perfection of health and spirits, but if one is
fairly content with a certain amount of imperfection, one
can get on and accept the life God sends one.

I wonder if it is the Devil who makes one ill, and how
is it one is able to get through the troubles of life and
make the best of it? That must be the secret of Providence which is hidden in the heart of things and feelings,
as well as in the light of the hills. . . .

To Mrs. Gerald Ritchie (in India)

Kingsley Lodge
Wimbledon
[1889].

I wonder if anyone has turned up for you in your solitude? I do so hope so—anyhow things turn up, *one-self* turns up, and one has no idea of the unexpected corners one has, until one's been alone a little.

I am becoming a second Miss Clare (did you ever hear of her?). The garden is a real delight to me. I prowl round counting my weeds and shoots, and nailing up the ivy.

Last night I enjoyed myself immensely at the Richmonds'—Marie Stillman and Mrs. Morris sat in that wicker bower, Henry James was there and the Andrew Langs who told me, of all people in the world, that Becky Sharp is still alive, at least Miss Tizzy Revis who was supposed to be Becky is, and she is now no less a person than the Countess de la Torre, and her cats one reads of in the police courts.

We have seen a good many people one way and another, Lady Airlie and Mrs. Kemble have been to tea, and Mrs. Wister from America, to whom I suddenly lost my heart.

To Miss Browning

Kingsley Lodge
Wimbledon
December 16th [1889].

How blind I was to the gravity of the bad news.[1] I *couldn't* believe it somehow, and when I wrote to you, I seemed alas! so convinced that what I had read was exaggerated, and that such vigour and delight as his could not succumb. Now I am beginning to realise the dark-

---

[1] The illness which resulted in the death of Browning.

ness and sorrow which has fallen on you, and yet his noble farewell words [1] are in one's heart—in all our hearts.

. . . I can only thank God for having counted him among those who live in my soul's life, and you too, dear friend I love, whom I am grateful and proud to count my friend. And to think of him who is with us all, though gone, is like thinking of the sunshine which survives and warms; and I for one who am so far on in life, feel that before the warmth of this light has ceased for me I shall have reached beyond all aching cold and dark.

. . . I think the only help to one's sorrow is to feel more and more the priceless treasure of those who made one's life what it was, and who *still* make it. Did this ever apply to anyone more than to Mr. Browning? I do too feel what you say, that life and vigour and strength seem so personified in him, that all this [2] seems far away from him. I feel as if we had him still, while the tributes are to his genius and goodness.

You are a Browning, and your courage and steadfastness make me cry. I was stupefied when I lost my sister, and I grudge it now, and feel how near I might have been to her, to the greater life, and I only thought of my own pain, and not of that blessing of love and tender devotion which was and *is* still, I do believe.

I only say this to you, for your mention of my sister did go to my heart.

. . . Do you remember that day I came with the children, when there were people in every room in the house? and you said we must come in all the same, and Mr. Browning came in and said, "Well, what can I do for you?" and I told him it was my birthday and I wanted him to give Hester and Billy each a kiss.

---

[1] *Asolando*, Browning's last book, published on the day of his death.
[2] The public mourning for the poet.

We have a hundred records of his kindness and of yours too, dear old kind friend, and I send you my old love and am your affectionate,

ANNE RITCHIE

To Mrs. Gerald Ritchie (in India)

Friday cum Christmas Day
[1889].

I have been to the Martins' where I found Mr. Froude, who was looking very handsome and who was certainly very kind.

. . . Then dear old Sir Theodore [Martin] came in, very pale and sad; he is going to be one of the pall bearers at the Abbey [1] on Tuesday and he had just come from the Brownings'. I was going to de Vere gardens, when I went in to the Martins', for one has a hankering after one's old friends at such times. Poor Miss Browning was ill in bed. There was a light in the drawing-room window, and in the ground floor room was the dear old friend's coffin, with its purple pall and the great Italian wreaths spread at its foot. I wanted to say goodbye and I dreaded the Abbey.

To G. F. Watts, R. A.

Wimbledon
Feb. 26th [1890].

Here is my little article—my enormous long article rather—about Ruskin which they have at last published. I am grieved to think that he is so ill. I needn't alas! have been so afraid of saying anything he might dislike, and how very very kind you both were in helping me.

. . . We send you our love and look at all your kind tokens of friendship on our walls—I wish I was hanging up on *your* wall, and could have a talk. We are in very

[1] Browning's funeral.

fair condition after that winter storm of influenza which
raged at Wimbledon. It was almost ludicrous to see the
people collapsing on every side, and our helpless conster-
nation. I had my four maids, my husband, my two children, and the man who cleaned the windows, all laid up
at once. But everybody is quite well, so it is no use
dwelling upon the sneezes of the past. . . .

To Mrs. Warre-Cornish

Kingsley Lodge
[1890].

Pinkie's delightful letter about you all has come this
morning, but I must send you my love, before I write
to her. . . .

Here am I suddenly overwhelmed by the realization
of what letters are to us all. I wonder which is more important, flesh and blood or paper and ink in the course
of ages? I am reading Lewes's *Life of Goethe,* and a
disquisition upon Shakespeare's attitude to his contemporaries first set me off wondering.

I suppose *men* are more important than what they feel
and say, but only to themselves perhaps. . . .

I have just felt like Carlyle himself, for being worked
up to a spurt of genuine ink-splashing, in comes Amelia
the parlour maid. "Mr. Witting from South Wimbledon particularly wishes to see you," and says I, "How can
you bring such messages to me, how *can* I see anybody?"
I resume ink spurting. Enter Amelia carrying this.[1]
"Mr. Witting wishes you to buy this basket for plants,
ma'am; he has made it himself." Yes, dearest Blanche, I
nearly exploded; all my ideas were crushed by that awful
basket, and I'm soothing myself by a note to you. I have
explained to Amelia that if ever she writes a book, she

[1] My mother drew a picture of the basket.

will find that anybody coming in like that will send all
her ideas flying out of window.

"Grrrrrrrrrr" is the most expressive line Browning
ever wrote, and I find myself always quoting it on every
possible occasion.

To Emily Ritchie (in Paris)

[1891].

I have been imagining you in my favourite corner of
my favourite city. Have you opened your windows and
looked out, does it smell—rumble—taste—Paris? I'm
sure it does. Even the little tin water cans are unlike any-
think anywhere else.

. . . Now I must tell you of Billy's repartee, which I
think will amuse you.

Billy to his Mama: "Tell me a story about when you
were very young."

Mama: "I went to see Mr. and Mrs. Browning at
Paris, and Mr. Aïdé who was there said to me, 'Well,
Miss Thackeray, and when are you going to write a
book?' Mr. Browning answered for me, 'All in good
time. The Roman ladies sat at home and spun wool.
Nowadays, too, every woman has wool to spin of some
sort or other.' "

Billy: "I don't call that a story, Mama, I call that a
yarn!"

To Emily Ritchie (in Rome)

Kingsley
[*April* 1891.]

Your letter came in with a burst of sunshine, so that
we nearly had to pull the blinds down. How delicious
does your Lucca sound. Mrs. Sartoris used to say that
of all her favourite spots Lucca was the most favoured.

I can't remember, but the Storys will tell you, and do ask them from me if they were not there with the Brownings and a whole colony of dear past spirits?

I remember your hotel perfectly, and I went there and either did or didn't leave a large bouquet of rosebuds for George Eliot. It was in my mind to do so, and I bought the flowers and went to the door with them, and then I think my courage failed and it seemed to me affected.

Though I'm not in Italy, I can see such a lovely white snowy range of peartree as I write, and my own tulips are sprouting; everything came out like a Private view yesterday with a blessed shower of rain.

. . . I can't tell you how I enjoyed a reading of *Luria* [1] on Easter Sunday. I'm not littérateurising now, but isn't the real sacrament of our life when something Godlike raises us for a minute from stuff to spirit? and *Luria* is a noble flash of great spirituality.

To Emily Ritchie (in Rome)

Kingsley
[*April* 1891].

It seems the wildest Romance to me, that anyone belonging to me should be standing upon the cornerstones of Rome. I think in some former existence I was a Roman matron; such an odd string tugs at me after twenty years and forty years, and a sort of odd feeling of former existence I can't describe. Paris is all my youth, but Rome is some indefinable association.

. . . It is dazzling, cold, cheerful, irritating Easter weather here. Mrs. H——, calmly literary, called the other day, and stayed and stayed, till I rushed off in despair, and found Billy in a grand draught and shirt-sleeves

---

[1] *Luria* by Robert Browning.

and open window, performing hairbreadth antics and refusing to appear till our company was gone.

There is something very ludicrous in discussing whether
my father's memoirs should or shouldn't be written, while
his grandson is catching influenza in the next room. Not
that he is. He is very jolly and in the seventh heaven with
Arthur.

To Rhoda Broughton

Wimbledon
May 9 [1891].

I knew you would be very indignant with me, but I
couldn't resist coming, having suddenly made up my mind
to the extravagance of a victoria and a treat to my daughter and her two friends. We went to Lady Russell, to
your enchanted home which "Cometh up as a flower,"
which I love "Not wisely," and how do you always secure
Dowager Countesses to open your front door and greet
your guests? Your Mansfield Terrace really is a triumph
of delightfulness.

I wound up my expedition with a horrible sad little
visit to such a brave noble old lady, Mrs. Thompson of
Trinity, who lives in a dreary roadside villa on the way
to Kew, too old to read, all alone after her brilliant
reign, and never saying one word of complaint—it is
really heroic.

Then we sailed through millions of white blossoms,
home by Roehampton Lane. But I was disappointed not
to see you, for coming earlier I had hoped to catch you,
and I *didn't mean to bring the little girls in*.[1] Richmond
has just come home, in utter scorn of *Hedda Gabler*. Au
revoir, you know we are always at luncheon on Sundays
at a quarter to two, but it is simply impossible for the car-
riageless, I know. Lady Lindsay said she always had had

[1] An allusion to Rhoda Broughton's well-known dislike of children.

her eye upon your pretty house when it was to let, and promises to *send* for me, and then I shall try and combine better, and find you as well as your house.

To her Husband

84, Plymouth Grove
Manchester
November 14 [1891].

O what kind ladies![1] O what a delicious dinner! O what a nice room! O how extraordinarily rejuvenated and cheered I feel!

I only wish you were here too, for I become quite ashamed of having all these delicious little attentions to myself. I am writing to catch the early worm! Meta met me at the station in a beautiful brougham. Pheasant, jelly, Apollinaris for dinner, champagne on the side table. It is very funny of what consequence one feels when one is paying a visit. The best of everything is not too good for one. The sun is shining, the air is delicious! I like the climate of Manchester!!! I arrived far less tired than when I started. I do wonder how you and the children are getting on.

Sunday 12 o'clock. Only just down! Don't know where the ladies are. You are an angel to have written again for I was fussy somehow and am thankful to hear all is well.

. . . I went to see a church yesterday built by Hansom, the most beautiful thing you ever saw. Julia says that she heard there a very fine sermon on Heaven and Hell not long ago, but by some nervous slip the preacher always said Hell for Heaven and Heaven for Hell, till it was all she could do to keep her countenance. After that we went to the Town Hall, and saw the beautiful

[1] My mother was staying with the Misses Meta and Julia Gaskell, daughters of Mrs. Gaskell, the authoress.

Maddox-Browns. The frescoes quite lovely. Then we drove on to the canal which was looking like a fresco too, with the sun dropping over the distant waters.

To-day there has been a luncheon party, Mr. Wilkinson, Prince Kropotkin and others, and an absurd little incident happened. Julia Gaskell said to me, "There is a charming man going to take you in, he is a self-raised philanthropist, a frame-maker, who has done so much for the poor people. You will be interested in him," and I being sent in with a little man made myself as agreeable as I could.

I. What a striking city this is!

He. Indeed.

I. What a magnificent Town Hall!

He. Really, I never have been there.

I (nervously). How proud you must be of the great work and achievements of Manchester.

He. I take no interest in them.

I. Not in that lovely new church I saw yesterday with Miss Gaskell?

He. I am an Atheist!

I (still more nervous). And do you care for the great canal?

He. Not at all, I am an Anarchist!

I. Good gracious, would you destroy everything?

He. Yes, I am a Nihilist!

Mr. Wilkinson here burst out laughing—I had mistaken Prince Kropotkin for the self-raised philanthropist!

However after this terrible beginning Prince Kropotkin and I became great friends, and he gave me a description of Anarchy that was more like Heaven upon earth than anything else, with laws of order, peace and beauty enforced by a vast army of Christian-hearted atheists.

To Mrs. Oliphant

Kingsley
July 16 [1891].

I have just written to Madame Villari and told her what I could about you, and this makes me want to *touch* you yourself.

How I have admired your Pilgrim's Progress of a book.[1] You have to my mind flashed him into your pages, and I sat up until I don't know what o'clock, and finished with a feeling—thank God, life doesn't depend on sanity or success or fulfillment; it is living *towards* the best one can which is the secret of it all.

I've so often felt *that,* talking to my mother. There is her loving humble generous life quite clear—through all its incompleteness. Suppose she was a strong-minded woman, or a leader of fashion or anything else, what more would she be in the kingdom of heaven?

I never could come and see you, though I longed to. . . . But I often am with you in thought, and always in love and affection, and indeed I don't forget what your courage has to endure.

To Mrs. Douglas Freshfield

Littlestone
Kent
[*August* 1891].

If your Browning[2] delays, let me know. I will send it off as I have done with it. But read Laurence Oliphant first; it seems to me such a striking and cheering biography. It shows how true the impulses towards Hope and the Unseen are. I don't think anything ever struck me more. Laurence Oliphant may be cracked, he may be

[1] *The Life of Laurence Oliphant.*
[2] *The Life and Letters of Robert Browning.*

affected, he may be unsatisfactory, but you feel the genuine true atmosphere through it all, just as you do in the Browning indeed, but then to feel like Browning one has to have something of his vigorous, strong nature. Now Laurence Oliphant is made of the same uncertain stuff one is oneself, only he has this beautiful generous aspiration, which carries him on real wings over the sloughs and oceans of life.

I can see him so plain in the summer evening, looking up and laughing so courteously and prettily, when my father apologised for having forgotten a second time that he had asked him to dinner.

. . . Except Sir Walter Scott's Journal, I can hardly think of anything written at length in detail which gives a very clear impression to one's mind of another person. It seems to me it is the short, natural, by-the-way things which are most vivid. I am trying to write a column for the *London News,* with a picture of my father which they are publishing—I don't know why—just because the man asked me. He wanted me to say what I thought of my father's biographies, and I began to think that three words of Mr. FitzGerald's put him more vividly before me than pages of disquisition. "There the door opened and Thackeray came in, grand, gay and white-headed." I know that phase of him so well.

To Miss Browning

Littlestone,
August 18th [1891].

I am just sending the last page of my little article [1] to Mr. Harper's agent, and asking him to send a proof to you, care of Messrs. Smith and Elder.

It is only a very slight thing, but a record of a great

[1] On Robert Browning, republished in *Tennyson, Browning and Ruskin.*

deal of happy remembrance. It is rather egotistical, as I had to tear up all I tried to write that wasn't personal, for I thought it so dull: and my article became only personal reminiscences at last. I hope there is nothing you will object to, and I send you my love, and to Pen and to his dear Mrs. Pen, who is always a pleasure to think of, especially with you.

Goodbye, dear, I'll never write about anyone I knew and *really* cared for again, for it is so complicated; and yet at the same time it is a very *proud* and grateful feeling to say to oneself, "And *this* was my Friend." I can only say thank God, for having known such dear and noble people.

To Mrs. Douglas Freshfield

Littlestone
Kent
[1891].

It seems such a long time since I have heard about you, but as Pinkie is going to see you she will send me word. Mlle. Souvestre wrote very touchingly about you. It was like one of Madame de Sevigné's letters, some of which (when they are not about old Grignan) do somehow seem to me the most touching and feeling letters that ever were written. Do you remember the very last she ever wrote? I have not read it for years, but it seems to me to concern you, when I think of it.

I wonder if you can tell me anything about Mme. D'Aulnoy? I have promised to write a short preface to her fairy tales, but my head has been so bad, I have had no chance till now. She is a parrot-faced little person, and has written some idiotic travels in Spain. Do you think the British public would allow me to quote the fact of the Dame du Palais, the Princesse des Ursins, escorting the King to bed, carrying a sword, a lamp and a pot de

chambre? I am afraid not, but it is the only fact I have
been able to gather as yet.

I send you Mr. du Maurier's letter to whom I wrote
about his two very beautiful opening numbers.[1] They
were like Ruskin, or anything akin to one. The story
nothing, the description of my and (as I find) his childhood, so extraordinarily vivid.

To Emily Ritchie

Wimbledon
[1891].

. . . I had an interesting visit to the British Museum,
found a fire, an armchair and a volume of memoirs, and
read and read and read as hard as I could, until luncheon
and Sidney Colvin appeared. Madame d'Aulnoy is a
humbug. A long farrago about her lovers, Vicomtes and
Marquises, and their jealousies and her family's unkind-
ness. She sounds exactly like Heloïse; not a word of her
children, nor her journey nor anything to the point in
any way. I have just made such an extraordinary dis-
covery in a footnote, while I was on her track: Madame
de la Fayette was a sort of spy! A political secret agent
to the Court of Turin. I feel inclined to go off to Italy
to read it all up.

. . . We have been reading the *Princesse de Clèves*.
Oh how dull it is! What saints of modest toleration were
our great great great French grandmothers who thrilled
so easily.

To Mrs. Oliphant

Oct. 16 [1892].

I have been wondering about you, ever since we parted
at the Abbey door,[2] and I fear from what Miss Lawless
tells me to-night that you are very tired and worn out.

[1] *Peter Ibbetson.*
[2] Tennyson's funeral in Westminster Abbey.

I came home feeling out of gear and out of spirits, and
I am only now shaking off the feeling of almost despair
which came over me, as I looked at all that should have
been of comfort and help. . . . It seemed to me like my
whole generation passing away. I think the great strain
of feeling so deeply and of seeing a public sight at the
same time is too much, and I will go to no more funerals
unless I may cry comfortably by myself and say my
prayers, and then comfort does come, and that is all I
know.

I was really touched by Ellen Terry's genuine grief,
though I think, if I had only been alone with you, I
should have felt in better harmony with that, to me, most
wrenching scene.

To *A. C. Swinburne*

Kingsley
[*December* 1892].

Here is a small volume to wish you a happy Christmas.
Wish us one with all your might and perhaps you may
exorcise the Fiend [1] who has gripped me here, and my
beloved husband in London.

We are so *longing* to get well for our boy's holidays,
who writes by every post, "On the 21st I arrive at Euston.
Send me the journey money at once. Please be well in
time."

I have the greatest faith in a friend's good wishes,
yours even if you were not an old friend!

What news have you of Bertram Brooke? I have
heard nothing since they left.

I send this to neighbour Frost's.

[1] Influenza.

To Emily Lady Tennyson

Kingsley Lodge
1 *Jan.* [1894].

It was dear of you to write to me about my mother's death, and I liked Hallam's note which I found when we came home from our sad solemn journey.

My dearest mother did not suffer; she was speaking of Billy and his school when she fainted. They carried her to her room, and she rallied for a very little, and then became once more unconscious. She did not know me when I got there, but I could sit by her bed and hold her dear little hand, and feel it was her and me still.

And in the morning, after that long strange night, something came into her face, something great and wise and beautiful beyond words or even remembrance. I thought the sun had broken thro' the clouds, but when I looked at the window it was dull twilight, and this great distinct light and beauty was in her face. I should like to think the children could feel as little sorrow and as much love when I go from them and their father. They were very sad, poor darlings, and cried and cried, but they have cheered up now, except that to-morrow is black Friday and Billy is going back to school.

I will write again very soon for I seem to have so many other things to say, but just now I will only give you a loving hug.

To Lady Bell

Kingsley Lodge
Wimbledon
Jan. 20th [1894].

Somehow I don't write to you because I am so sure with you, and I know you know how I love you and yours, and what a joy in life it is to be *at home* in the

hearts that come natural. Just at first after my mother
died every word I wrote seemed like struggling against
a great weight. And yet it has been more of thankfulness
than sorrow—she had no pain, and those who saw her
die, now know her, and what she was within the tranquil
person of her life. Dear Mama, so silent, so undemand-
ing, so loving, so contented. As she lay there, she looked
wise and strong and full of peace, and one couldn't feel
sorrow, and yet I shall miss her day after day. The
children cried bitterly and her poor friend and companion can't be consoled. I went back and found her
sitting all alone in the middle of the room quite broken
and overcome.

To Mrs. Warre-Cornish

January [1894].

Pinkie will have told you about my mother. Her
death was something far beyond peace. It seemed to me
like a reality of Life and Knowledge and her dear face
looked translated, supreme. I have no words to tell you
how great she seemed to me. Richmond and the children,
and Julia and Edward Thackeray came and laid her in
her grave—my kind, sweet, patient mother.

To Emily Ritchie

15 June [1894].

WE are coming home Monday after an absence of many years.[1] I find England very little changed, though of course my long residence in Ireland has modified my views. O how they hate us—it's awful—simply awful.

Edgeworthstown was exactly what I expected. One of Miss Edgeworth's own groups was at the railway station, an emigrant family going to America, and Mrs. St. George going off fishing. She has the most splendid diamonds, although she is nearly starving. "Where is Mr. St. George?" says Mr. Edgeworth. "Oh he couldn't be bothered, we are going out for the day." Mr. Edgeworth says he had far rather see the French and Americans in Ireland, than the English and Home Rule; so do lots of other people. It frightened me. They all like Mr. Morley and Lord Houghton.

To Emily Ritchie

The End House,
Wimbledon
4 o'clock
[*June* 1894].

You will like to hear that we are triumphantly through the travail of a new home, and the home is born![2] A

[1] A fortnight in Ireland. My mother was writing her introductions to Miss Edgeworth's novels.

[2] The End House was built by my parents.

242

van arrived before breakfast and carried off the drawing room. Here sit I in the comfortable chair by the fire, in perfect raptures! To-morrow the remaining dining room and bedrooms follow, and then comes Mr. Lee and his hammer and nails. It is more like Rosary Gardens than anything else. It feels quite dry-ish already, and we have been in luck with our van-guard, a magnificent retinue of "Porthoses," with the minds of d'Artagnan and the noble manners of Athos, have brought all the furniture in procession. I said yellow room, blue room, green room, as they came in, and that was all.

To Julian Sturgis

[*July* 1894].

Thank you for *your* thank you, dear Julian; what a delightful cheering fillip to warm my old and failing steps. I *love* my recollections, and I now understand why everybody writes them. One begins to dance again, and lark, and frisk, and thrill, and do all the things one can hardly believe one ever did. I'm sure some of our happiest joys and carols were under your kind kindest home, and I think of Mount Felix as Mount Happy indeed.

Jealousy of the Miss Whites (and how they detested us! I can't help laughing now when I remember the amenities which passed between us) was the only shadow, but that gave point to the dial.

I think it very likely indeed my father wrote at Mount Felix, but he finished *Esmond* before he went to America the first time, and it was *after that* I think you went to Mount Felix, and we used to come over with the Synges. There was a house at Richmond [1] or somewhere there-

---

[1] "Little Marble Hill," the Sturgises' country house before they moved to Mount Felix.

abouts we used to drive to, where I once saw Hawthorne, who didn't speak and looked grim, and where Howard was an infant running away without any clothes on, but that was more like *Esmond* times. I will try and look it up and tell you, if I can find anything. I shall so value the book; another thank you for *that*.

To Julian Sturgis

July 21 [1894].

Your kind thought of us touched me very much, and when the book [1] came I read it straight off, and thought it so well done, and so sincere a picture of your lovely home and its dear inmates. I *thought* to you—I do hope I wrote what I thought, and felt and feel, but I have a vile way of thinking my letter, beginning it, and long afterwards asking myself if I ever finished it, and ever sent it off?

Whether I did or not, I am very grateful and glad to have this little bit of my own past safely written down and printed by you. I think some hours at Mount Felix were almost the happiest of all my life—I can breathe it back still, the fresh mornings, the delightful five o'clocks; and I can see your father so plainly, so handsome, so upright. Once we went with him on the four-in-hand, I think the only time I ever was so majestically placed in all my remembrance. Thank you again if I have not thanked you already.

To Emily Ritchie

The End House
September 27th [1894].

To my joy I have just packed Maria [2] into an envelope, and registered her off to Mr. F. Macmillan. I feel as if

[1] *Books and Papers of Russell Sturgis* by his son Julian Sturgis.
[2] Introductions to certain novels of Miss Edgeworth.

she were as glad to be rid of me, poking and prying, as I
am to be rid of her. It has been a real window opening
in some ways, chiefly Irish ways.

Lord Knutsford told me he knew Miss Edgeworth
very well, and she said she couldn't bear *Patronage,* but
that *The Absentee* represented her herself. "Look for
me in *The Absentee,*" she said. He said she was very
French and sprightly.

You two dear travelling ladies, are you basking and
floating and pirouetting in blue and lilac? We actually
have a fine day again which we are all enjoying. Lady
Castletown has taken me a turn in Paradise with her two
white horses.

To Emily Ritchie

Eastbourne
[*November* 1894].

This is such a four-post-bedstead of a place, sleepy
invalids, nonagenarians and schools, bath-chairs and
young ladies' schools, alternately. My parasol blew
away yesterday, as I was reading the account of the
Czar's [1] death—poor, poor Czar—and the young ladies'
schools and bath-chairs pursued it down the Esplanade—
it was a public benefit.

Richmond brought down that maddening book the
Lys Rouge which has oh! such clever things, and oh!
such revolting things. He also brought some more of
St. Amand, and we are deep in the Duchesse de Berri's
adventures. Joan of Arc was nothing to her. I have
bought *Marie Amélie* cheap at Mudie's, which is great
fun, but makes one hate Louis Philippe. I am no longer
an Orléaniste.

I'm going out in my bath-chair, and for the first time

[1] Czar Alexander III died on November the 1st, 1894.

don't feel like the bolster at starting, so that I hope the turn has come.[1]

We went to the Huxleys', but it kept me awake all night. He looks very charming and unchanged, with the six portraits of his daughters hanging round. Mrs. Huxley was ill. He has built his house, and does a great deal of gardening, and says he never expected to recover as he has done. Farewell, dearest, and I long to hear about the cottage.

To her Husband

Brighton
[*August* 1895].

. . . This is the most *piping* day of all the days we have had. I am just back from my lunch at Mr. Willet's. He showed me the most exquisite little prayer-book to-day, every page illuminated. Louis XVI gave it to the Abbé Edgeworth on the scaffold, and when the Abbé died in America, all the jewels on the sides were torn off, to pay for his funeral.

The Pooles thoroughly enjoyed coming. Hester and I took them to the station after dinner and drove back. Brighton might have been Grenada or Bagdad or anything romantic you please, thousands of people, of electric lights, and Zephyrs and shimmers. Brighton becomes beautiful after sunset. All day long it burns and blazes, but it has answered my purpose very well, and you certainly get enough seaside for a year in a fortnight here.

I hope Lucy Broadwood sang every one of your favourite songs. All the lodgings were on music yesterday—a regular Saturnalia.

[1] To Lady Bell she wrote, "Eastbourne wound me up, and coming home has set me ticking again."

I have been spending the morning with Tisey,[1] and reading some very interesting letters, Shelley's and others', to her father. Shelley is just starting for a sail, and raving about Spezzia and the friends who have lately joined them. His wife wants to go away, he says, and doesn't like the place. It gives one an odd turn to see it all in black and white, and then they all want to borrow money of Horace Smith.

To Mrs. G. F. Watts

The End House
Oct. 7th [1895].

Why have I never been to see you? I wonder if you have seen my bundle of wishes walking in again and again! I go to that station, I do something I have on my mind, my head begins to ache, I come home again or I go to Leslie, or I meet somebody, or am not sure that you are in town. I can't describe all the things which happen, but the best consolation I have is that, whether one walks in or not, one goes on existing in one's secret self alongside with certain people who are always kind and unchanged when one thinks of them.

I also live every day with my two pictures, with that head of my sister which is my treasure, and the picture you gave me of the not ungrateful person who wishes she came to see you, and who sends you both her love.

I was so glad to hear yesterday from a neighbour that Signor was going to paint Mrs. Josephine Butler, for hers is certainly a very noble Leonardo sort of head, and what a picture Signor will make of her!

Richmond is at the Priory with the Curzons. I had a

---

[1] Eliza Horace Smith. She could remember Keats and Shelley. Her father, Horace Smith, told her to look at a gentleman "in ambrosial dark," sitting beneath a wide-spreading ilex tree. "Do you see that man? That is a poet," he said. It was Keats, who had come from Hampstead to Fulham for the day.

very great wish to go, and wondered what pictures of Signor's I should find there, but as usual I had a headache and couldn't start. We are going to Dresden on Thursday for a month. I am very busy packing away and tearing up old scraps.

To Emily Ritchie

Berlin
[1895].

. . . What a contrast is this grim spot to smiling Dresden—it is like a shabby Paris, and is my idea of Chicago, but what delicious contents! We did so enjoy the beautiful opera last night, white, gold and electric, crammed with officers and Berlin, and the beautiful music, gold and electric too. Yes, that is what it is—not daylight. Cecil Spring-Rice came with us. We are going to see pictures with him, so I will write no more now. . . .

All Richmond said was not one word too much. I came home from the picture gallery, happy and grateful, and set off again about tea time, for the rehearsal at the Hoch-Schule, which was a thing to make one happier all one's life. Joachim's kindness and his benevolent rule, the young musicians struggling with their new-fledged wings to fly, and the beautiful music and the completeness of it all were impressive.

A little American girl, straight, light, sixteen, stepped up and played first fiddle to the whole orchestra. You never heard anything so lovely—full sweet tones, suavity and spirit. *All* the orchestra clapped when it was over, and Jo turned round benevolent, clapping, delighted. He came down to say goodbye, and to send many warmest messages to you; and all England; he said, "You cannot stay for the concert?" but we had to go back, and pack and dine at seven.

We go tomorrow to Magdeburgh and take our tickets from there to the Hague.

To Mary Millais

The End House
[1895].

Give my best love to your dear father, and tell him *how* glad I am I was born into the same age as he was. I have been making immense hankering friends with enchanting people at Dresden, Holbein and Lippo Lippi specially, and others too; and three hundred years hence, people will come and long to have known *him*.

Meanwhile, as I am in his golden age, I should like to see him sometimes. Could you ever spare time to come all this way and lunch? You can't think how fresh and nice it is; the children whirl round and round on bicycles and I look out of window at the Jesuits next door and listen to the thrushes.

To Hallam Lord Tennyson

The End House
Wimbledon
December 11th [1895].

I have just been tearing up some papers, and among them is a note I wrote down one day after a walk with your father. The first part of the note I used for my little article, the second will possibly interest you, and I daresay you may have heard him speak of it.

Your father began by saying that, as he walked thro' Eaton Square at night with Carlyle in the moonlight, Carlyle looked up at the houses round about, and said, "Acrid putrescence." Then the note goes on to say that your father was stopping at a coffee-house in London, and Carlyle came to smoke a pipe with him of an evening, and Mr. FitzGerald was there. They had some talk about the immortality of the soul, upon which Carlyle began to say, "Eh! old Jewish rags! ye must clear your mind of all that. Why should we expect a hereafter? Your traveller comes to an Inn and he takes his bed, it's only for one night, and another takes it after him."

To which Alfred answered, "Your traveller comes to his Inn and lies down in his bed almost with the certainty that he will go on his journey rejoicing next morning," to which Carlyle only replied with a grunt, and presently went away.

And then Mr. FitzGerald, who was a man of great humour, said, "You had him there." "Which proves," said your father, "how dangerous an illustration is."

I like the little scrap so much I can't help sending it off with my love.

To her Son

40, Park Lane, W.
[1895].

God bless and keep you and all of us, and make us love each other and other people, too. I always feel as if everybody had to make some *good* in the world, and to give out love and help to make other people's lives more easy.

I feel very much made good and easy at this moment, the Smiths [1] are so kind. Henry James, Mr. Guthrie, Mr. Gibbs, all dined last night and asked after you, so did Mary Millais, and they were all very nice and there was a most delicious and shiny sort of dinner. Mr. Thompson has given me a picture of Mrs. Hemans. I think I must write an article about her. . . .

[1] The Murray-Smiths, with whom my mother was staying.

To Mary Millais

The End House
[1896].

I send you this little egotistical note to *Punch;* it is almost the only tidy one, but I will copy out some more for your dear father. How I hope he has had a more easy time and that he slept last night. He seems to me like his own knight [1] crossing the ford in the sunset, and helping others to value the light in the sky overhead. I always loved that picture beyond most of his beautiful noble pictures.

. . . I am so touched that your father should have thought of me—I do better than admire his genius. I *love* my old friend, and you his daughter.

The following recollections of Sir John Millais were written by my mother for his biography. Mr. Millais kindly allows me to reprint them here.

Soon after your parents' marriage, my father took us one day to see them. I do not remember being shown any pictures on this occasion, but there is one I can still see. Your mother was recovering from some illness, and she was extended straight in some beautiful flowing dress upon a sofa, with her head resting upon a round gilt leather cushion, which made a "background of pale gold" to her face.

I remember once taking a picture to your father that an importunate friend was most anxious he should see. "*You* know better than to bring me such a thing as that!" said he. "Take it away." And to this day I blush when I recall that work of art. Simplicity and the

[1] Sir Isumbras crossing the Ferry. Sir John Millais died August 13, 1896.

directness of his blame took away the sting of it; for it is not so much criticism that people resent generally as the spirit of censure in which it is given.

Almost the last time I ever went to see him in his studio, that beautiful picture of "The Old Garden" stood upon the easel. I said how beautiful I thought it.
"Do you like it?" he answered rather sadly; "I can tell you that a bit of my life has gone into that picture."

I once saw an artist at work in a little wood near Knole on a certain day in July, when we all started on a happy expedition Mrs. Millais invited me to join. Her sister was there, and the Trollopes, and Mr. Charles Clifford. We had found sunshine everywhere, and a drag at Seven-oaks, and as we walked through the woods, we came upon this painter at work under the trees. Our host stopped for a moment. "Why," said he to the painter, "you have not got your lights right. Look, *this* is what you want." And he took the brush out of the painter's hand, and made a line or two on the picture, and then nodded to him and walked away.
Mr. Trollope laughed, and said, "The man looks be-wildered; he ought to know it is Millais," and he ran back and told him. Then some one else laughed, and said, "He ought to know it is Trollope." So a second message was conveyed to the unfortunate painter, and greatly amused we all walked on through the woods to where the carriage was waiting.[1]

The last time I sat by your father at dinner, was at the house of my husband's sister, Mrs. Freshfield. It was a very great pleasure to find Sir John there, and still more

[1] My mother does not reveal that it was she herself who conveyed the second message—and that another member of the party then ran back, saying: "Now he must be told that that was Miss Thackeray."

to find that my place was to be by his at dinner. After a long talk on books and pictures, he told me a ghost story, which, as he assured me it was true, I venture to repeat here.

It was of an old manor house in the north, standing in an old Scotch garden. A London lawyer, who liked to go to Scotland, happened to see it one day as he was driving across the moor, and he expressed a wish to the friend with whom he was staying, for some such retreat to come to with his wife. She was out of health, and he wanted to get her away from London, and he added it was just what they would both like; only that he feared he would never be able to afford it, and he named the sum he could give. The friend answered that he might get such a house well within the price he named; this one was going to be put up for auction, but there was some ghost story about it, and no one up there would bid.

Then the lawyer went back to town; but shortly afterwards he received a telegram from his friend in Scotland telling him that the house had been put up for auction, and finding it was going far below its value, he had secured it on the lawyer's behalf.

The lawyer's wife was no less delighted than her husband to hear of this purchase. She had been for some years past suffering from strange hysterical attacks, and was longing for change.

Her attacks came on in her sleep, and she would wake utterly exhausted. She always had one dream of an old house that she never remembered to have seen when she was awake. She used to find herself hurrying up and down the corridors, and along the paths and terraces of the old-fashioned garden. The place was all perfectly familiar to her, and she knew every yew hedge, and turn of the paths. She could not stop herself though she would be sinking with an exhaustion which unnerved her for hours after she awoke.

When the autumn came, the family set off for the North. As they drove up the avenue leading to the house, the lawyer noticed that his wife was looking very strangely but he put it down to fatigue. When he rang the bell the door was opened by the housekeeper, to whom he introduced himself, and said a friendly word or two of greeting, and almost immediately he began to ask her whether anything more had been heard of the ghost—whether it had appeared lately.

"What sort of a ghost is it?" said he.

The housekeeper did not answer, but stood quite still, looking hard at her new mistress.

"No one can answer that question better than the lady here," she said at last, slowly.

As for the poor lady, she gave a sort of cry, for as she came into the hall she saw the house which she had always dreamt of—and where she herself had been seen again and again. The end of the story, I believe, was that the lady got quite well in the fine Scotch air and quite gave up dreams and astral bodies.

To Emily Ritchie

Brighton
[1896]

Observe a new pen—calm and no blots! It produces a limited state of mind, and is I think exactly what I want. I filled my fountain pen at 5 a.m. and went back to sleep feeling that life was easier all round, and that stylographers pervade the universe.

. . . Our Brighton has been a triumph rather than a success. I don't think in all my life I ever saw anything more lovely and vast than yesterday morning. Proud, capering, beautiful waves dashing against the beach, a divine light in the horizon, and exquisite lights on shore and on the clouds overhead, and all the tribes, Christians and Jews alike, dancing before the Ark.

We wound up the day by a delightful play. Thrilling —Mr. and Mrs. Kendal—revenge—banter—gambling— white parasols.

. . . I have been doing some work, and I will take it to the post and drop this scrabble along with it. How are you? Is it finer? I do hope and trust it is. Here it really hardly matters as the sea is always dry, or perhaps I should say wet. Brighton is to me the most blessed spot.

To Emily Ritchie

Brighton
[1896]

I am now going back to Quills! One's self vibrates through a quill pen far more easily than through iron and wood; do try.

The sun is shining and everything looks very balmy. The thousands of excursionists look like nothing but barrelfuls of shrimps. I *hate* being of so little consequence as I feel when I see the crowds, but again I comfort myself by thinking that every atom is eternally divisible.

This afternoon I was told Sir Henry Cunningham was at the door, but couldn't leave a card because his coat *was buttoned!*

I went out much surprised and found Herbert Spencer as rosy as ever.

"Goodbye," he said immediately, "goodbye. Don't stop out, goodbye," and off he went.

To her Son

The End House
[1896].

Last night we all walked out on to the Common and heard the nightingale sing to the moon, then we sat on the loggia and wished you were there too.

Today Hester and I went to London to three dress-makers, and to see poor Dutton in his hospital. I can't think why people are thought frivolous for going to dressmakers; it is most serious and exhausting, I think, and yet one must have clothes and the tidier the better. It is much more trouble to look tidy when one is old, I find, than when one is young.

To her Husband

Hôtel St. Romain
Paris
March 20th [1897].

. . . I have two delightful things to tell you about, *Don Giovanni,* the most merry, romantic performance. Nobody, except Zerlina, had any voice to speak of, but they did it so gaily and conscientiously, and as for the Commendatore! his notes boomed out of his white boots. The theatre baking hot and we galloped home after the performance in two little carriages.

If only Nelson's statue and the Duke of York would sing to you like that, as you come and go to the India Office, what a good time you would have! The Duke of York might produce a splendid note up the column.

Then this afternoon I have been to George Duck-worth's box at the Français, to see the *Cid.* I couldn't have believed it possible, the whole Français crammed, all the schools, all the Lycées, all the head masters, and I and the two girls, and the 3,000 people, simply vibrating with excitement as to whether Miss Adeline Dudlay was going to get over the blood of her father and marry the noble young warrior; the court and the King and all the attendant knights were absorbed too in the love affair. And oh! dear me, how well they acted and how they spoke it. I didn't stop for *Les Plaideurs,* for I find it pays so much better to do less. But it is certainly a treat to hear such lovely French rolled out.

We mean to travel all day Sunday and to get to Cannes on Monday afternoon. But I think the coming back to see you will be nicer than all the going abroad.

To Mrs. Warre-Cornish

Bordighera
March [1897].

We all three took a real walk yesterday; we wandered through the old town and saw a peasant woman and told her we were tired and wanted to rest in a garden; she flung open the first gate crying, "Entrate, entrate," so I said, "Is it allowed?" And she answered, "Per Bacco! yes."

Wasn't it delightful to hear the Gods called upon in this Christian spirit? Bacchus took us into a divine arbour, flowers starting, butterflies flitting. Oh blessed Bacchus!

To her Son

Bordighera
March [1897].

Hester brought home crimson and white anemones from an olive wood. I can't think how the flowers grow as they do, for everything is so dusty and dried up, but the flowers blaze away quite contentedly. We had a great storm of wind yesterday, and the palm trees were

bowing and bobbing. There never was anything less
suitable to a high wind than a palm tree.

Yesterday we lunched in a green field with violets and
anemones, a ravine, an old castle in the distance, and
having lunched we went on to the castle and the fortified
village. My gracious, it was like Dante and Browning
and all the Cossas and Van
Eyks boiled down, the winding black zig-zag steps, the
arches, the long passages.
Then little holy families
having meals beyond the
shadows in lighted-up inner
rooms, and girls feeding
goats, and old crones spinning, it seemed as if all the
fairy tales had become alive.

There was a ruined palace
of the Doria's at the top of
the rock, and miles of sub-
terranean passages down below, and the people looked
at us, and never moved a
muscle, as if they were ghosts. All their windows gave
into these black, narrow defiles on arches. Two nice little
ragazzi showed us the way with their arms round one
another's necks.

. . . My favourite person here is a baby called Walther von Winter, a German baby, who generally posts
my letters for me and who stuffed your last card into the
box. I hear Walther von Winter roaring. He is very
particular as to which hat he wears. His nurse wears
bare arms and a sort of cap with long ribbons; she is a
German, not an Italian.

I don't know where the Italians are. Mrs. Fanshawe's villa is more Italian than anything else. The two nuns who look after her hospital are Italian, and the gardener and the footman. The dogs are Danes, Danish boar hounds, but they understand Italian, and jump upon you in any language. They are most alarmingly affectionate, and peculiarly horrible—but Rosa adores them.

To her Husband

Villa Guicciardini
Florence
April [1897].

Abbiamo arrivato—Imagine—no you can't imagine! We find ourselves in a palazzo 500 years old.[1] Hester and I in bedrooms with painted ceilings and a private sitting-room, a mixture of (I should imagine) the Palace of Delhi and Henbury, with green still gardens and birds out of windows, and Sir John coughing in the distance.

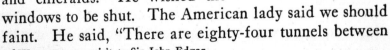

We had a wonderful journey here, first in and out of tunnels, divine seas and sights for an instant, then more tunnels. Hester must tell you about Bulbo and his carpet-bag. Then he slumbered beside his umbrella; the carpet-bag was in worsted work and the jewels embroided alternate rubies and emeralds. He wished the windows to be shut. The American lady said we should faint. He said, "There are eighty-four tunnels between

[1] We were on a visit to Sir John Edgar.

this and Pisa." I said, "Then you shall pull up the window forty times and I will pull it down the other forty." He gave me a look of fury. The American lady went off laughing. "It's no use trying jokes with such people as that," she said. Bulbo merely slept on scornfully.

. . . I don't know where to begin or to end or how to go on, everything is so interesting. Sir John has been taking us round the garden and showing us his sacred shrine lined with books, with a back door by which he escapes from bores.

I paid him a solemn little visit in his study last night. We invented a book, *The Seven Champions of the Victorian Age.* It would be a fine subject, wouldn't it? Nicholson, Gordon, Laurence, Outram, John Bright, Newman (this is Sir John's hero, also Parnell). People who didn't care about getting on for themselves.

To her Son

Florence
[1897].

To tell the truth these little horrors of Florentine tea parties seem a desecration on the lilac hills. I shall write a story about it some day. Friendly converse, remembrance and humanity are as lovely as the lilac hills, but why do they always seem to have to be mixed up with stuffy tea and bread and butter?

Hester is steadily mending and the rest of us are gradually recovering from our influenza. She is going to have some farina cooked by the chef who drives up in a donkey carriage every day to cook the meals. The dinner gets more and more invalidish as they all get more and more ill, entrées of gruel, of beef-tea, of fried pills. The man-servant, Eusebio, pours out different mixtures and we all go to bed at nine o'clock! Viva la bella Italia! it's very nice notwithstanding, not so very unlike Sedbergh.

Sir John has been too *enchanting*. He would be delightful in a cockle-shell. He tells stories of India like Kipling, only better. He is very unwell, and just as delightful as if he were well. He seems to me more like a generation of Englishmen than one man. Vivid, wise, delightful company he most certainly is.

To her Son

The End House
Pre-Jubilee Sunday [1897].

I am out of spirits and very sad, for my dear Mrs. Oliphant is too ill ever to get well again. She sent for me and kissed me and sent you and Hester her love. I think she is longing to go. They sent to borrow Alfred Tennyson's poems last night. There was one that she wanted. In it he says Death should have another name and that is "Onward." [1]

. . . It was Mrs. Oliphant who bestowed on me my first review when I was twenty-three. It was summer time and I opened *Blackwood,* and my father beamed with satisfaction.

It is so curious how all one's life remains—things don't go, we fade not they. It is all there.

To Rhoda Broughton

The End House
June 29 [1897].

I took your note to Denny Oliphant and her sister, it said so truly what all our hearts are feeling.

[1]   . . . Death's truer name
Is "Onward," no discordance in the roll
And march of that Eternal Harmony
Whereto the worlds beat time.
Ode to the Duke of Clarence.

I am going to get ready now to go to the funeral. I have lost a life-long friend,[1] and the world too, in that wise, tender and humourous woman whom all delighted to love and appreciate. She was to me one of those people who *make* life—so many un-make it. As I think of those who *make* life for us, I think of those I love, and may I think of your sister at this moment? who used to remind me of my own, in her understanding and sincerity and sweet reserve of her nature.

Mrs. Oliphant said to her girls, "Make things look *comfortable* after I am gone."

To Denny Oliphant

Wimbledon
[1897].

. . . I, who am near the end, can only tell you who have a busy life of work and love and solicitude before you, that death is *no* parting; and God's will is that we should be faithful and love, and yet love again and again, and I think the meaning is that He is in all true feeling, and that our dead love is not gone but lives again in the present.

I can't explain, even to myself, how it is that I hardly ever hug my children without a thought of my sister.

To her Son

The End House
October 2 [1897].

This morning the first proof of my Edition[2] has arrived. I haven't read it yet. I was shy—can you

[1] Mrs. Oliphant died June the 25th.
[2] A new edition of the works of Thackeray with biographical prefaces by my mother. Of these Introductions Swinburne wrote:—"To the exquisite genius, the tender devotion, the faultless taste and the unfailing tact of his daughter, we owe the most perfect memorial ever raised to the fame and to the character of any great record by any editor or commentator or writer of prefaces or preludes to his work."

understand that odd sort of hold-off feeling, which seizes one about the things one most cares about?

I can't tell you how I do feel more and more what a courageous tender-hearted father I had, and how proud I am of him.

When I have done six more introductions I shall go to Brighton and bask for a week, and when you first come back I mean to do no work at all until the end of January. I love doing it and it makes me very happy, but it certainly disagrees with your excitable Mama.

To A. C. Swinburne [1]

[1902].

DEAR OLD FRIEND,—I have just seen your kind words, which made me very happy and grateful to you. My daughter found the *Quarterly* [2] and came and read it to me!

As Tennyson once wrote to my father, "It is because you are the old friend that you are, and also because you are the great man that you are, that I feel all the fullness of your praise."

These were not quite the words, but it was the sense, and I who am grateful to think that I am the daughter of a great man, and the friend of great men, send you my love and my thanks for this bit of new life and pride and happiness for mine and me, and I am yours—decorated by you——

Affectionately,

ANNE RITCHIE.

[1] This letter is inserted here in order to complete the series of letters about the Biographical Edition. Swinburne's article on Dickens in which he mentions that Edition appeared in July 1902, and was the first signed article published in the *Quarterly Review*.
[2] See note on the preceding page.

To Mrs. Gerald Ritchie

Brighton
December [1897].

The last of the MSS is despatched and the notes go off to-day, and this great and, to me, very real event is a cause of most genuine thankfulness and gratitude. I love to think of my Father's unconscious protest against the coldness and flippancy and silliness of the present fashion, and I think it may add something good and simple, as he was himself, to the thoughts of those who are yet to read and to love him. It is a finer standard than this hateful low standard of today.

To Reginald J. Smith

The End House
April [1898].

. . . Hester, recovered—removed and thought unin-fectious—is allowed to hold the *Vanity Fair* in her own hands, and her exclamation of pleasure and delighted approbation is so cheering that I long to carry it on to you. . . . I had a charming letter from George Russell, and Richmond sent me the best compliment of all. He says Lord George Hamilton was very much interested *indeed,* and said he could remember Dizzy saying to him that he couldn't understand Dickens, but that my father's style was so magnificent that he would never cease to be read and to be admired.

I am longing to know *how* the Edition is selling.

To Bernard Holland

12, Kensington Court Gardens
April 9 [1898].

I have just had a line from Gussie to whom I sent your beautiful book.[1] I then saw Pinkie looking with such

[1] *The Letters of Mary Sibylla Holland,* first published in 1898.

longing eyes that I could not resist giving her another
copy, and I sent your letter with a third to India. I do
not generally treat my sisters-in-law so liberally, but
somehow I feel as if this dear message of your mother's
ought to be given—not bought by each. I am sure the
book will live on—don't mind what anybody says to you.
It is a gift for those who have hearts to feel with. Richmond told me the *Times* was churlish, but what would
you expect of a hurried review? It is little by little that
her noble influence will spread. How far it has reached
already! I think your introduction is such a true picture.

Do you know that you never came to dinner on Monday—Mr. Lushington, Edith Sichel, and your empty
place?

To her Son

The End House
July 31 [1898].

In the garden—by the fig tree.
The most heavenly sunshine and pretty shadows; there
the shadow of a bird flew by, now I hear your father's
steps, now he wheels by his bicycle. There are flies buzzing and a persistent French horn which has been going
on and on ever since I came out.

I have been reading Renan, who says how can people
dwell as they do on their own small troubles, when there
are such astounding things to interest them everywhere—
suns—moons—colours—velocities—calculations—discov-
eries—and it is really a very sensible suggestion. I had a
bad day yesterday and couldn't appreciate suggestions,
but to-day is delicious and I'm enjoying every minute
(jackdaw chatters over the Jesuits' wall).

I came back, as Hester will have told you, and I am to
go thro' this new treatment, which it is much better to

face than to go on waiting and waiting and not getting any better but rather the contrary.[1]

We laughed out loud over your pictures, and the "Pardons" and "ces bons Bretons" and "ces horribles English," and I was much impressed by the Kissells' brilliant tour-de-force getting you up at 4.30! Tell Mr. Kissell I am waiting to be better to write to him and give my kind compliments to Mrs. Kissell, and tell her how glad I am you are staying with them.[2]

To Her Son

August 18 [1898].

Mrs. Ritchie presents her compliments to Monsieur Denis. She also hugs him and gives him a kiss.

His father has piles of maps of Normandy and Brittany and is making out the very most delightfulest tour.

All the Madame de Sevigné country I do envy you. Would that I were Madame Kissell to mount a bicyclette and fly after you—Les Rochers where she lived—the avenues she planted—Rennes where she used to visit in her big coach. I can't help posting my book of Madame de Sevigné for you to read. I'm sure you will like the place all the better if you have read about her. I wrote it when you were a baby and proudly dedicated it to my Chevalier. Stupid Madame de Sevigné only cared for her daughter, who was odious. Madame de Grignan was just like her name Madame de Grognon, Madame de Grignotant. (There is some word for stinting, something like Gringnan but I can't quite remember it.) But dear jolly generous loving Madame de Sevigné, I love

---

[1] My mother's letters give no impression of the constant ill health from which she suffered; she never dwelt upon this, nor did she allow it to interfere with the ordinary course of her life.

[2] Her son was learning French with a French family in Brittany.

her, and I always imagine her something like Mrs. Freeman.

Our dinner was a very great success, and Henry James
not only ornamental but useful and really and truly kind.
Arthur and Adeline enjoyed themselves extremely and
appreciated his stories and descriptions. He is going to
take us to see a cinematograph at the Palace—a flying
train—and you see the country spinning before you, and
then you plunge into tunnels and come out again to more
scenery. I asked him if he had read Sarah Grand's
books; he said, "It may be Pride, it may be Prejudice,
but I have *not*," so I said, "Perhaps it may be Sense or
Sensibility," and Henry burst out laughing and said: "I
only need Persuasion!"

. . . We have had some delightful days in the garden,
and now I am thankful to say I am going to have my
final doctoring done, and I hope you will find a nice new
Mama on your return.

The English moon has been most glorious, quite as
lovely as your French moon, and The End House has
been flooded with silver. I shall certainly be very glad
to see The End House again by moonlight, or sunlight
or even paraffin! God bless you my darling beloved boy,
and "He will!" as the old apple-woman used to say to
my father.

To her Husband

Brighton
10 *January* [1899].

You will be glad to hear that Brighton is a most agreeable place and that we are enjoying it.

Two rather amusing things happened. One was that I
took Pinkie to call on Herbert Spencer. He was much
pleased that she should play to him, but said the worst
of Beethoven was he never knew when to leave off. The

second movement of the Sonata he stopped. "Thank you, I'm getting flushed, that will be quite enough. Thank you." He was rather nice, very absurd, and very discursive.

The poor remaining companion nearly wept on the stairs as she let us out. "Now happy Agnes Shinner is departed, life is scarcely bearable," she says. I have invited her to lunch on Tuesday by way of making life worth having.

The second, that I went to see Tisey Smith who sang to me. She says there are four notes, head notes, throat notes, chest and stomach notes, and Charles Kean, who taught Charles Kean Junior to act, shouted at him because his O in Romeo was so dull. So young Charles Kean said, "Why it's from my stomach," and his father roared, "It should come from your bowels, Sir."

The sky was like a divine parrot's breast just now with a deep deep flapping sort of sea. Herbert Fisher strolled by looking like a philosopher.

O how nice it is to be going to do just as I like all this evening!

. . . They have asked me to join the "William Black Memorial Fund," and I was very glad to do it, for I love some of his books.

Rudyard Kipling told us when he was in America he went salmon fishing, and in the middle of a vast stream a man in rags arose upon a great rock, also with a fishing rod, and the man said, "Are you an Englishman? I have been to England and stayed there, and there is only one man in England who can write a book and his name is—" Mr. Kipling said he began to wonder what was coming.

"*Black,*" says the man.

To Reginald F. Smith

116, Marine Parade
Brighton
21 *February* [1899].

It *was* kind of you to send me the Browning Letters;
how glad I am to have them.   I feel as if I ought also
to have a little casket to keep them in, with their warm
record of great love and true hearts.   It is not so much or
not *only* because Mr. and Mrs. Browning were poets
and world-known, as because they were beloved friends
that I prize it all.   I am trying as I write to remember a
line by Mrs. Browning, "Euripides the human" was it
not?
The Brownings are like noble simple people of the
past whose life was in their genius, ~~& their genius was to
love too.~~ I scratch this out for it is too like a phrase.
Sometimes I rather long to lock the casket up, but life *is*
so difficult, and a great feeling like this one is such gain
and happiness and interest that I am glad indeed to be
one of those to hold the key to it.   I am sure that Miss
Browning will feel as I do, and I can so well realise
Pen's loving pride in his parents' history—never was
there such a story, except my dear Tennysons' indeed,
and she too was a poet in her life and fervent feeling,
though she did not write it down.   Again thank you
—I needn't say that I have hardly read more than the
beginning.
How delightfully the very *first* letter leads it all off.

To her Husband

Brighton
[1899]

. . . The day began with cats and dogs and howling
wind and snarling seas.   Then in the late afternoon the

storm subsided, and great mountains floated about in the sky, and balmy winds blew gently, and Dorothy and I took a long walk all the way from Sussex Square back home. We were carried along by wild excitement. Herbert Spencer has invited Dorothy to succeed Miss Shinner as his companion, and to my amazement and pleasure Dorothy accepts. She is delighted. She is going up to play to him tomorrow, and to see if it is possible. Even if it lasts three weeks or three months, it is something to be companion to Herbert Spencer. All your mornings to yourself, and to play the piano to him of an afternoon, never longer than ten minutes, when he feels his pulse and desires you to leave off. He is extremely cross, but also extremely kind. It is certainly very amusing and unexpected.

Yesterday we drove to Lady Burne-Jones'. Her house is all done by Willy Benson, with one or two beautiful frescoes on the nursery wall by E. B. J. His studio is a lovely broadside of a window with a deep sill, and just outside, the old church and the Kiplings' ivy manor house. It is a very delicious home indeed.

Lady Burne-Jones is most touching, tender, and courageous. She says all her life she has made the greatest mistake of being too reserved. She said George Eliot once said to her, "Ah! say I love you, to those you love. The eternal silence is long enough to be silent in, and that awaits us all."

I have hardly recovered from my tea at the K——'s, a cup of friendly sand in the desert of the Sahara, or a conversation at the North Pole. They have, however, lent me an enchanting book, for which I bless them, *My Official Wife;* do get it.

To Mrs. Henry Hart

Holmrook
Tunbridge Wells
March 17th [1899].

Your dear kind letter shall go to Billy who will be back next Tuesday, I hope. We don't get home till just after Easter. It is so delightful for the children to have your never failing kindness and welcome to look to and your invitation seems almost a part of the feeling of holiday and coming home.

The spring here is most wonderfully irresistible. A sort of down-pour of buds, and then birds flapping and singing, and sweet copses flowering all round about in the country.

As for this ridiculous little toy-town, it makes one feel like a lady in an automatic machine winding up the narrow path and coming round the artificial rocks and putting up a parasol with a click. And now Farewell, with another Thank you.

To her Husband

Holmrook
March [1899].

Home-*cook* would be a better name for this lodging! I have begged the land-lady not to send us up such delicious meals in future. Howdoyoudo this morning? Did you have a less foggy fussicating day yesterday? We had the very most lovely drive imaginable thro' Eridge Woods, with all the beautiful mist of little buds everywhere, instead of the ugly east-wind mist which has been spoiling everything. We had a little carriage and a plucky hump-back boy to drive us, and a frisky pony who made nothing of the hills and took us into Arcady.

To-day we had an expedition to Southborough. The old Inn [1] has been pulled down, but the delicious spring has not been pulled down, the millions of buds, the floods of light and the birds and the songs.

The sun was setting, and every tree and branch seemed whistling up. In the middle of it all, coming out of a little coppice, we met two smut-black chimney sweeps. I believe they were probably gods in disguise. I'm sure *we* were for five minutes.

To Mrs. Gerald Ritchie (in India)

36, Grosvenor Road
[*November* 1899].

. . . I awoke before six in the dark yesterday and I thought I was dreaming still: I heard cheers and cheers and music and more cheers. It was the regiments going off to the war,[2] and I suppose they were crossing Vaux-hall Bridge. It was all so sleepy and so dark and so puzzling, that it was not till I read the evening paper that I realized what had happened. The crowds were up at five o'clock to see them off. It all seemed like something one had read of, rather than a real, true, actual thing. . . .

To Emily Ritchie

36, Grosvenor Road
[*Dec.* 1899].

What a glorious burst of sunshine this is, and I'm sure it is wanted. I never saw a more impressive heart-aching sight than all the people's faces yesterday, hundreds and hundreds of people with their newspapers. Hester dragged me off, saying, "Don't read!" But after I had left her, a little newspaper boy jumped into the omnibus.

[1] Where Thackeray stayed and wrote part of *Esmond.*
[2] South Africa.

I said to the man next me, "There's nothing here," and
he with a grubby finger, without a word, pointed to the
fatal added paragraph at the end.[1] As I write, I look
up and see the people still passing, reading newspapers.
The only consolation to me is that it is not England
crushing poor innocent farmers, but fighting a great and
long planned revolt. I hope the Boers will build a wall
and keep their beastly gold mines and leave us at peace
in our Cape.

I have so often thought how thankful I was not to have
been born in the time of Nelson and Wellington, and now
I see England is full of heroes and wonders and splendour, and it has all caught one up, alas!

[1] English defeat at Colenso.

To Mrs. Gerald Ritchie (in India)

Florence
[1900].

WE mean to stay another week in Florence, and then go back in *another* week, taking it easy by Milan and Lucerne. The birds are singing in the garden as I write, and Billy says the Oxford birds are all tuned up—do birds sing in India?

. . . Yesterday we went to see Sir John Edgar and found him just as usual, groaning but looking younger, and the kind ladies, and the sunset in the sky, and lo! in walks a neighbour across the garden with the last evening news—another victory for Lord Roberts along the Modder, 3,000 offering to surrender. Can it be Joubert? It is all rather mysterious, but O what a blessing to see Peace coming over the mountains.

Can't you imagine yesterday? and the two old friends, Sir John and his neighbour, exchanging telegrams and beaming, and us ladies all twittering and beaming too?

It has been the most dramatic good news for me and Hester all the way along. The first we heard was on the steps of the Cathedral at Genoa, where the newsman was selling *Naziones,* and we could hardly understand how good it all was, and what "Resa di Kronje" amounted to. My child, every word you say is what I feel about the war and about politics and about fighting. Last night I lay thinking about our noble Dandies and "Cooks' sons," and of that wise old man Lord Roberts forgetting his own overwhelming grief, to plan victory and moderation and success for his country. And then I thought of over-riding, conquering Kitchener working with him so loy-ally, and the people waiting so courageously and patient-ly, and Zebul coming at last. I do thank God that life is not only bad and hard, but strong and kind and endur-ing.

To Rhoda Broughton

36, Grosvenor Road
[1900].

Half a loaf is better than no bread, and your kind letter extracts a penny roll from me. If each of your many ad-mirers send a guinea, you will have more than enough.

We are all preparing to return home on Monday week and then I shall come soon. Hester and I got to Florence and got back again, with such a luggage of rivers, deli-cious hills and galleries and marble steps. How lovely things *are,* and curiously enough it seems to me that the five minutes of later life and the passing glances, are ,worth all the nice bountiful twelve hours at a time of one's youth.

I'm so glad I was such a young idiot, and left *some-thing* for now—I brought back Leonardo da Vinci's "Cena" from Milan among other things, which I declare I never saw before, though I have *looked* at it at intervals all my life long.

Hester radiated, and I often thought of your sight of the Flower City, but we never got to the Certosa.

I am now preparing to go off to the Gosse-Crewe-Burghclere luncheon. I suppose a *Wet*suntide is good for the country, but as soon as the trees have drunk enough I do hope it will leave off raining.

To Emily Ritchie

Brighton
[*June* 1900].

This is Saturday, Golden day, anything exquisite you can think of. I imagine that this will arrive about the same time as my family, and how I wish I could also come in thro' the letter-box, and listen to the heavenly conversation of your good company.[1]

. . . I have been going to sleep over George Sand and trying to think of *literature* as music, or rather to hear the music of literature. I really and actually come upon bits of Beethoven in George Sand. George Eliot is to me only Mendelssohn (*Romola* is Kalkbrenner's exercises). My father—yes, and Dickens too—seem to me at times to belong to Mozart. My father when he is moved, and Dickens when he is irresistible. Micawber and the Kenwigs are Mozart, and that scene out of somewhere—*The Old Curiosity Shop?*—where Kit takes his Mother to the play. When you write next tell me how it strikes you, and how the musical party goes off.

To Mrs. Gerald Ritchie (*in India*)

The End House
[*August* 1900].

Mrs. Ritchie has come into the garden to cut a cabbage leaf, to make an apple pie, and to write to her Miggs. She is extremely hot, but only hot. Yesterday was suffocating too, and if you touched anything it began to smoke!

To-day is poor Richmond's Budget,[2] and he won't be home till midnight. Yesterday he was back at eight-thirty; we dined at nine and we sat comfortably cooling

[1] A musical party.
[2] Indian Budget Debate in the House of Commons.

down in the garden till past eleven, with such *stars*—
The Wain and some other great shining wonders.

On Monday I am going for my expedition on Mrs.
Watney's yacht, the *Palatine*. I have a new grey serge,
and boots with gutta-percha soles by command! It is
like a page out of Stevenson. At 7.25 on Monday, two
sailors are to meet me with *Palatine* on their shirts and
caps, by the steps leading to the pier and to convey me
on board, whither oh whither? And if I don't write
next Friday don't be surprised.

Richmond came back rather cheerful last night. He
says the Budget was very interesting, and I am waiting
for the newspapers to know why. I hate to read the
papers; it is like the Book of Revelation, seal after seal
broken and misery and pestilence, but what courage and
noble endurance. Now I will post this and return to
Mrs. Hemans, if I could but get her done before I go!

To Mrs. Gerald Ritchie (in India)

The End House
August 9th [1900].

This isn't in the least bit where I am! My present address (which mind you don't write to) is S.S. *Palatine,*
Dartmouth, Devon—with the *Britannia* and all the three
hundred little midshipmen at one side, and cliffs, white
gulls, pouring rain at the other. I have come up to a
dear little deck cabin; it is 10.30 on the 9th of August,
and there is just time to catch the mail and answer your
welcome letter.

My most adventurous adventure has ended in doing
me more good than I can tell you. I feel a perfectly
different person since I came, and except one day, we
have really escaped the storm miraculously—the fearful
storm—by being safe in port. The *Palatine* is 500 tons

and very, very steady, and oh! so neat and clean; *Pinafore*
is nothing to it. There are twenty-six crew and servants,
four visitors and the Dr., and Mrs. Watney. The visitors
are an authoress, an admiral, a schoolmaster and a Squire,
my old acquaintance, Mr. Milnes-Gaskell. His son took
him to the stores and rigged him up with yellow india-
rubber shoes. This is the authoress [a drawing], also
india-rubber shoes and a grey costume. They are all
most extremely kind, and I shall stay on until the 14th,
when I rejoin my deserted family. I have been made
very happy by the most delightful trinity of a letter from
Richmond, Hester and Billy, all deeply sympathetic over
the terrible storm. But in Portland Harbour, with the
great ships coming in (a great line of twenty-five battle-
ships) and all the crowds of boats and launches, it was
the most wonderful and amusing and elating sight, and
I never realised what the Navy was before, except once
with Billy at the moving pictures at the Polytechnic.

To Emily Ritchie

Mrs. Watney's Yacht
August 9th [1900].

Since I wrote, we have been safely anchored and seeing
the most beautiful sights in the world.

It was like Turner yesterday in the sunset, when one,
two, three, six, eight great ships came with state, sailing
into the harbour. Out of the mist, some sudden gleam
lit up all the labyrinths of spars, and the sailors up aloft,
and then it all became mist again, with huge forms still
advancing. When it was dark there were all the lights
over everything.

Our admiral is a delightful companion, and so is our
Milnes-Gaskell; they started in a gig for the shore and
a walk to Weymouth. Mr. Milnes-Gaskell talks always

with racy fun and is an enchanting gossip. The gig is
going off, and I shall send this by the nice Matthew,
Mark, Luke and John sailors, who put on their tarpau-
lins to row ashore. The boat is here, à demain!

To Mrs. Gerald Ritchie (in India)

[*Jan.* 1901].

. . . We have been reading a page of history.[1] I went
to see Laura yesterday, and all the way from Victoria to
St. James' was lined with people waiting. The blinds in
Buckingham Palace were down, as in every club and
office. All the people were in black, interested and
gravely excited. I said to the cabman, "What is it?"
He said, "The King, ma'am, it's the King coming up."

When Richmond came home, he told us Lord George
[Hamilton] went with the others to St. James' to swear
allegiance. There were crowds of people there. (Can
you imagine Mr. Lecky on one knee kissing the Royal
hand?) The King was very out-coming, very much
moved and overcome, and they all felt for him very
sincerely.

When I came back, the crowds were flowing out of
St. Paul's and waiting in front of the Bank and the
Mansion House.

To Beatrix Paul

[*March* 1901].

BELOVED GOD-DAUGHTER,—How I *do* like it![2] Aunt
A., Beatrice., Christening! Almond Birthday Cakes!
Apple-tart, Barley sugar, Cream ices!

It seems to me everything nice is expressed by A.B.C.,
to say nothing of its making my favourite places such as

[1] The death of Queen Victoria.
[2] An A.B.C. sampler.

Aldeburgh, Brighton, Cromer, quite easy to reach. It is
a delightful present, and I shall always be using it, all
the more that Sir William Broadbent strongly recom-
mends Brighton! . . .

I have been reading *Much Ado about Nothing,* and
when I read to where Beatrice "like a lapwing runs," I
sent you all my love, but I did not imagine you at work,
but flying thro' a garden.

Your loving
Aunt A.

To Emily Ritchie

Brighton
[*September* 1901].

. . . As I drove home I met Herbert Spencer in his
carriage with his two recalcitrant attendants. I got out
of mine to speak to him. He looked about thirty-six,
and is coming to call to-morrow.

Then I went to Tisey[1] who will be ninety on the 15th.
of November. "The Fifth act, my dear," she says, "but
not the last scene. Oh! no."

She has lent me (with a good deal of reluctance) Ain-
ger's *Life of Charles Lamb.* She said to him, "I hope
you had plenty of mint sauce with your Lamb."

She suggested an article for me to write, *Frederica
Bremer.* I think I shall go to Sweden and get it up some
day; Bremer *v.* Ibsen might be instructive.

I am not enjoying myself as much as if you and Edith
were here. It is being like a newspaper with little paragraphs and then a good deal of nothing particular, but
I am thankful to have come, and I feel already a great
deal better.

[1] Miss Horace-Smith.

To Reginald J. Smith

109, St. George's Square
25th July [1902].

What a *Jack* Thomas Carlyle was, with his attacks upon giants. Do you remember his calling my father a Cornish giant? as if it were a liberty of tall men to be taller than short men!

. . . At this moment I am furious with him, cross-grained, ungrateful, self-absorbed old nut-cracker. He who could have such beautiful thoughts should have lamented not his fellow man but his own egotistical puerilities.

To her Daughter

Sedbergh
[1903].

The wind is up again to-day, but yesterday was a day of days; I basked, he golfed, they golfed.

I have invited Miss Dormer to dine and go with us to Donald Tovey's Concert. She plays delightfully, and is really a dear creature. I can't get over old Mrs. Weisse's extraordinarily fine performance the day before yesterday. It was really very pathetic, the old musician pulling herself together and playing like a young disembodied spirit. She used to teach Mrs. Sidgwick and Lady Blanche Balfour.

Mr. Crawford has sent us two brace of grouse, and writes a long affectionate letter. Did I tell you I wrote an answer to him, and said at the end, "Grüssen," German for grouse!

Yesterday, when they were all out, I arranged the tea, but I forgot to fill up the fire in the kitchen and it went out. Comes Smith with her head on one side. "I think, Mem, I can light a fire! I do believe that it is a thing I understand. I have brought up a chicken from the egg, fed it, looked aafter it, killed it, plucked it, trussed it and roasted it here on this very kitchen fire, and served it for a gentleman and lady in the dining-room before one o'clock all by meselff! So I think ye can trust me to laight the fire for tea."

To Edmund Gosse

Feb. 29th [1904].

Thank you for your kind letter and for your sympathy and warm expression of feeling for my dear brother.[1] For brother he has been for years and years of constant goodness and faithful affection. I, who am used to love people who *do* things, may be forgiven if I think even more of what they *were,* than of what they accomplished. Only it is a sort of comfort to hear him praised, and all these truly appreciating words of friendship will make his children feel less parted from him. Again, thank you.

To Emily Ritchie

[The New Forest]
9th June [1905].

It should be ashamed of itself for pouring so, but we are getting acclimatized, and we are quite reckless as to fires.

Yesterday we had an expedition in Thena Clough's victoria and spirited horse across the common, and all the way we were meeting carts, vans, barrows, coal-drays loaded with happy people on their way to Auberon Herbert's tea—"Oncommon good tea tu," said our coachman. Anyone can go. They were taking children and grandmothers and all going themselves; it really was great fun.

[1] Leslie Stephen died February 22nd.

Then we passed a dream of an old house, Moyles Court, standing among great trees, with a low wall over which we could see the beauty of the ancient garden. Then we reached Margie Poore's Vicarage, by a beautiful old church tower—the Vicarage modern, but in a *bower* of roses—I never saw anything like it, the paths pink with the fallen leaves and the fresh buds coming out thro' the rain. She told me that Dame Alice Lisle, who had her head off at seventy-two for taking in two rebels who appealed to her, came from that exquisite old Manor we passed. She went to sleep in Court, while Jeffries was condemning and rating her. She is buried in the little churchyard with her daughter.

As it is my birthday I am sending you a copy of Dr. Johnson's prayer which I love. It is a prayer too old for you, but which speaks from that beloved man straight to one's heart, to mine most certainly.

"O Lord, my Maker and Protector, who hast graciously sent me into this world to work out my salvation, enable me to drive from me all such unquiet and perplexing thoughts as may mislead or hinder me in the practise of those duties which Thou hast required. . . . And while it shall please Thee to continue me in this world, where much is to be done, and little to be known, teach me, by Thy Holy Spirit, to withdraw my mind from unprofitable and dangerous inquiries, from difficulties vainly curious, and doubts impossible to be solved. Let me rejoice in the light which Thou hast imparted, let me serve Thee with active zeal and humble confidence, and wait with patient expectation for the time in which the soul which Thou receivest shall be satisfied with knowledge. Amen.

Notes of Happy Things [1]

How much I might have written of beautiful and happy things all this time—and vexing things too! only I intend to keep this book full of sunny cheerful happenings.

Last night I had an odd dream that a message, some joyful good message came to me, and I awoke with a sort of happy shock. Amen,—my message is nearly over now, but I mean to enjoy old age as much as I can, and I feel that the happiness of the old makes peace for others, and, as Huxley said to his wife, "It should be the cheerful acceptance of the inevitable."

I still love my own life and the lives of others very much indeed.

Tea at Mary Cholmondeley's. She had asked us, and we went into a most intelligent, cool, handsome drawing-room, off the Kensington High Road, with sofas and recesses and pictures, like a country room. Victoria Cholmondeley is a most charming, outcoming creature, Diana poured out tea; Mary received the company. Elegant ladies came floating in with feathers, hats and a pretty stateliness of manner. There were plenty of flowers and a most delicious tea. Mr. Julian Corbett and I discussed the difficulty of disposing of tea-cups without a table.

First lady, earnestly: "Do come to tea with me one day."

Second lady, passionately: "Yes, yes, I will indeed."

[1] The following extracts are taken from a little MS. book of my mother's named by her, *Notes of Happy Things.* These notes are undated; they can however only refer to the years between 1902-1905.

Pinkie and I, departing, found a passing omnibus and whirled off to the Watts', where I had long tried to go.

Holland House was over-flowing with people and flower-shows, streams of carriages were rolling by. Little Holland House was, as it always is, calm and delightful with pictures and flowers. Watts was in his studio among his beautful dreams. He looked more like Titian than ever. He gets up at four every morning and starts work, and he paints all the noble fancies which come into his mind. "Better to wear out than rust out," he said. I told him how I admired his picture of Joachim, and he said: "I tried to put some music into it." Then he told me a story of a sort of poem he had suggested to Donald Tovey, who sat down and began to play the poem. "That is Beethoven," said Donald, "but is it not exactly what you told me to play?"

The most charming thing was his delight over the work of a boy of sixteen—Brian Hatton, I think the name was. "I have shown it to Riviere; he is perfectly astounded," says Watts. "Look at the instinct for beauty, look at the sheep lying in the grass, look at this child sitting in the twilight; it is like Sargent."

We met Mary Watts coming from the Flower Show, and called at the Holman Hunts'. Then we stopped more omnibuses, and after Pinkie left me, a nun got into mine, a nice jolly woman, who told me she was from Hammersmith. Then a poor woman with the dropsy came in. I paid her fare and the sympathetic old nun with her many crucifixes escorted me across the road, seeing that I was frightened by the many wheels of fortune or misfortune.

A crowd of ladies in lace and diamonds, of gentlemen mostly in uniform with stars,[1] Richmond with his orders and his gold lace, Hester with a little veil over her head, I, agitated and befrizzed, glimpses of a lighted up house, a crowd, cheers, a royal carriage. We waited and waited, and at last in weary despair walked away up the quiet back streets to that one where we had made a league with the coachman. We followed a diplomat, covered with orders. "That is the great Sir Thomas Sanderson, of the Foreign Office," said Richmond.

Next day we met the same crowd, but it had changed its clothes. It stood under the lovely trees at Osterley. The grass was like a psalm; it was so green, and so fine; so was the weather, so were the ladies, but the train was too tiring. "Never more will I go by train," quoth the raven.

Sunday morning; lovely, but exhausting. Hester putting out the flowers; the doors and windows all open, cool and reposeful. Richmond calmly occupied, Billy invisible.

All the way to Rottingdean I was staring in wonder at the poppies. They blazed along the chalk downs and in places turned to violet, and then came massed dandelions and white celery, dazzling too, and then gorgeous poppies again. The beautiful shields of colour caught the light. I then found Lady Burne-Jones reading an old painted missal in her garden, where sweetness upon sweetness seemed floating. The Church bell was ringing across the green, the birds were flying out to sea. It was Sabbath weather, and is delicious to think about, and write down.

[1] A party at Londonderry House.

As I left the Hotel, the old deaf gentleman came up.
"What's the good of being Pope," says he, "if he fights
so hard for life?"

"He may not be going to be Pope in the next world,"
says I.

Hester and I drove by appointment to fetch Mr. Nowlan (the picture restorer), whom we had promised to
take to Leighton House. I was touched to see how smart
he had made himself with a beautiful shiny hat and neat
gloves and shirt. It seemed like Samuel Titmarsh over
again. As we drove down the shabby street, our dear
little man set to work to amuse us. He told us wild Irish
stories, made gentle little jokes and recounted ancient
histories, and when we reached Leighton House he
jumped down and handed us out.

Mrs. Barrington in a hat and feathers met us at the
top of the stairs, and took us straight to the drawings
which Nowlan had come to see and report upon. There
they were, those lovely designs and sketches, each delightful and suggestive, and half of them badly scarred
and blotted with those spreading yellow spots of mold.

Nowlan ceased to be Titmarsh when he was brought
face to face with the drawings. He became the man of
the hour. He was dreadfully busy, he said. He could
not undertake a great deal; two pictures he eventually
carried off, one desperately mottled girl's head, and the
Florentine senator with the distracting marks across his
nose. . . .

One of the pictures there which always strikes me very
much, is a terrific but admirably drawn head of Mrs.
Sartoris. I remember her coming into a room once, when
I was a girl, looking like this very picture. She had
"great blobs" as ornaments (so my father called them);

she looked very noble and stately and alarming. Leighton laughed and beamed in admiration. "How beautiful," he said, and hurried to meet her.

It is horrid, being old and remembering all these vanished visions as Ruskin says. Some I like to dwell upon, others I try to forget. . . . My last visit to Leighton was one Sunday, with his beautiful picture on the easel, of the Fawn teaching the boy to aim his arrow, and Leighton gay, courteous, laughing and telling me of his wonderful new doctor, who had done so much for him. I am glad he never failed, glad his charming looks never left us (for people's looks are for *others,* like their kind welcomes and friendly greetings). I don't think I knew Leighton, but we were always friends, and I go on caring for him in that strange medley of death in life, in which elderly people are all living.

It made me really happy to be able to do something for the drawings, and to bring our little fairy man, Nowlan, to save them from the moth and dust that corrupt. . . .

To Mary Millais

109, St. George's Square
November 2 [1905].

Every day when I pass by, I look up at the veiled statue of your father.[1] It *stands* well, and that is all that I can see. I shall take a wreath as soon as it is uncovered, from an old and lovingly admiring friend. I shall take it under my cloak. He would think it absurd, but all the same I think it will be, for me, a gratifying and right thing to do, and there are so many guardians about, that it will not be allowed to lie and spoil.

Thank you for writing to me, and do come and see me when you get back.

[1] The statue of Sir John Millais in front of the Tate Gallery.

To Mary Millais

109, St. George's Square
Nov. 28 [1905].

Hester and I took our wreaths and placed them at the foot of your dear father's statue. Sir Charles wrote a nice letter, and said, "Thank you for the wreaths, they add a human touch to the monument to the great man we have so recently lost, to whose noble work we all owe so much." I think those were the words. . . . I have stupidly mislaid Sir Charles' note, but I wanted to tell you I had done what I said.

This is the day my sister died, and it always seems to me a Saint's day.

To Gerald Ritchie

[*May* 1906].

. . . Your letter made me wipe my eye. It is so nice to be happy, and we all are at our Bill's happiness.[1] How I did like your description of him—my dear, dear boy, and now you have added to the happy *cairn* of hoping and kind blessing.

To Mrs. Gerald Ritchie

Gracedieu Manor
Whitwick
August 7 [1906].

I must tell you how the house is overflowing with family and kindness.[2] There are chauffeurs without number and three or four motors, and the villagers come up for suppers and cricket matches. The "Foresters" on horseback with a band appeared this morning, fol-

[1] Her son William Thackeray Denis's engagement to Margaret, second daughter of the Rt. Hon. Charles Booth, D.C.L., D.Sc., F.R.S.
[2] We were staying at Gracedieu, the Charles Booths' country house, for the marriage of my brother, which took place on August 8th.

lowed by crowds who disperse across the cricket field and
climb the slopes.

The household of Sir Thomas More is the only thing
at all like it, and O! the kindness of it, and the gentleness
and courtesy. They are the dearest people, and I wish
you were here—how you would enjoy it, and how Peggy
would enjoy it. She must have some wedding-cake.

I am taking it easy upstairs, and I hear the voices outside, and the cricket and the clappings through the window. I write this now, for the wedding is to be at 10.30
to-morrow morning and we go home in the evening. I
shall keep back this letter until after the wedding of Mr.
and Mrs. Denis Ritchie, and hope it will catch you before your start for France.

To Mrs. Gerald Ritchie

[1906].

. . . Solomon (the cat) has been purring messages,
tell Peggy. He purposes to write, but he says it is supurr-
fluous to say how much he misses her and that he is purr-
fectly lost without her to stroke his back. He has tried
my lap but he doesn't much like it; he finds it too purr-
pendicular and he sends his love purr me.

To Reginald J. Smith

109, St. George's Square
18th October [1906].

. . . I forgot to say about the picture [1] that it doesn't
convey very much to me. I remember Charlotte Brontë
wore a dress of a little mossy *light green* pattern; she had
no curls or loops such as ladies wore then—she did not

---

[1] This portrait of Charlotte Brontë had been purchased by the National Portrait Gallery; doubts, however, were thrown upon its authenticity. My mother
was appealed to, as one of the few people who could still remember Charlotte
Brontë.

look pleasant as she does in your picture, and I remember how she frowned at me whenever I looked at her, but perhaps it was specially at me—at least so I imagined. There was a general impression of *chin* about her face which doesn't show in this picture.

Light green as the colour of her dress I can swear to, and that interests me very much. I only saw her once, perhaps twice. I think the party and the dinner-party were the two occasions.

To Mrs. W. W. Vaughan [1]

109, St. George's Square
[1907].

Hester tells me how kind you and Will have been and are being to her. I like to think of her in my old haunts. I was telling her how I used to write *Old Kensington* at Settle when I was a little older than she is now. How I wish you and Will had been born and had been living at Giggleswick in those days! I blush to say I have even forgotten my own books, but I had a Squire Anley who was Mr. Birkbeck, whose joy it was to be mistaken for Tennyson. He used to wear a big hat and clothes made by a Swiss tailor-guide and he always walked like Robinson Crusoe with mysterious strides.

To Emily Ritchie

[1907].

I have been reading William James on Transcendentalism. Things *in* it I delight in, and I agree that one might get through life very well in a sort of balloon of Supereverythingness. His absolute want of the spirit of *awe* and holiness I dislike.

I go back to my father's religion. If I am to be

[1] Daughter of J. A. Symonds, and wife of the present headmaster of Rugby.

annihilated, I prefer, while I live, to love reverently.
I don't want to live in a trance if I can help it; and, as
Leslie used to say, annoyances make us wholesomely
alive, so let us make the most of them. I haven't nearly
done the book so it is too soon to write about it. . . .

To her Husband

R.M.S. *Tasso*.[1]

Calm isn't the word, it is smoother, softer, serener
than anyone could imagine. Who wouldn't be at sea!
The ship is full of lean elderly men who are all going
to fish salmon, and who all look exactly alike. There are
two little Miss Bolithos who talked to us in the train,
one was taken ill and wept and then recovered. They
know Florence and Constance Thackeray and are going
to stay near Edith Cole. They asked me if I was Miss
Thackeray? and I said, "No, I was Mrs. Ritchie;" and
then as the ship had started, I told them I believed I
would be Lady Ritchie to-morrow morning!

Hester and I are longing to see the Honours List with
your biography, and to know who are the other K.C.B.'s.

While we were at dinner the Channel Fleet crowded
with sailors passed by the port holes. We sent you picture post-cards from Hull, anything less like Hull than
the cards you can't imagine. I never saw such a dismal
city. We walked and walked between shabby little
houses and asked our way to the Tender, and presently
like the Pilgrim's progress up came a little man running
who said, "Are you Mrs. Ritchie? I wrote to you yesterday."

Lady Ritchie is getting rather twaddlesome! but we
are most happy and comfortable and wish you were on
board going to catch salmon.

[1] My mother and I were on our way to Norway to stay with Miss Edith Cole.

To her Husband

Lilledal, Sundalsören
Norway
4th July, 1907.

I send my love to you from this wonderful new world; it is like being *eternal* for one instant, as you come into the heart of the great mountains and look and look. It is so solemn one can hardly admire, and one finds oneself building an altar in spirit—and then by degrees kind every day comes in.

Would that you were preparing to go out fishing with Hester. You must bring her some year. Your holiday would be twice as long, for one goes to bed quite fresh at midnight, and gets up again quite brisk; and the per-petual daylight instead of bothering as I expected, be-comes a sort of alabaster lamp-light—most healing and soothing. Hester is writing hard as well one may, when it takes a week for a letter to reach. Please write back here the very moment you get this, for we leave on the 18th., which is just a fortnight off, and I think we shall give up Trondjem and return to Bergen, the birthplace of Ibsen and of *Lady Ritchie!*

Yesterday we floated in the Viking life-boat. Next week Annie Cole[1] arrives, and, I hope, Miss Vivian. We took a little private steamer and came straight here, instead of zigzagging up the fjörd in the public boat all day in the pouring rain. But though it rains it doesn't get into one's throat, and we arrived quite dry at the landing, the sören with little dots. Our journey after leaving the steamer was the most adventurous of all. It was so rough the boat couldn't land. Then a cart came out for us, and finally we walked up a fragrant hillside and arrived at a fragrant wooden châlet, with wood fires

[1] Now Mrs. Neville Chamberlain.

in deep stone chimneys, and comfortable chairs, and a
dining room decorated with ornamental fish and old
Norwegian cups, and the most exquisite dinner, and dear
Edith Cole—and two spacious pine bedrooms opening
on to a gallery, and this noble new world all round about.
It is like Switzerland, but softer and bigger and not over-
run. The snow lies on the hills, there are seven waterfalls tumbling down the rocks. The flowers and leaves
and mosses are quite indescribable; Edith Cole has books
of botany and knows them all. She has an old attendant
fisherman who goes about with her. She calls him Ole,
and I asked if this was his family name. It is his Christian name, Ole, and his son is called Oleson, and so they
go on; Billy would be Richmondson and his son would
be Billyson, and so on for ever and ever.

Good-bye, good-bye.

To her Husband

Bergen
1907.

. . . *Haakon II,* the boat in which we came here, had
a programme of the day at Bergen for the travellers,
winding up with "at 11 o'clock the ship will sail and
then for a jolly roll on the North Sea, home to old England."

We began with a "jolly roll" from Christiansund and
at dinner we were put next the Captain, and found out
that we had rashly slept going North, between Bergen
and Christiansund, just when we should have been
awake, while passing a certain defile; so Hester and I
got up at 11.30 and hearing four bells came on deck. It
was dim luminous twilight, the great rocks with pointed
spires rose sheer up on either side, the end of the pass
opened into floating opal Monte Rosas, and suddenly

at a break in the great wall, a round red moon hung over
a gigantic pass. We had not seen it all the time at Lilledal, for the moon doesn't go so far North. But I can't
in the least tell you how magnificent it all was; we longed
for you to see it, and wondered whether to rush into the
saloon and call all the people out from their bridge, but
while we were hesitating, the supreme moment was past.

I shall be enchanted now to get home again and to
face the North Sea and its "jolly roll." We had a most
tremendous experience in the fjörd with Edith Cole, who
sat calm and like a reassuring rock with the elements
thundering around us, and what I thought was a wave of
the sea in my perturbation, was a flock of white gulls
swooping over us. Hester and I sat calm, but it was
very impressive and when we landed I could hardly stand
with excitement. As usual the whole population came
down to see us land, and saw us off again the next morning. I can't think how they have time. The little boys
here are much to the fore, dear merry natty little boys,
who help to pull in the steamers and to carry the bags
and who scull about in huge boats.

The dinner is over: first we had salt mince something,
then soup, then boiled fish, then dishes looking like the
map of Europe in different colours. They cook very well
indeed and we get the most delicious tea. We look out
on a really fine statue of Ole Bull standing playing in a
fountain with a nixie coming up to listen. Ole is pro-
nounced Ulla. I have thought of a little bit of a story.

To her Husband

[1907].

We landed last night, after a delicious progress up
the Fjörd with a huge approving red moon looking at
us over the tops of the rocky battlements. We made

friends with a little old German music master, who had
hurt his foot, and we gave him a lift in the carriage which
we had telephoned for. Our little German professor
kissed both our hands at parting and said that Ritchie
was a "berühmter" name. We didn't go into it. (Did I
tell you of the American young lady who burst into tears
when I told her my father's name?)

It was 12 o'clock at night when we got here and the
sky was a lovely faint rose colour and the dawn was coming in yellow from that horrible place we had fled from,
where we found the King of Siam and 400 tourists, and
cross, exhausted, Norwegian maids and exasperated porters, and nothing to eat. We got away in a little carriage
from this nightmare of a place, and my heart sank into
my boots as we came down agonising precipices and
waterfalls to the flatness again, and from the flatness to
the fjörd steamer here. Our coachman down the preci-
pice yesterday could only say, "All ri," and when I said,
"Stop! let us get out," he said, "All ri," and cracked his
whip of doom. I can't draw it [picture]. The rocks
are like great Indian juggernauts, the waterfalls are really
stupendous. Then came the evening, and I trust our
adventures are now over.

Husum, and another astounding drive up cataracts,
moraines, mighty stony places. Dante isn't in it, or the
Pyramids or any of the wonderful wonders. The Harts
met us along the road among rocks and rushing rivers.
They were kindness itself, and much excited about you
and delighted with your letter.

They have been suggesting an expedition, but we have
firmly said, "No!" A day's drive there, then three hours'
walk, then the Laps with hundreds of reindeer. The
Norwegians are furious with the Laps because they are
let off conscription. They only rush off to the ice-fields

when they are called to enlist. Mrs. Hart says they are short little creatures, with a strut.

To Lady Robert Cecil

109, St. George's Square
October 1 [1908].

I was so much touched and interested to get your kind note—I puzzled and puzzled in my mind over Galsworthy and his problems. You put them so vividly and incisively that I couldn't forget them. I once saw his *Silver-Box,* which haunted me for days, it was all so exactly like some of the poor people I had met, but *not* exactly like the rich or the middling people. We are not good for much but we are good for something, and we *have* got souls, though Mr. Galsworthy hardly recognises this fact.

Forgive me for sending you this note from a woman who has been an old angel, without wings, alas! and only a bad leg to get about with for years, and who is now going off dignified and independent to the infirmary where she is sure to make friends and find something friendly to do and to say, and to enjoy. I first knew her looking after eight grandchildren—when one little grandchild died she nearly broke her heart.

Even Wordsworth doesn't stir my hope, as does such a generous unconscious life as this one, full of trial but brimful of tender affection. She has never begged or made phrases.

We are all artists sometimes, and we respond to the call of sincere and true things, and one has not to mind feeling a little desperate at others. You have life before you—I should like to feel a little clearer before I die, but I am sure you will write many many more true things that vibrate and reach your readers.

To Mrs. G. F. Watts

19th July [1908?].

I thought I had many more letters, but I can only find these three. I can never trust my own impressions of place or time or quantity—only I can feel the essence which is there and which does not vary. If I find more letters I will send them. These were in a book; the others must be scattered in those beloved packets of the past which I am slowly sorting as I read them. I think the Past somehow was not so *present* at the time as it is now. Shall we ever look back at life somewhere in God's Kingdom to come? and thank Him with new thanks for all its wonderful blessings. How much of what is the Holy Psalm of Life, your dear great Signor made clear from his place in God's Kingdom upon earth.

To Emily Ritchie

Freshwater
Easter Sunday [1909].

Swinburne is dead. Yesterday came a telegram from Watts-Dunton which was sad, sad to get. As I said to Hester, the one thing which would be worse than death would be to live on and on after everyone one cared about had gone. The poor young poets, who shall I say?— Davidson, any of them—may die and I don't cry for them—but I did cry for Swinburne—who wrote *Atalanta* and the letter about James.

The following letter from Swinburne is the one to which my mother refers:—

To Anne Ritchie from A. C. Swinburne [1]

The Pines
Jan. 22, 1908.

DEAR LADY RITCHIE,—I do congratulate you cordially on being a grandmother. To have a baby at hand or within reach is to belong to "the Kingdom of heaven" yourself. I met this cold morning on my daily walk, a fair friend not yet "well stricken in" months, who beamed and chuckled inarticulately (being still by necessity "an inarticulate poet") at sight of me, from the depth of her pushwainling (I hope you never use the barbaric word "perambulator"?). Don't you like the late Rev. W. Barnes much better as a lexicographer (though I fear Miss Pinkerton might have demurred to his claims on that score) than as a poet? The happy term "pushwain-ling" for a baby's coach of state is what makes him immortal in my eyes.

Many thanks for sending me Miss Coleridge's poems. They are full of beauty and charm—a charm which does not belong to all beautiful writing and delicate execution. It is high praise—from me—to say that they often remind me of Mrs. Shorter's (born Dora Sigerson) which I hope you know and admire as I do.

Sir Theodore Watts-Dunton belongs to the same order of creation as Mrs. Harris. But Mr. T. W.-D. is none the less grateful for your so kindly misplaced congratulations.

Ever sincerely and cordially yours,
A. C. SWINBURNE.

[1] This letter is published by the kind permission of Messrs. Heinemann.

To Anne Thackeray (*in Rome*)

[1910].

What a joy to get your letter and to think of you in Rome, the best place in all the world.

Stamp on the beloved ground for me, and *drink* a gulp of the waters of Trevi for me—and O, that shining toe in St. Peter's! Minny and I both kissed it in our excitement, and O the smell! and O the shine! and O the state of mind! Mind you never move without a shawl, and avoid chills and Roman fevers.

. . . Did I tell you that they were thinking of bringing out a Centenary Edition of the Biographical Edition— probably two volumes at a time, beginning in November.

It will be a comfort when it is done. My memory is a worry. I remember, but so slowly that it is most provoking and irritating.

It's a good thing one didn't make oneself, and that one has to put up with being what one *is* and not what one might aspire to, like the German Emperor who imagines himself the voice of God.

To Emily Ritchie

Freshwater
[1911].

Your words about Gussie [1] were very true and very heartfelt for me, for us. I am glad you wrote. Last night in my dreams I was crying and crying about *Death*. Now that I am awake, I wonder what I cried for and why I minded so much, and now here is the daylight and the green fields and the sea from my window, and the wind-blown Freshwater trees. . . . I keep saying to my-

[1] The death of Mrs. Douglas Freshfield, May 26th, 1911.

self about death what the Lieutenant on board the *Titanic* said, "It doesn't matter very much."

Thank God we have lived—and lived about the same time. But my heart aches for you and for all of them.

XIII

1912—1919

O<small>N</small> October the 12th, 1912, my father died. Of the pain and sorrow of this time there is no need to speak. Those who were with her will never forget my mother's noble courage and constant thought for others in the midst of her own grief.

After a while we left the big house in St. George's Square and went to live at 9, St. Leonard's Terrace, Chelsea, that we might be near my brother and his wife.

To Reginald J. Smith

9, St. Leonard's Terrace
10th November [1913].

. . . I am also writing to you about two memorials which belong to my life.

I. I want to send this guinea to dear Andrew Lang's memorial; I cannot remember where to apply, and I felt sure you would kindly help me.

II. I have heard from Bishop Welldon,[1] and I am grieved I cannot help him. The few letters I kept of beloved Meta Gaskell's were loving greetings not for print, only the kindest and most tender personalities. They were *clasps* rather than letters, in that lovely handwriting of hers.

Last night I saw Miss Broughton, who said to me, "I

[1] A proposed memoir of the Misses Gaskell.

hear you have a new book coming out," and I said, "You shall most certainly have a copy!"

Yet one more thing I have to ask you. On Wednesday next there is a meeting of the Literary Fund. If you are able, will you go there and please support poor Mrs. ——; she is left with *nothing* but her good courage. I am hoping enough may be granted to pay for the funeral and also to keep her through these first sad months.

All this do not please trouble to answer for I know you will respond with or without writing.

To Lady Battersea

9, St. Leonard's Terrace
[1913].

How kind of you to write, and how pleasant it is to hear a friend's voice come out of the envelope—it is nearer than a printed page!

My printed page [1] has done very well, and is going into a second edition. I liked putting the scraps together, re-writing some of them and thinking of the beloved past. It seems so great a boon to live back again.

Let me know when you come up, and either come to luncheon or let me come to you one evening. Lunching out doesn't suit me somehow, but tea or dinner I should gratefully accept. I am 'very well on the whole, and except for sadness I am happy in a way. The children are away but they will soon be back. I want to say to you, dear Connie, that it was an ache to me when Blanche Lindsay died, all the more that I felt I had not gone as often as I might, but one gets so soon tired when one is my age. All the same it made me grieve to feel this, and to think how kind she had always been.

[1] Her book, *From the Porch.*

To Lady Bell

9, St. Leonard's Terrace
Dec. 31st [1913].

Hearing of you through Antonia Macnaghten and Imogen, makes me want to cross pens, shake nibs, hit you with a piece of paper to attract your attention!

Here is a nice game! one person (it or she) sits down with a bit of paper and some dark-coloured fluid, with which she traces your name, also those near and dear to you, and to herself too. Then she thinks (she needn't speak), "Old friends" and remembers "all sorts of things" as Betsinda used to say. Then the game isn't over: the other side nods back to you in a friendly way. . . .

In July, 1914, Mr. Sargent made a beautiful portrait of my mother to which the following letters refer. The drawing was made at the request of her friends, who afterwards presented her with the picture.

This letter from Henry James tells the story.

Henry James to Anne Ritchie

21, Carlyle Mansions
June 30, 1914

DEAREST ANNE, admirable old Friend and illustrious Confrère!—It is altogether delightful to think that this happy thought of your likeness being "took" by our all-responsive and all-ready Sargent is on the way to be effectively arranged, for such a Public Treasure shall the work appear destined to become, if all goes well with it.

The happy thought sprang up in the breasts of the Protheros—to them alone I more than suspect belongs

the grace of having first thrown it off. I doubt whether
it will seem wise to invite you to take your place on the
sitter's throne before the autumn—the reason of this
being that all your friends of every size and shape ought
to have the chance to join in the demonstration according
to their ability. I have taken the liberty of urging that
consideration out of the depth of my own experience—
my heart was so wrung by the plaints of those who had
not been notified by my two or three acting friends when
Sargent turned out *my* simulacrum! The lament of
those who had been unknowingly overlooked distressed
me almost more than the pleasure of the others gratified,
and I should wish for you that everyone without exception who would like to add a pebble to your cairn shall
have been communicated with, which is in course of
being seen about.

I rejoice for you meanwhile that you are not swelter-
ing with us here in the heavy Cockney heat, but sitting,
I hope, in the flutter of the Porch, and getting better of
the indisposition of which you speak. Porches and airy
flutters do me more good than anything in the world when
I (more ponderously) droop—and even as I write this
I am almost hanging out of my 4th. floor window into
the stuffy darkness of our Thames-side, praying for a
stir in the night that doesn't come. Don't exchange your
headland over the deep for this sorry state without due
circumspection. You have written me a most beautiful
and touching note, and only this hell-broth of the great
London social Pot has kept me from thanking you for
it more instantly.

Have patience with us all and believe me your stoutest
and fondest old adherent

HENRY JAMES.

To Mrs. George Prothero [1]

The Porch
Freshwater Bay
[June 1914].

I can only send my loving, grateful, spiritual hug to
you, for your amazing thought to give me pleasure and
content and pride and delight.   The feel of it all—the
kindness—has cured me I do believe of my attack of illness, and as long as I am alive and well, I shall feel all
the more alive, for having been made a *Sargent* in the
army of—occupation?—appreciators of what is fine—I
don't know what to call it.

I shall be home on the 3rd. for a week or two, and I
may come back here for part of August.

Will you come to tea on the 4th. or any day convenient
to you?   Mr. Sargent says Tuesday the 7th. for my sitting.

Naturally enough my first thought was how pleased
Richmond would have been—and my father—and sister—as for my dear family it is radiant.

To Mrs. George Prothero

9, St. Leonard's Terrace
9 *July* [1914].

I have just come away from Sargent's studio.   It is
the most lovely, *fine* picture—I can't tell you how I have
loved the gift, the givers and the devisers, or how I have
enjoyed the sittings.   I could only tell Mr. Sargent that
I thought that when I came away, the picture itself
would—could thank him for me.

I am sure it ought to thank you, sweet and kind en-
chantress, who have devised all this, and your husband

[1] Now Lady Prothero.

and kindest Henry James. I write *now,* for I am going to Freshwater to-morrow; if I can I shall come late to-night or early to-morrow to see you a minute before I start.

To Rhoda Broughton

9, St. Leonard's Terrace
July 30 [1914].

It really is an enchanting picture. I am more touched and interested and grateful than ever.

I went for another sitting yesterday and he said, "I like your bonnet so much, may I add it?" and so my poke bonnet is there supreme.

I am asking the photographer to send you a photograph of my picture to say thank you for me better than I can myself. . . . I feel quite shy before my portrait, it is *so human,* and I feel so like it, yet more *grim* alas!

Your devoted, indebted and grateful
A. I. R.

To the Friends who gave the Portrait

Such a beautiful gift is almost beyond any poor thanks of mine. It has come bringing gracious sympathy and comfort and kindness—May others find the same help in their lives as that which has been given me and mine!

With a grateful heart I sign myself
ANNE THACKERAY RITCHIE

August 11, 1914.

M. F. Prothero to the Subscribers

24, Bedford Square,
August, 1914.

The following is a list of the subscribers to the portrait of Lady Ritchie, by Mr. John Sargent:—

Blanche Airlie
J. M. Barrie
Constance Battersea
Florence Bell
Hugh Bell
Gertrude Bell
Hugo Bell
Maurice Bell
Arnold Bennett
Mary Benson
Augustine Birrell
Eleanor Birrell
George M. Booth
Margaret Booth
Mary Booth
Stopford A. Brooke
Rhoda Broughton
Katharine Bruce
Marion Bryce
Annie F. Chamberlain
Basil Champneys
Lucy Clifford
Eleanor Clough
T. J. Cobden-Sanderson
Edith Cole
Louise Creighton
Margaret Creighton
J. W. Cross
H. E. Cunningham
H. S. Cunningham
Ariana R. W. Curtis
Lionel Cust
Sybil Cust
Elizabeth Darwin
Horace Darwin
Ida Darwin
W. E. Darwin
M. Llewelyn Davies
W. H. Deverell

A. V. Dicey
E. M. Dicey
Emma du Maurier
Arthur D. Elliot
K. E. Farrer
Jane Fletcher
E. H. Flower
Douglas W. Freshfield
May E. Gordon
W. Wilson Greg
Anstey Guthrie
Elizabeth Haldane
Sophie V. Halsey
Florence Henniker
Alicia Eliza Hill
Mrs. W. H. Hughes
Bernard Holland
Augusta Julia Huth
T. G. Jackson
Henry James
Peggy James
Ellen Joachim
Rose Lamb
Walter Leafe
Constance Leslie
H. E. Litchfield
Anne Low
Susan Lushington
Elizabeth Mathew
Alexandra Micholls
Bella Middleton
Peggy Middleton
Monteagle
Claude Montefiore
Eveleen Myers
Helen Shore Nightingale
L. H. Shore Nightingale
Emily Norman
Philip Norman

Richard Norton
Bessie Olliffe
Frances M. Paley
Charles E. Perugini
Kate Perugini
Pierpont Morgan
Frederick Pollock
Georgina H. Pollock
Dighton Probyn
Barbara Prothero
G. W. Prothero
M. F. Prothero
Emily Wyndham Quin
Mary Rawlinson
W. G. Rawlinson
Clara Richmond
Elsa Richmond
Adelheid Robertson
Elizabeth Robins
Elizabeth A. Rodd
Rosebery
Alys Russell
Margaret of Sarawak
Louisa Lee-Schuyler
Georgina Lee-Schuyler
Adela Schuster
Walter N. Senior
Edith Sichel
Eleanor M. Sidgwick
Constance Hugh Smith

Alick Murray Smith
Elizabeth Murray Smith
Ethel Murray Smith
E. T. Murray Smith
Elizabeth Babington-
  Smith
Henry Babington-Smith
L. Pearsall Smith
Isabel M. Smith
Reginald J. Smith
Agnes Spring-Rice
Cecil Spring-Rice
Georgina Spring-Rice
Maude Stanley
Herbert Stephen
Katharine Stephen
Lisa Stillman
Marie Stillman
Jane Strachey
Howard Sturgis
Tennyson
Charles Tennyson
Ivy Tennyson
Mary Trevelyan
Margaret Vaughan
W. W. Vaughan
Josephine Ward
M. S. Watts
Margaret Woods
Annie Yorke

The portrait has been completed, and sent to Lady Ritchie. A silver inkstand and a pair of candlesticks with the following inscription: "Presented to Anne Thackeray Ritchie by her friends, August, 1914," have also been given her, together with a cheque for the residue of the subscriptions, to be used as she may desire.

M. F. PROTHERO.

To Miss Lee-Schuyler, New York

Tadworth
Surrey
9th Sept. [1914].

Your letter came last night and I loved it, for I felt that if you were here, you could not enter more completely into all that this awful experience of war brings into our life. I long for Richmond every hour, and feel if he were only here, he could help more than anyone. Strangely enough when Sir James Dunlop Smith (the Military Attaché at the India Office) went there the other day, going from room to room trying to help my nephew Arthur Ritchie to get to the Front, he said wherever he went, whoever he saw, each said, "If only Richmond Ritchie were here! Nobody could give such good counsel as he."

My part is waiting and doing. London is too moving and agitating to stay in, the garden in front of our house is full of soldiers and horses. The friendly *bores* who are left stranded, are impossible to avoid, the people we care for are away, and with this awful strip of news coming in, I felt I must *touch* Hester and join her at Tadworth.

Arthur Ritchie is gone. Charles Thackeray is drilling morning, noon and night. They are all so cheery, so full of honour and noble courage, that it is as much thank God in one's heart, as horrible dismay. I can only pray for peace, that peace which passeth all understanding.

Give my love to Georgie. How can I ever say what pleasure my *beautiful* testimonial [1] gave to me. It came just before this horrible thunderbolt. How dear it was of you both to subscribe; any money over will enable me to give your help and others—kind people—to the wives

[1] Her portrait by Sargent.

and children of the soldiers at the front. It is appalling to hear of the thousands of refugees from Belgium and France arriving every day, but everyone is helping.

It warms my heart to know that you in America realise the truth—the lies the Germans publish are fantastic. I am well, only troubled at heart.

To Mrs. George Prothero

9, St. Leonard's Terrace
[*January 30, 1915*].

O what a delight! After being bombed out of our sleep, defrauded of Billy and Meg at dinner, then befogged out of a morning's meeting with the grandchildren, generally rubbed up the wrong way, I come down to see a little parcel waiting which I open with languid interest and lo! Peace, Pleasure, Plenty surround us all, your grateful friend in particular, whose ways you smooth and shine upon. Thank you, thank you, dear Fanny, and once more I feel in a gentler mood, and once more it is you I thank, and am yours affectionately and over again gratefully,

ANNE RITCHIE.

To Rhoda Broughton

The Old Vicarage
Ware
May Day [1915].

Songs of Birds. Opening chorus—then solo by distinguished performers, Signor Cuckoo and others. Then general burst of specialists.

Audience—daffodils, young vegetables and myriads of little buds.

I wish you were here, my dearest Rhoda. The square comfortable house seems like a palace—the entrance is so pretty, first across a field with Caldecott views, then a hill, and behold The Old Vicarage with its weather-cock windows.

Ware itself is exactly like Caldecott's John Gilpin; he must have come here to do the pictures.

. . . I want to tell you of our afternoon with Charles Lamb. One could almost see him standing by his "granddame's" grave in Widford Churchyard; Lady Buckmaster took us and she showed us the house Charles Lamb used to go to, such a quaint, prim, dim little house, all overgrown by trees and creepers, but the owner will only let it to people who will sign a promise to cut nothing down, and nobody will agree to this, so the house is turning into *one* large laurel bush,—like Daphne, wasn't it?

Then we had tea under the apple-trees in Lady Buckmaster's garden, where Charles Lamb used also to go. There was an American lady who so adored him that last year she came over with her intended to be married at Widford Church, and the pew-opener gave her away.

It was the strangest combination of Elia and us, and the hundreds of soldiers from their billets, and the hospital close by, and a lonely drive home in the sunset.

To James Bain

The Old Vicarage
August 23rd [1915].

I owe you a real, great pleasure and interest and *emotion* reading the life of that dear and wise person Alexander Macmillan and getting still more to know him and enjoying his presence once again.

The life is indeed admirably done; how many familiar voices speak out of its pages. Perhaps none more familiar than yours, dear Mr. Bain, kind friend as you have ever been.

. . . I am reading Sir Alfred Lyall, and that clever, *clever* novel of Arnold Bennett's, *Whom God Hath Joined*. He has discovered *how* interesting uninteresting things and people are.

. . . Everything is so sad and unnatural that to fly away into one's youth and the youth of one's friends and companions is the best calmer and comforter. I wish you could get younger and younger, and I too! and that one could go off via childhood again.

To Rhoda Broughton

9, St. Leonard's Terrace
Sept. 30 [1915].

What a blessing a friend is on a day like this, to light up the darkness and cheer up the damp and be an umbrella to ward off the rain! and I bring down a book,[1] (short and well printed to read in) and as I open it I come upon a dedication to Miss Broughton and a kind little inscription: "To Mrs. Richmond Ritchie with the author's best wishes and apologies." He has certainly made me laugh out, even on a day like this. Mrs. Casaubon's letter to Belinda is the funniest of them all, I think. Dear Andrew Lang!

We are going a little sooner than we intended; there are always two thousand little reasons and unreasons for what one does. Last night in the middle of the night I remembered I hadn't set the drawing-room clock and came down accordingly. Early this morning Hester was struck by the same idea and she also put the clock an hour back. Then came Ada, the cook, who had forgotten all about summer time, crying out against the milk and

[1] *Old Friends* by Andrew Lang.

baker and the paper boy. I don't know where we are any more, and what is expected of us by coupon or otherwise.

The clock says three-thirty, it is growing darker and darker, is it five-thirty? Please when you write tell me what o'clock it is, and I am your loving

ANNE RITCHIE.

So poor Mrs. Cramb is relieved from her dreary experience of life. She wrote me a nice letter not long ago.

To Charles P. Johnson

The Old Vicarage
Jan. 22nd [1916].

It was very cold and quite dark when Billy arrived, and after he had had his tea and settled down by the fire, he said, "Now children," and they rushed away and came back bringing in the hamper and opening the lid, and lo! there were the beautifully bound books![1] Did any authoress in her old age ever see such a droll, touching sight as her beloved grandchildren, and Belinda in particular, eagerly turning over the leaves of all her past days, exclaiming at the pictures, and obediently putting the books down when their father cried, "Beware of fingers"?

What a kind, old friendly God-paternal thought, what an apotheosis for my life-long chatter to find itself so kindly honoured and decorated.

I hardly knew which were the grandchildren and which were my stories, so much of the past was written in each one of my books. And Walker's lovely drawings and George Leslie's and Mrs. Allingham's illustrations all seemed alive too, and thank you and thank you, dear

[1] A complete set of my mother's books in first editions given by Mr. Johnson to his god-daughter Belinda Ritchie.

Mr. Johnson. Richmond would have been so glad for Belinda, and responsive and pleased for me.

You have given me the order of the Pen—the ancient Pen—and I shall send you the order of the K. T.—not Thistle, but Kind Thought!

To Miss Lee-Schuyler, New York

9, St. Leonard's Terrace
Dec. 13th [1916].

Do not be alarmed by Miss Bosanquet's beautiful typing.[1] I see her blush! I have had letters from her which she used to indite for dear Henry James, and now that my eyes are rather groggy I do enjoy the luxury of talking to a friend instead of blotting my affection.

I am going to get another opinion about my eyes. One doctor said I had decided cataract coming on. Another said I hadn't. I have heard of a third, whose address I have unfortunately lost, who cures cataract by reading three hours a day, which will suit me very well. When I have found the third doctor's address I will let you know what he says.

I am glad we are not at war with you, but I wish your President, while preserving peace, had found a word of indignant flame for the organised horrors the Germans have perpetrated, not in fair fight. Better would it be for them that a millstone could be tied to their heads— a million millstones. How dare the Germans talk of the Peace of God, while perpetrating their bloodthirsty attacks on Belgium and Poland, and accuse unprepared England and France!

I wonder if you are installed in your new home? Your letter came the very day of your move, and our love will

[1] This letter was dictated to Miss Bosanquet at the typewriter.

find you out. I delight to think of all the honours and dignities, my dear, which pursue you wherever you go.

I have just read your beautiful preface.[1] The concluding paragraphs go to my very heart. You were moved to true eloquence, and to the song of the Heart when you wrote this last and most lovely *grace*. A bit of sunshine indeed, a sound of running waters.

I am writing to you in a thick damp fog; I sat down dispirited, feeling how incapable old age is to come and go, to help others, to be grateful for the innumerable blessings of life, and as I read your Introduction I forgot everything but your dear and noble words flowing on, and the example set to others by those who have kept on clear and serene to the very end. It is a *treasure* in life to count on such a friendship as ours, and when we are both promoted, we shall have had this best possession ("Le meilleur de tout est un ancien ami," says Victor Hugo), and whether we are 50,000 years old or 80 or 30, as we were when first I loved you—thank God for his blessings in this life.

To Edmund Candler (*in Mesopotamia*)

9, St. Leonard's Terrace
Feb. 16th [1917].

What interest your kind letter rouses in us all! I have nothing to add to your friendly and most unexpected studies,[2] and if you quote anything out of my letter please let it be that I know it would greatly touch my father that at such a time and under such circumstances, you should find rest in the (good) company of his books. I remember he told me that when Sebastopol fell, a *Vanity Fair* pierced by a bullet was picked up in one of the bar-

[1] An Introduction written by Miss Lee Schuyler to *Recollections of a Happy Life* by A. C. Hobson.
[2] An article on Thackeray.

rack rooms, and now after more than fifty years the story is heroically repeated.

. . . Except for a friend who sent him an occasional turkey, I cannot remember any connection that my father had with Norfolk, and I am ashamed to say that until I read your letter I had never realised the presence of the Bungays in his writings. It will be most sympathetic to find your notes in the *Cornhill*—and thank you for writing and believe me,

Your grateful reader,
ANNE RITCHIE.

To her grand-daughter Belinda

April 30th [1917].

MY DARLING LINNY,—It is eight o'clock and here is my breakfast, and for a treat *butter* instead of margarine. I have read my Psalm for the day; it is one I like, "One generation shall praise Thy works unto another: and declare Thy power." I am one generation, your father and mother are another, and you a third, and a very nice one too, say we grandparents. Some of your generation are rather wild. There is a nice little boy here called Oliver Woods; and a nice little girl at Farringford called Anne, and Oliver says to *his* grandmama, "Do you think Anne ought to thump little children she doesn't know?" So all the grandmothers say, "Certainly not." Anne has not got a grandmama to teach her manners, only a kind old Nurse who cannot catch her up when she runs about. I am so glad that none of you "thump children you don't know when you meet them," but I must say Anne rushes up to me not thumpingly but with her little arms out.

Bless you darling Belinda. Give the second generation and the third generation hugs from the first generation.

My first is a letter of the Alphabet.
My second is part of one's legs.
My third is very small and tiresome
but necessary during the war,
To keep my whole alive.

To Mrs. Charles Thackeray

The Old Vicarage
[1917].

Hester is going down to telegraph our pleasure and delight over the new Director of Submarines.[1] Oh that he on sea and our Colonels on land may set us free from this loathsome Kultur!

I wish, how I wish, I could be cut up into four active young women of twenty to come and go. I should like wings to fly with, and intelligence to know what might be of use.

I always come back to Belinda's wish, "God only made me a little girl, and not a fairy as I should have liked," and he has made me an old woman to send you my love.

All the poor Yeomanry are clanking about utterly disconsolate. Their horses have been taken and there they are left with their saddles and bridles on their own backs. They can't even get their food in, which comes from a distance, and the poor elderly Majors are condemned to bicycles.

To Thomas Hardy

The Porch
July 24 [1917].

I have just finished *The Dynasts* with *awe* and with absolute admiration. It is a relief for my excitement

[1] Captain, now Rear Admiral, W. W. Fisher had been appointed Director of the Anti-Submarine Division, Admiralty.

to write to you and I feel as if I were one of your spirits speaking. I have almost forgotten the war for a day or two, in wonder at your inspired history *of now,* written in 1907.

Are our poor, poor grandchildren to go through it all again? Let them read *The Dynasts* and have chained copies fixed up in every home.

How Leslie, how my sister would have admired, as does yours sincerely and sadly and gladly too for many things.

ANNE RITCHIE.

To her grand-daughter, Catherine

THIS SWEET CATHERINE
IS MY VALENTINE

To her grandson James

Your birthday is getting very near. This is nine-thirty o'clock on November 2nd and the soldiers are sounding their go-to-bed horns and I am sending you my love. I remember how all the squibs and crackers were sounding and going off on Guy Fawkes Day when you were born ten years ago; is it possible it is ten years already? I am so glad to hear the cake went right this time. I shall send one once a month, and please give George Ritchie a slice for his name's sake.

We had squibs and crackers and banging and thunder-ing on Wednesday night. [1] Hester and I came down to the drawing-room and Hester fetched a rug and we poked up the fire. It was a lovely moonlight night. I have been having drives in a bath chair these last few days. A nice little boy called Whitworth who is living next door came to speak to me yesterday as I got out of my chariot, and I invited him in to have a ride on the rocking horse, he seemed surprised that a quite old lady like me should keep a rocking horse, and I had to explain that it was for my grand-children and small nephews and nieces. Most of them are away now to be out of the raids.

Darling James, God bless you, and I am your loving, loving

GRANDMAMA.

I have been writing about a hospital and I hope they will print my letter in the *Spectator* and that some money may come to help my friends the nurses.

[1] An air-raid over Chelsea.

To Mrs. Herbert Paul

The Porch
[*January* 1918].

. . . I wish we could all be at our best all our life long, instead of the contrary so very often. What makes me happy is that I think I have discovered at last, that wrong and failure and irritation and selfishness are part of the texture of life, not the Devil nor the Hun so much as the very condition of existence, but that with all this comes God, the Spirit of good, walking on the face of the waters, and making bad things into peace, goodwill and courage.

Journal (1918)

The Old Vicarage.

June 30th. "I am an old man, who lived thro' many fears and troubles, most of which never happened at all." And this most assuredly applies to me! Billy told me the little history just now, when I said I felt like the old woman in the fairy tale who sat weeping in the cellar for fear the mallet should fall on her future grandson's head. Little Belinda wondered what we were talking about. She is reading her book beside me in a garden chair, and Billy is digging at the weeds. Now and again a young bird up in a tree gives a little mid-day croak. The flowers seem to give an extra flash of colour in the gleam of the sun, the little dog rolls over on his back and stretches out his paws: distant poultry cluck from beyond the hedge and a fly buzzes across my paper. Kind minute, tranquil peaceful hour, for which I can still thank God, before I go my way.

To Mrs. Gerald Ritchie

The Porch, de mon Coin
[*Autumn* 1918].

We had a delightful journey, friendly young soldiers, (not too many of them) who lunched with us off our sandwiches and buns—We had a dream of a crossing, grey soft skies parting to show blue of every faint and shining depth, and finally Miss Gillan and the motor to meet us.

I have been thinking of my *dear* month in London and all the friendly people, things, meetings, and not the least my Miggs and my Nan and all their loving-kindness.

I found on arriving the book from Mr. Murray with the Sartoris article which will do very well indeed. There is such a funny letter from Mr. Brookfield quoted in it. He asks that two pair of shoes he forgot at Warnford may be returned to him. He says as it is Lent nobody is surprised to see him going about with bare feet, but that it will look odd at Easter!

I have seen nobody yet except the caretaker and the cat, both so overjoyed to see us that it made me feel quite ashamed.

I am so engrossed by all the things I have to think about, and the news and the peace one is longing for, that I feel as if the room was crowded with hopes and blessed realisations too.

There was a little pile of the *Echo de Paris* awaiting us, giving the French quick, definite accounts of the advance each day.

Hester has also settled down, and we had a delicious little fire, chiefly sticks we had picked up and brought in from the shore.

To her grand-daughter Maisie

The Porch
[*November* 1918.]

MY DARLING MAISIE,—I have not written to you for a long time and I think I must write to-day.

It is raining; I want it to leave off for we are going for a long drive if it is possible. Yesterday was so beautiful it seemed to make one *fly* with joy and when I thought of Peace coming it made me say my prayers of thanks.

Last night Nelly Elias read out loud how the English came to Lille and how the happy free people cheered and cheered and waved flags and *kissed* the English out of gratitude. It was *delightful* reading, and it almost made one cry to think of their happiness, poor things. This morning I met James and Rachel Tennyson [1] picking up sticks for the fire, and I told them about Peace coming. James laughed and said, "I am a crocodile," and I don't think he understood. They come running to meet me just as you do, and I always think of you all when I see them.

How happy we shall be when we go to meet you at Yarmouth, and the steamer comes up with you all on board, and then we shall trot home. Daddy must draw a picture of you all in the coach, for I never can draw horses, not even a donkey can I draw. Do try and learn to draw horses and donkeys too. It will be useful when you are a grandmama.

The one over-fed animal here is Miss Gillan's donkey which goes off at a hand-gallop and is—terrific—and won't ever stop on the way. The Government have forgotten to cut down his oats, and he has more to eat than any of the horses, and that is why he is so fresh. I do

---

[1] Great-grandchildren of the Poet.

hope you will have a donkey some day, but not quite such a velocipede as this one.

Goodbye, my darling granddaughter.

To her Daughter-in-law

The Porch
[1918].

I cannot tell you how happy your letter made me. It was like suddenly *going up* in the air to hear of you all.

Who has sent me a beautiful flower which *open* is a parasol and which folded is a useful support, and which to look at is a pleasure? It comes from Peter—Jones—Robinson—one of them. It arrived by post and is a mystery.

I would have taken it to vote with but it was pouring lions and tigers. At the voting booth we displeased a clerk. I said, "I hope I have done it all right." He said severely, "This is vote by ballot, you have no business to show your paper." Why Hester and I have each a vote I do not know,—anyhow we both stepped behind the screen and both voted Coalition, and Hester grins and says now we counterbalance A——, and Sir F——, who has travelled all the way from London to give his vote to Sir Godfrey Baring.

The taxi took us off at two o'clock, so we escaped a crowd, and the disapproval of the Court was concentrated on my undignified behaviour. There were about twenty people sitting in a double row and our neighbour, the tall policeman.

Dear, have you got back? Have I ever told you how your *butter* eased the wheels of life when Adèle arrived very hungry?

Ever your loving,
VOTARINA.

To her Daughter-in-law

The Porch
[1918].

We have had a great deal of weather the last few days. The wind whistles and scrimmages, the water washes, the storm is everywhere, and I feel all anyhow, and only wonder what I ought to do?—*Nothing* is the best answer.

On Saturday night Hester called me to come out on her balcony and look at the moon. The moon was red, very red and angry, and quite round and galloping along into a great cloud.

Since writing all this the storms are over and gone, and I wish I could pack up all the breath off the downs and all the light off the sea, and the beautiful sight Hester and I have been watching, six fine pairs of cart-horses dragging ploughs along the great field leading down to the Bay, the old men driving them and a little bit of a boy with fair hair leading one of them. I said to Hester, "Well done, James." She laughed. The little boy turned sharp round, and stared. His name must have been really James.

Beloved daughter-in-law,
Farewell and Bless you.

To Lucy Broadwood

The Porch
December 4 [1918].

How grateful I feel for your letter. As I read it, I seemed to be listening again with Richmond to your music. Your words came to me like a song sounding through the door of the past.

. . . Ryde is a very long way from Freshwater, but I will look and see how the trains fit; with longer daytime there may be possibilities, and as Peace grows there may be luncheons fit to offer, and we could, as you know (anyhow Hester could), show the way to Farringford.

One thing about you still often haunts me, which is that somewhere on the lawn of The End House your beautiful diamond is hidden away.

Another thing I shall hate to think of, is that you may be leaving your kind nest where we have all sheltered in turn. I have to stay more and more by my own fireside, but I think the quieter old people keep, the more their spirits roam and fly.

To Mrs. Gerald Ritchie

The Porch
[*Dec.* 1918].

. . . Have you read Macaulay's life lately? I cannot tell you how I have enjoyed reading it and my father walks in and out of it in the most amusing way.

There is a story of the Zoo, two ladies visiting the newly arrived hippopotamus. My father hears one say to the other, "That is the way in; and Oh! there is Lord Macaulay coming *out*—which would you rather see?" First Lady, "Lord Macaulay,—never mind the hippopotamus," and they rush after Lord Macaulay. Later on he meets my father, who tells him of the conversation, which he (Lord M.) says is the greatest compliment he ever received.

. . . Pelman tells Hester not to misuse the priceless gift of imagination picturing troubles, but to go higher, and he is quite right—not picturing impossible rainbows but accepting. I always go back to "Sing sorrow, sing sorrow, triumph the good."

To A. B. S. Tennyson

The Porch
16th December [1918].

To our great pleasure the enchanting portrait of Clemenceau has arrived, shrewd, courageous Clemenceau able to hold his own, to wave that hat to the delight of all London, and to give a cachet to our modest home! We have pinned the admirable picture up by the door, and we proudly show it to your family and our visitors. Yesterday we had a tea party, most agreeable and successful. "Crackers, Oh and scones!" says James, approvingly. James asked about M. Clemenceau: and I said he was a very good old man who had helped the French and brought about Peace and made us all very happy. "He hasn't made me very happy," says James; so I say, "Oh, yes, he has, he has made your Mama happy, and helped to bring your Daddy back from the War." "But he hasn't made me happy," says Rachel. She was quite convinced, however, when we assured her he had. . . .

To Mrs. Gerald Ritchie

6th January [1919].

If you think my letter *cold,* it is the weather not I!

The great event of this week has been reading Mrs. Barnett's book![1] How good it is! How fine he is, and how well she tells the story of his generous, beautiful life. Some parts made my tears break out unexpectedly.

I simply laughed out loud when I read of Herbert Spencer with his umbrella in the desert beating the donkey boy. His brown kid gloves, his tie, his umbrella! How well I can see him at Wykehurst tripping angrily

[1] The *Life of Canon Barnett.*

along the terrace. I told you he had been ordered to rest
and to travel with unintellectual people, and he asked if
he might join us as he thought we should not tire his
brain in any way! . . .

To her Daughter

15 *January* [1919].

. . . All yesterday I was tearing up old letters, and it
seemed like living through the past once more and parting from it all again. I felt the beloved rush of the
tempest of life, to which I still seem to belong, far more
than to *now*.

Who says, "Youth's a stuff will not endure?" It lasts
as long as we do, and is older than age. For those moments of eager life, of seeing and being, come back to us,
and we babble of green fields and live among them to
the very end.

Anne Thackeray Ritchie died at Freshwater on February the 26th, 1919. A tablet to her memory in the village church has the following inscription:

Her writing reveals the inheritance of genius
Her life the inspiration of loving kindness.

APPENDIX

CHRONOLOGICAL LIST OF LADY RITCHIE'S BOOKS

1863. The Story of Elizabeth.
1867. The Village on the Cliff.
1868. Five Old Friends and a Young Prince.
1869. To Esther and other Sketches.
1873. Old Kensington.
1874. Toilers and Spinsters.
1875. Miss Angel.
1876. Introduction to "The Orphan of Pimlico," by W. M. Thackeray.
1880. Introduction to the "Life of Anne Evans."
1881. Life of Madame de Sevigné.
1881. Miss Williamson's Divagations.
1883. A Book of Sibyls.
1885. Mrs. Dymond.
1887. Little Esme's Adventure (a story for children).
1891. Introduction to "Cranford."
1892. Records of Tennyson, Ruskin and Browning.
1892. Introduction to "Madame d'Aulnoy's Fairy Tales."
1893. Introduction to "Our Village."
1893. Introduction to "Lord Tennyson and his Friends."
1894. Chapters from Some Memoirs.
1894. Life of Lord Amherst (in conjunction with Richardson Evans).
1895. Introductions to the following books by Miss Edgeworth:
  Popular Tales.
  Ormond.
  Castle Rackrent and the Absentee.
  Helen.
1898. Biographical Introductions to the Biographical Edition of W. M. Thackeray's Works. 13 vols.
1908. Blackstick Papers.
1911. Biographical Introductions to the Centenary Edition of W. M. Thackeray's Works. 26 volumes.
1913. From the Porch.
1919. From Friend to Friend (published posthumously).

INDEX

THE END